The Disenchanted
Island

THE DISENCHANTED ISLAND

Puerto Rico and the United States in the Twentieth Century

Ronald Fernandez

Foreword by
William M. Kunstler
and
Ronald L. Kuby

New York
Westport, Connecticut
London

Library of Congress Cataloging-in-Publication Data

Fernandez, Ronald.
    The disenchanted island : Puerto Rico and the United States in the
twentieth century / Ronald Fernandez ; foreword by William M.
Kunstler and Ronald L. Kuby.
      p.   cm.
    Includes bibliographical references and index.
    ISBN 0–275–94096–9 (alk. paper)
    1. United States—Relations—Puerto Rico. 2. Puerto Rico—
Relations—United States. I. Title.
E183.8.P9F47 1992
327.7307295—dc20   91–41618

British Library Cataloguing in Publication Data is available.

Library of Congress Catalog Card Number: 91–41618
ISBN: 0–275–94096–9

First published in 1992

Praeger Publishers, One Madison Avenue, New York, NY 10010
An imprint of Greenwood Publishing Group, Inc.

Printed in the United States of America

The paper used in this book complies with the Permanent
Paper Standard issued by the National Information Standards
Organization (Z39.48–1984).

10 9 8 7 6 5 4 3 2 1

a mi hermano, Luis Nieves Falcon

Contents

Foreword

On August 25, 1989, Filiberto Ojeda Rios, acting as his own attorney, gave his closing argument to the jury in a U.S. court in San Juan. The indictment, drawn in the name of the United States of America, charged that Ojeda Rios had shot at and assaulted agents of the Federal Bureau of Investigation. The prosecutor had been appointed by President Reagan, the judge by President Carter, and the American flag stood in the courtroom, but the jury was Puerto Rican.

Far from denying his actions, Ojeda Rios embraced them, and asked the jury to uphold the right of the Puerto Rican people to use force, in self-defense, against the unwanted, foreign presence of the United States of America. Said Ojeda Rios:

You heard several members [of the FBI] tell you how much they feared for their lives when they heard shots. They, who came attacking, shooting, breaking down doors, shattering windows. . . . They, with all their experience as members of a unit that specializes in assault operations, say that they were afraid. And I, alone with my wife, listening to their screams and deafening blows, their shots, their battering and destruction . . . ,[they] in their war uniforms with their weapons and painted faces—I was not supposed to fear for my life. I was not supposed to do anything to defend my wife's life, or my own.

This is typical of oppressors. The oppressed are never supposed to think and act according to our own human nature, because for them, we are not human! And much less should we, according to their mentality . . . have the audacity to prevent their abuses, attacks, and assassinations.

In concluding, Ojeda Rios told the members of the jury that he placed absolute trust in them, their moral valor, and their sense of justice. He told them that their decision would define what it means for "the more than century-old struggle of us Puerto Ricans seeking our Puerto Rican identity. What matters, above all, is that you do justice for this Puerto Rican homeland. You can judge me. History will judge us all."

Just a few hours later, the jury unanimously found Ojeda Rios innocent of all charges, including even illegal possession of weapons. It was the first time in the history of federal prosecutions that a defendant successfully claimed self-defense after shooting at agents of the FBI.

The verdict has not changed the course of Puerto Rican history as much as ratified it. It was one thing for Ojeda Rios, a radical *independentista* advocate with a deep admiration for the Cuban Revolution, to preach the doctrine of armed resistance to the United States. But how could twelve citizens of Puerto Rico, drawn at random, the beneficiaries of a U.S. cultural, political, and economic presence, agree with him?

In this eminently readable work of history, Ronald Fernandez provides detailed and complex answers to this question. Fernandez meticulously documents the evolution of American colonialism in Puerto Rico, mercilessly exposing the lies, cynicism, economic pretensions, racism, and denial of democratic rights that have so often characterized American domination over Puerto Rico. From the conquest of Puerto Rico as a spoil of war in 1898, through the current continued suppression of its independence movement, the actual wishes of the Puerto Rican people remain irrelevant to American planners.

Whenever Puerto Rican wishes have threatened to become an obstacle to American political or economic interests, the FBI has gone to work with ruthless and sometimes murderous efficiency. The FBI's infamous COINTELPRO operation, designed to disrupt, misdirect, and neutralize legitimate opposition groups, targeted all of Puerto Rico's independence leaders and advocates.

One of Fernandez's most original and fascinating contributions is his uncovering of a previously-secret Carter administration review of the FBI's operations in Puerto Rico. The review confirmed what independence activists and civil libertarians had known for decades—that the FBI had conducted extensive and prolonged "dirty tricks" operations against legal, nonviolent political groups in Puerto Rico. The Carter review concluded that "the entire record leaves the United States highly vulnerable to an attack by both independence parties. . . . The U.S. has repeatedly and pridefully declared its policy on political status to be that of self-determination. Yet here is a record of a decade of hanky-panky. . . . What is not acceptable is a campaign of disruption of what functioned as a legally constituted party." The results of the review were immediately suppressed and the Carter administration, like its predecessors and successors, again made the requisite annual trip to the United Nations to "pridefully declare" that the Puerto Rican people had freely chosen their status in a democratic manner.

There are no American heroes in this book, nor is there a happy ending. Yet it is imperative for Americans to know our own contribution to the perpetuation of colonialism, particulary as some prepare to celebrate Columbus Day 1992. When the sun rises on October 12, 1992, marking 500 years of colonialism, Americans would do well to take a look at Puerto Rico and the destruction wrought there in the name of "democracy." The island today has a per-capita income of one-half that of Mississippi, the poorest state in the United States. Its rates of suicide, mental illness, drug addiction, crime, alcoholism, and sterilization of women are among the highest in the world.

The land, water, and air are polluted by multinational corporations to which U.S. environmental and labor laws frequently do not apply. U.S. military bases occupy 13 percent of Puerto Rico's land, including the beautiful island of Vieques, used by the Air Force as a practice bombing range. The people of Puerto Rico are governed less democratically now than they were a century ago under the crumbling Spanish empire. Tragically, eighteen Puerto Rican political prisoners and prisoners of war are incarcerated in U.S. prisons, for long terms and under barbarous conditions, for fighting for the freedom of their homeland.

As lawyers, we have been both proud and privileged to have represented some of these defendants in politically motivated criminal trials. We have witnessed, at first hand, their anguish over the colonization of their native land and their determination to see their country become what it ought to be—a free and independent nation. To attain this goal, they—like the rebellious American colonists in 1776—have been willing to risk "[their] lives, [their] fortunes, and [their] sacred honor." Mr. Fernandez's book superbly documents the background of their struggle and provides an indispensable tool for understanding the justness of their cause. We hope that it gains the widest currency possible.

William M. Kunstler
Ronald L. Kuby

Acknowledgments

My greatest debt at Central Connecticut State University is to June Wel-
wood, Steven Cauffman, and Kiyomi Kutsuzawa. They managed to
graciously and efficiently provide more than one hundred requests for
books and articles via interlibrary loan. Thank you.

I was also lucky enough to work with the staff and resources of the
Connecticut State Library. This is a great facility, run by a group of
exceedingly capable and always friendly librarians. My thanks to Julie
Schwartz, Al Palko, Nancy Peluso, Steve Kwasnik, Joy Floyd, Susan
Harris, and Doreen Di Bonis.

The U.S. system of Presidential Libraries is a remarkable resource for
scholars. My thanks and gratitude to Dennis Bilger at the Truman Library, to Regina Greenwell at the Johnson Facility, to Leesa Tobin at the
Ford Library, and to Martin Elzy at the Carter Facility. My thanks too,
to the staffs at the Kennedy and Roosevelt Libraries. It was a privilege
to work at these institutions, with such a dedicated group of archivists.

Cesar Carmona first got me interested in Puerto Rico. He helped
change our family's life—and we all thank him.

At Central Connecticut University Karen Bayard, Richard Pattenaude,
George Clark, and Burt Baldwin all provided essential and continual
assistance. Thanks.

Brenda Harrison was my partner at a number of the Presidential Libraries. More important, without her love, patience, understanding,
intelligence, and support this book would not exist.

The Disenchanted Island is dedicated to Luis Nieves Falcon—with all the affection and respect I can muster. He is a wonderful person and a great Puerto Rican.

I wish I had somebody to blame for any mistakes the volume contains, but, unfortunately, I alone am responsible for any errors or weaknesses.

Chapter 1

Puerto Rico:
Prostrate and Paralyzed

While we are conducting war and until its conclusion, we must keep all we can get. When the war is over we must keep what we want.

William McKinley

Senator Edmund Pettus (D., Alabama) was astonished.[1] Did his Republican colleagues really mean to make the Puerto Ricans reimburse us for hurricane relief? And, adding insult to injury, was the U.S. Senate actually going to make islanders pay interest on the costs of the food and other supplies we had rushed to the island after a storm's fury flattened it in August 1899?

Reject the Republican bill, pleaded Senator Pettus, because the reimbursement provision "puts the United States in the unseemly attitude of generously relieving the sufferings of some of its citizens . . . and then taxing those people to get back a generous donation. That is a thing which this government never did before and I hope Senators will not allow such a thing to be done. It is illegal and hardly decent."[2]

Rising to meet the Democratic challenge on March 8, 1900, was Senator Joseph Foraker (R., Ohio), chair of the just-created Senate Committee on Pacific Islands and Puerto Rico. Foraker agreed that "our armies have been marching over their soil and have interrupted their business and vocations and pursuits; and, as a result of it all they are in a distressed condition." Indeed, "ever since we took possession in October of 1898," the island has been "absolutely paralyzed and prostrate." What the hurricane did was to greatly exacerbate an already terrible situation, which meant that Congress owned a possession in which "direct taxation was impossible."[3]

Foraker's idea was to achieve reimbursement by tapping into the new wealth our involvement would inevitably generate. The soon-to-be-created colonial government would simply issue bonds, payable when funds appeared; and this was just because critics like Senator Pettus completely neglected Puerto Rico's unique and peculiar political status. Different moral rules applied in the Caribbean because this was the first time in U.S. history that Congress had tried to legislate for a territory that, while a permanent possession of the United States, was never intended to be a state. In Foraker's words, "Puerto Rico belongs to the United States, but it is not the United States, nor a part of the United States."[4]

Under Spain, Puerto Rico was a province, with representation in both houses of the Spanish legislature. Under the United States, Puerto Rico was a national nobody, an "unincorporated territory" to which the Constitution did not apply.[5] Thus, not only an "unseemly" measure like the reimbursement bonds but a variety of other un-American political practices were also legitimate when applied to Puerto Rico and its people.

Explaining U.S. behavior in Puerto Rico, legislators often used terms like "destiny," "duty," "inevitability," and "grace." The United States would resurrect Puerto Rico, like Lazurus, creating, in Senator Foraker's words, "a new era . . . a new life . . . and prosperity far exceeding any hopes that have been excited or any anticipations that have been entertained."[6]

What actually happened was less graceful and never inevitable. In fact, from the day William McKinley decided to annex permanently what his soldiers had so easily conquered, Puerto Rico was stranded in a sea of ambiguity, racism, good intentions, whimsy, audacity, contradiction, indifference, and political compromise.

People—not destiny—made policy in Puerto Rico. And people were responsible for what happened on and after July 25, 1898.

Using iced coffee to ward off both sleep and the heat wave in Washington, D.C., Jules Cambon worried about the future of Africa. As French ambassador to the United States, Cambon had a sworn responsibility to protect real and possible threats to French power and influence. His problem was that as of July 5, 1898, the Spanish had already lost the Philippines and Cuba. What, Cambon asked himself, if the war lingered on for another two or three months? Would McKinley, egged on by his "bellicose" constituents, demand that Spain cede control of the Canary Islands?

Cambon believed that Americans in Africa might threaten the French colonies in Algeria and Senegal, so he offered his services to the Spanish government. If the war could be stopped at once, he and France would gain ample prestige for their efforts, while France, passing Spanish colonies to the Americans, would more easily keep control of her own. As Cambon's biographer noted, the ambassador had accepted a mission "unique in the history of French diplomacy."[7]

On July 22, 1898, Spain decided to press for peace. Cambon eagerly tried to deliver the Spanish feeler the moment he received it, but he was unable to do so. Somehow no one had given Cambon the code key to the Spanish message! That essential item was in the hands of the Austrian ambassador, who could not be reached for four days. So while Cambon impatiently sweltered in Washington, U.S. soldiers invaded Puerto Rico.[8]

On July 25, troops commanded by General Nelson Miles landed at Guanica, placing a military stamp on what was formerly a diplomatic matter. In fact, within three days of the invasion, Miles already controlled the city of Ponce. Knowing a Spanish surrender was only a matter of time, Miles happily made this pledge to the Puerto Rican people: "We have not come to make war upon the people of a country that for centuries has been oppressed but on the contrary to bring you protection . . . to promote your prosperity, and to bestow upon you the immunities and blessings of the liberal institutions of our government."[9]

The following day McKinley dictated these terms to Jules Cambon.[10] Spain had to relinquish sovereignty over Cuba, and as a territorial indemnity for the human and financial costs of the war, Spain had to cede Puerto Rico. Cambon protested, acting under orders from the Spanish. In a meeting on July 31, he argued that the "demand" to keep Puerto Rico as an indemnity was actually an attempt to hide "a conquest by arms." McKinley, said Cambon, was caught in a contradiction. How did the president reconcile the taking of Puerto Rico with his public posture that the United States had no territorial ambitions in the Spanish-American War?[11]

Cambon said that McKinley never answered his questions. Instead, the president simply repeated his demands, noting that had Spain requested the peace after George Dewey took the Philippines in May, the United States might have settled for less. Now Puerto Rico was a war prize the Americans meant to keep.

Cambon advised the Spanish to accept McKinley's terms: "If you did not resign yourselves to sacrifices like Puerto Rico, McKinley might demand even more onerous conditions." So, with Spain's approval, Cambon settled the essential terms of the peace on August 4. In a two and one-half hour meeting with McKinley, he drafted the key elements of what would later be the Treaty of Paris.[12]

To conduct their negotiations the two men used a translator. In French and English they dictated terms for the Spanish. No Puerto Ricans were

ever part of the negotiating process, and neither the president, nor
Cambon, nor the Spanish took note of the 1897 constitution in which
Spain established self-government in Puerto Rico. That constitution specifically mandated that no changes in island government could occur
"without the consent of the Puerto Rican legislature."[13]

On the island local politicians quickly grasped that "through the fate
of war"[14] and the force of arms, their constitution was now irrelevant.
But despite a declaration of martial law, the general reaction to the U.S.
invasion was still quite positive. For decades the "colossus of the North"
had been an admired political and economic ideal; or, as *La Democracia*
told its readers, "from a people who are descendants of Washington,
no one should expect a sad surprise . . . we trust, with full confidence
in the great Republic and the men who govern her."[15]

To islanders General Miles's pledge meant that U.S. actions were
married to U.S. ideals; thus, despite losing one constitution, island politicians expected to write an even better one as soon as the military
government was quickly abolished. Meanwhile, Puerto Ricans began to
add three new letters to the addresses they put on correspondence:
Puerto Rico, U.S.A.[16]

In Washington, McKinley and Cambon quickly ironed out the final
details of their White House negotiations; in a short, late afternoon
ceremony on August 12—with Cambon wearing a top hat, frock coat,
and patent leather shoes—the U.S. president and the French ambassador put an end to the Spanish-American War. McKinley formally ordered a cessation of hostilities as he signed a protocol stipulating, among
other things, that Spain would cede Puerto Rico to the United States
and order her troops to evacuate the island and its environs immediately.[17]

Puerto Rico now belonged to the United States. The unexpected political issue was what to do with her. Many democrats said it was bla-
tantly unconstitutional for the United States to have a colony.
Republicans were more open to the idea of imperial possessions, but
even they had no predetermined plan to resolve questions like citizenship, tariffs, and education.[18] While Americans argued what to do with
their new possession/colony/territory, Puerto Ricans lived under a military system that undermined one way of life, albeit tenuous, without
replacing it with another. For almost two years Puerto Ricans would be
ruled by policies that often substituted whimsy for intelligence, expediency for political and economic development.[19]

On August 19, 1898, President McKinley formally established tariffs
on Puerto Rican commercial goods. The stated purpose of this policy
was to obtain the funds needed to administer the military government,
but its actual result was to make a significant contribution to the devastation of Puerto Rican agriculture. In 1898 that enterprise depended,

in descending order, on two principal crops: coffee, 65.8 percent of foreign trade in 1897; and sugar, 21.6 percent of foreign trade in 1897.[20]

In Europe many coffee connoisseurs thought that Puerto Rico's brew was the best in the world. Aromatic and strong, yet somehow sweet, Puerto Rican beans were a favorite in France, Germany, and Spain. Ironically, the island's industry had received its principal stimulus when, in the mid-1870s, the United States opened its doors to tariff-free imports from Brazil. That country shifted its emphasis from Europe to the United States, which preferred the weaker Brazilian beans, and Puerto Ricans happily and profitably filled the hole left by the Brazilians.[21]

What McKinley neglected to consider was what the Puerto Ricans would do with their principal crop if the Spanish and the Cubans (also favoring the Puerto Rican brew) did the same thing as the Americans. While a Spanish colony Puerto Rico had enjoyed preferential treatment in Cuban and Spanish markets; as a U.S. possession, however, Puerto Ricans suddenly discovered that their new and old masters had independently united to create a situation in which, because of postwar Spanish and Cuban taxes Puerto Rican coffee was no longer competitive in Europe and the Caribbean; and due to McKinley's August 19 decision, it was also unable to compete with the Brazilian coffee that dominated the U.S. marketplace. Within eighteen months coffee would represent no more than 6 percent of Puerto Rico's foreign trade.[22]

Sugar also had problems because of the tariff—and because of organized opposition on the mainland. The last thing Louisiana producers wanted was free trade with an island full of fertile land and cheap labor. Echoing McKinley, mainland sugar producers lobbied for a continuation of the tariffs that limited productive possibilities. As many potential investors saw it, why risk substantial sums of money until they first created the free markets that would yield large profits in sugar?[23]

Because Puerto Ricans had so much trouble selling the crops that sustained their economy, many farmers suddenly found themselves on the verge of bankruptcy, while all Puerto Ricans tried to deal with the substantial increase in the cost of living. Even before the war the United States was Puerto Rico's second largest trading partner;[24] now the island was a captive audience for products that were subject to tariffs that had not existed previously. The price of basic foodstuffs like rice, wheat, and lard escalated as Puerto Ricans tried to pay for their necessities with currency that was halved in value within weeks of McKinley's decision to impose tariffs.

Before the U.S. invasion, islanders used silver pesos, valued at seventy-five cents to the dollar when they traded on international money markets. However, one American traveling with the U.S. Army argued that given their extremely high silver content, the actual value of the peso was eighty-five cents to the dollar.[25] In reality, no one had a scientific calculation of the peso's exact value when, shortly after the invasion succeeded, General Miles decided to base the exchange rate, not on the peso's value in silver, but "on the assumption that a peso was worth in bullion value less than half of one dollar, backed by a gold reserve in our Treasury."[26]

To General Miles this was an easy solution to the currency problem. To Puerto Ricans it represented an arbitrary, immediate, and substantial reduction in their net worth. Equally important, Miles's "short cut" had a ripple effect for virtually every man, woman, and child on the island. Salaries, for example, were cut to mesh with Miles's rate of exchange while greedy island merchants, many of them Spanish citizens, kept the same price structure in dollars and in pesos. Rice, four centavos a pound before the war, sold at four cents a pound after the Miles decree. The result for the *campesino* was an immediate 40 percent rise in *the* dietary staple of island life.[27]

When McKinley finally made the dollar the island's only legal currency, in January 1899, he set the rate of exchange at sixty cents to the peso. This was an improvement, but as William Dinwiddie charged in an 1899 study of the island, the U.S. Treasury still robbed the Puerto Rican people. Allowing 386 grains of silver for the peso and 412.5 for the U.S. dollar, Dinwiddie calculated a difference of 8 percent. Accordingly,

what argument can be advanced to defend our government against the severest criticism for having, through military power, set an arbitrary rate of exchange, whereby every peso collected at fifty cents [and later sixty cents] by our Treasury may be reminted, after the addition of five cents worth of silver, into one of our own silver dollars?[28]

No one ever answered Dinwiddie's question. But something had to be done about the abysmal condition of the Puerto Rican economy. Between the tariff and the exchange rate islanders had no way to pay for essential goods and services, not to mention find the resources needed to plant new crops. The new year saw banks threatening to foreclose on properties all over the island when the military suddenly ordered, again in January 1899, a suspension on all foreclosures.

Soldiers hoped that their well-intended gesture would protect small and large landowners from losing their most valuable possession. What they failed to see was that the foreclosure decree choked off the principal basis of agricultural credit. Without collateral, that is, land, farmers had no way to raise the money needed for the next crop. Freezing the land equaled freezing the economy. As a result, in a move that created great and lasting resentment, many islanders sold portions of their property to raise the funds needed to maintain a viable operation.[29]

Not surprisingly, the principal people with money were Americans in search of "opportunities in the colonies."[30] John Luce, for example, was a Boston financier representing the firm of Kidder and Peabody who in August 1898 managed to open an island bank that was immediately appointed fiscal representative for the occupying forces. All tariff funds were deposited in the Luce bank, which was also authorized to exchange dollars for pesos. Luce prospered to the extent that in early 1899 he and his colleagues bought a sugar estate of nearly 2,000 acres. Called Central Aguirre, it became a dominant force in an economy that would, if Luce and his colleagues had their way, engage in free and profitable trade with the United States. Luce assured Congress, "We feel very strongly that with American capital coming to the island the entire tone and the prosperity of the island would be very much increased."[31]

If there were free trade, this would be so; but free trade would never even be an issue if Congress failed to ratify the Treaty of Paris. On February 6, 1899, the Democrats had actually introduced a resolution "that under the Constitution of the United States no power is given to the Federal Government to acquire territory to be governed permanently as colonies."[32]

With McKinley in deep political trouble and John Luce and the Puerto Rican people on hold, Congress debated the political legitimacy of owning a colony the United States had already brought to the brink of economic ruin. As Secretary of War Elihu Root told Congress, "The principal difficulty now in the island of Porto Rico is that the transfer of the island from Spain to the United States has not resulted in an increase in prosperity, but in the reverse."[33]

In the Senate debates Horace Chilton of Texas wanted to amend the treaty. Colonies in the Pacific were certain to lead to war with Russia, Germany, England, or France; but closer to home, Chilton not only had no problems with colonies, he cited the "moral" authority of the Monroe Doctrine: "We will say to the powers of the Old World . . . [that] we will take Porto Rico and we reserve the right to take Haiti or Brazil or Cuba or any other part of North or South America when we think it proper to do so."[34]

Chilton knew that "few Senators objected to taking a cession of Porto Rico, which lies in the Western Hemisphere." The issue threatening to sink the treaty was the acquisition of the Philippines. From a fear of war, to a fear of cheap labor imports, to a fear of foreign "races," many senators had grave reservations about the wisdom of McKinley's Pacific policies.

On principle the president had no chance of success; senators would not be budged. McKinley therefore used offers of patronage and pledges of good committee assignments. On Senator Henry Heitfield of Idaho

McKinley's forces tried a bribe, but the young senator refused. Luckily for McKinley, he confined his criticism and indignation to the cloak-rooms, where, in Senator Henry Cabot Lodge's words, "we were down in the engine room and do not get flowers but we did make the ship move."[35]

Actually Lodge took more credit than he deserved. On February 6, 1899, McKinley's forces were still laboring in literally smoke-filled back-rooms when word of another war came over the telegraph. On Luzon Philippine nationalists had engaged U.S. troops; the Americans had suffered heavy casualties and the president counted his lucky stars. He told the colonel who brought him word of the battle, "How foolish these people [the Filipinos] are. This means the ratification of the treaty; the people will insist on its ratification."[36]

"Insist" was a strong word to use in this context. What actually hap-pened was that instead of a thirst for retaliation, the new war helped produce one more vote than the president needed.[37] The treaty squeaked through to ratification, the United States owned colonies for the first time in its history, and the Puerto Ricans saw their political and economic future linked not only to that of the United States but to the Filipinos who would so often influence U.S. policy making in the Caribbean.

McKinley signed the treaty four days after he received it from the Senate. In Spain the queen regent seemed to hesitate, but six weeks after the president she too put her signature on a treaty that was formally ratified in Washington on April 11, 1899. Standing erect in a White House reception room filled with every U.S. official space permitted, French ambassador Cambon and his secretary once again acted as substitutes for the never-to-be-present Spanish. The diplomats bowed, Cambon presented his credentials, the protocol to the treaty—in French—was signed, and, as a final gesture, McKinley and Cambon exchanged a "handsomely engrossed" morocco leather portfolio for a "handsomely engrossed" morocco leather box. Each container held a copy of the treaty, which finally ended the Spanish-American War.[38]

Cambon made one last appearance. On May 1, 1899, the French am-bassador went to the State Department to pick up $20 million in bank drafts as payment for the Philippines. As Whitelaw Reid, one of the U.S. treaty negotiators, explained, "Were the representatives of the United States, charged with the duty of protecting not only its honor, but its interests . . . to content themselves with little Puerto Rico?" Never! The United States demanded that Spain cede the Philippines, but in a face-saving gesture to the vanquished, the United States paid the Span-ish $20 million for their property.[39]

In Washington no one seemed to worry about face-saving gestures for the Puerto Ricans. On the contrary, though not a mean man,

McKinley presided over ceremonies that openly humiliated the Puerto Ricans and completely disregarded the opinions of a culture whose core values included a deep concern for *dignidad* and *respeto* (consideration and respect).[40]

To McKinley and to most Americans the Puerto Ricans were invisible; not contemptible, just invisible. When, in 1898, General Miles decided to make islanders spell the name of their country "Porto Rico," no one cared that the word *porto* did not exist in the Spanish language. And when, in 1899, McKinley extended U.S. navigation laws to Puerto Rico, islanders were not consulted about one of the most far-reaching and contradictory of McKinley's Puerto Rican policies.

To the president and his representatives in Congress Article IX of the Treaty of Paris—"The civil rights and political status of the native inhabitants of the territories hereby ceded to the United States shall be determined by Congress"[41]—gave them the legal right to legislate as they pleased. If Americans did see fit to consult Puerto Ricans, that was a sure sign of U.S. benevolence and generosity; but consultation was always a U.S. gift, never a Puerto Rican right.

Since the founding of the federal government the United States had always barred foreign ships from participating in the U.S. coastal trade. And every time the United States added new territories to its domain, the coastal laws were also applied. This happened in California, in Alaska, and even in Hawaii. The meaning of these laws was obviously strained when applied to Hawaii, but that *incorporated* territory had an open and accepted claim to statehood. It made sense, therefore, to argue that it was part of, or at least would be part of, the United States of America.[42]

Puerto Rico was different. Indeed, as Senator Foraker told Congress, "We understand that the effect of the treaty was to put the United States into possession of Puerto Rico. We do not understand it was intended or expected to make them a State, or to do that which entitled them to be called even a Territory. We understand . . . that we have a right to legislate with respect to them as we may see fit."[43]

Possession in this case was 100 percent of the law. Puerto Rico was not a part of the United States, nor was it ever likely to be anything other than an unincorporated territory. However, despite this status, Puerto Rico was a part of the United States when it came to supporting and sustaining the U.S. merchant marine and U.S. shipbuilders.

Before the Spanish-American War only 16 percent of Puerto Rico's exports and 22 percent of her imports were carried on U.S. ships. Although 80 percent of the island's imports were coming from the United States at the time,[44] U.S. vessels were little used to carry goods because they cost substantially more money to use. Once the United States included Puerto Rico (though not the Philippines) under its shipping laws,

however, Puerto Rico became a prisoner, not only of substantially increased costs for its literal lifeline but for U.S. products. Within a decade
virtually all the island's trade was with the United States. "Foreigners"
stopped coming because of the high tariffs and because of the restrictive
shipping laws.

In Congress Representative Thomas McRae of Arkansas accused
McKinley of perpetrating "an outrage upon these people."[45] McRae
thought the islanders had been treated in an un-American fashion, and
to the indignation of many McKinley supporters, so did many Puerto
Ricans. After all, the shipping laws were imposed on an economy already
in desperate straits. So, in a country still ruled by soldiers, Puerto Ricans
resorted to peaceful yet not so subtle reminders of their dissatisfaction
with U.S. authorities.

On July 4, 1899, *La Democracia* reprinted the U.S. Constitution, calling
it "a manifesto that is one of the most glorious pages of her institutions."
Read the Constitution, the editorial suggested, because "a people constituted on a basis so free and democratic cannot bring forth tyrants.
That is the reason why we trust in the justice that will be given soon to
us: the offsprings of these who signed that Declaration of Independence
can't do less than give liberty to our people."[46]

The president said no. Reports commissioned by the War Department
indicated that the Puerto Ricans had achieved nothing more than a
rudimentary stage of political development. As Secretary of War Root
suggested, "They would inevitably fail without a course of tuition under
a strong and guiding hand." Despite his good intentions, therefore,
Senator Foraker's plans for Puerto Rican participation in the colony's
government should be rejected. Let them first undergo a period of "probation," Root continued, and when and if they prove themselves, give
them small doses of democracy, one pill at a time.[47]

Senator Foraker protested. Acting on McKinley's behalf, he was about
to present legislation to Congress. Although he agreed that Puerto Ricans had "very crude ideas" about democracy, he believed, "a people
full of kindliness of disposition toward the United States" deserved some
symbol of democratic government. After all, U.S. representatives would
initiate and control all significant legislation that came from Puerto Rico;
why, then, not permit the "docile" islanders to have an elected Lower
House that would provide the tutelage required to turn them into good
and loyal Americans?[48]

The president hesitated. Not only Secretary Root but several other
cabinet members advised him to eliminate the idea of an elected House,
even one without power. Foraker, however, persisted, engaging in "a
number of conferences with the President." As a result, McKinley finally
agreed to allow the Puerto Ricans to elect a legislature. Years later Foraker
would boast that with this argument settled, the stage had at last been

set for Congress to consider what Theodore Roosevelt called "one of the best bits of legislation ever put upon our statute books."[49]

The debates were fascinating, especially because they revolved around, not the rights and powers of Puerto Ricans, but the rights and powers of Americans. In the Senate and in the House, U.S. legislators argued among themselves about themselves. Puerto Ricans assumed such a virtually invisible or irrelevant status that even when a contingent of island lobbyists came to plead for free trade, no native Puerto Ricans were represented. Americans, Spanish, and English dominated the files of those eager for the free trade supposedly so essential to the islanders' well-being.[50]

How did Congress manage to legislate for Puerto Rico without making the wishes and aspirations of the islanders a central aspect of the congressional debate? And why, when the Puerto Ricans sent an urgent plea to the Senate in the middle of its debates, was the plea utterly disregarded?

The elected (under Spanish rule) representatives of the Puerto Rican people expressly told Congress "that the acceptance of the fostering arm of the United States by the Puerto Ricans was based on the faith in the pledge and word of honor of an American General representing the highest government authority." Because to date Congress had not kept its word, the Puerto Ricans requested that the island "be instantly declared a part and parcel of the mother country by adoption, an integral Territorial district and not a mere tributary; her citizens in reality citizens of the United States and not subjects of an arbitrary and imperialistic power."[51]

For a people with no experience in democratic practices, the Puerto Rican legislators nevertheless manifested an admirable ability to "talk turkey" with the Americans. How could the Senate print the long, detailed, and cogent statement from the islanders and then, without comment, immediately turn to the next order of business, "the construction of a driveway and approaches to the national cemetery at Salisbury, North Carolina"?[52]

Three factors explain Congress's indifference to Puerto Rico and its people. First came the Philippines. In a heated exchange with Senator Foraker on April 2, 1900, Senator William Bate of Tennessee explained that "Porto Rico could be readily settled, easily disposed of, but for that which is to come after it. The embarrassing question is as to the character of government which we are to have in the Philippines and how it will effect certain interests. We are upon that line of battle today, under cover."[53]

In his memoirs Foraker admitted the truth of Bate's allegations: The Puerto Rican legislation was the precedent that would "enable us to legislate intelligently for the Philippines, which was, from the beginning, regarded as a far more serious and difficult problem than that presented by Porto Rico."[54]

Puerto Rico was a stand-in, a proxy that would allow Congress to establish the plenary power required to deny citizenship to the Filipinos, regulate their trade, and deny them entry to the United States if Congress chose to do so.[55] For example, in his original bill, Senator Foraker offered a form of citizenship to the Puerto Ricans. Because "we did not want to treat our own as aliens, and we did not want to have subjects, we adopted the term 'citizens.' " However, Foraker placed the status in quotes because in using the word "citizens," he explained, "we did not understand . . . that we were giving to these people any rights that the American people did not want them to have."[56]

To Foraker that kind of thinking solved the problem. But to his colleagues, especially those in the House, a grant of citizenship, however peculiarly it was defined, implied a pledge of statehood. Citizens belonged to a country, which made them a part of it, which meant that their territory was an incorporated entity of the United States.

Even without the Philippines in the background, whether the Puerto Ricans would "ever reach a condition where it shall be for their interests, or certainly for ours, to let them become one of the members of this Union was very doubtful."[57] But with issues confronting the Philippine people waiting in the wings (e.g., how could you tax Philippine imports if Filipinos were U.S. citizens?), the Puerto Ricans got another original status: In the revised Foraker legislation they were "Citizens of Puerto Rico," a nebulous classification that, like a piece of dough, could be twisted into whatever form Congress deemed appropriate.[58]

Race was the second factor that allowed Congress to treat the Puerto Ricans as an invisible force in the debates shaping the island's future. In 1900 no one knew how many races there were; one writer said three, another eight, and a third, who got carried away, argued for the existence of one hundred races. Still, despite disagreements about numbers and characteristics (e.g., skin color, size of brain, size of body), a widespread consensus existed that a god-given hierarchy of races numbered peoples in descending order.[59]

In U.S. eyes the first problem Puerto Ricans faced was their Spanish blood. In the United States this heritage is called the Black Legend and is the basis of prejudice focused, not on color of skin, but on cruelty of behavior. Lecturing his colleagues on April 2, 1900, Senator Chauncey Depew of Oregon stressed that

the government by Spain was oppressive. . . . The taxes were enormous, no roads were built, no schoolhouses erected, no public improvements maintained, but these great revenues were dissipated by the Spanish officials. . . . Arbitrary arrests were made and citizens lay in dungeons for years because there was no way by which they could get a trial.[60]

Depew's charges hit the mark: The Spanish overlords had often behaved in a cruel manner. The problem for the Puerto Ricans was that even when Congress made accurate charges, they had a negative impact on senators' perceptions of the islanders' rights and potentials. The Black Legend essentially symbolized the bag of undesirable characteristics that were Spain's terrible legacy to the New World. As early as 1816 Virginia congressman John Randolph announced that "you cannot make liberty out of Spanish matter."[61]

Randolph's successors agreed. And instead of arguing that a people subjected to tyranny deserved the chance to shape their own society, senators stressed that Puerto Ricans were an inferior offspring of an already middle-level race. Senator John Spooner of Wisconsin noted, "There is something pathetic about the island. Under the tyranny of Spain I believe they never rebelled." And to George Perkins of California, Puerto Rican civilization "was impressed upon [Puerto Ricans] by a nation in which the principles of freedom and self government have hardly even yet taken root. . . . Generation after generation must first be educated in the school of civil and religious liberty before they can fully appreciate the benefits they may enjoy under a republican form of government."[62]

If Spanish blood was one central reason the Puerto Ricans would take so long to educate, another was the color of their skin. "More than one third of the entire population was of the negro or mixed race; the balance was mostly of Spanish origin. . . . There were, of course, a small percentage of other nationalities but they are principally of Spanish descent, negroes, mulattoes, and what we in the United States call colored people."[63]

For Congress it took only two strikes to declare the Puerto Ricans unfit for democracy. In many cartoons of the period the Latino was presented as a "black child," whose low position on the racial hierarchy was underlined by introducing apelike features. In one especially obvious caricature Uncle Sam is holding the hand of a dumbstruck Puerto Rican child watching Cuba—portrayed as a black person holding a dagger and revolver—walk away. Uncle Sam says to Puerto Rico: "And to think that bad boy came near being your brother."[64]

Puerto Ricans had a chance. With a majority of their population boasting white blood, they might eventually climb over the barriers erected by their Spanish and Negro heritage. But as Senator Perkins stressed, it would take generations for islanders to escape and perhaps overcome their lowly past. Meanwhile, like all good children, the Puerto Ricans should speak only when they are first spoken to. Otherwise, instead of being pathetic for their docility, they would be "Cubans" because of their willingness to question their benevolent Uncle Sam. As General Guy Henry put it to the *New York Herald* when he closed a number of the island's newspapers, "Publication of articles criticizing those in authority and reflecting upon the government or its officers will not be allowed."[65]

The final factor that allowed Congress to disregard the Puerto Ricans was a taken-for-granted assumption. That assumption was the notion that "what America touches, she makes holy."[66] As Senator Perkins put it when he told the Puerto Ricans that it would have taken them generations to become Americans:

> Heaven is not reached at a single bound;
> But we build the ladder by which we rise
> From the lowly earth to the vaulted skies
> And we mount to its summit round by round.[67]

Congress's self-assurance, or, from another perspective, its conceit, had deep roots in U.S. history. Puritan settlers built a blessed "city on a hill," and Tom Paine equated common sense with the nation's ability "to begin the world all over again." At no point did Americans achieve a consensus about which characteristics exemplified the extraordinary uniqueness of the United States; but these differences of opinion never undermined the taken-for-granted assumption that the United States was superior, special, eternally young, and at all times uncontaminated by the sordid morals that characterized the "old world."[68]

Congress's self-assurance also helps explain the ability of many senators to deny the obvious. For example, in their statement to Congress in February 1900, the Puerto Rican leaders noted that based on a reading of the U.S. Constitution, they "were petitioning the government for a redress of grievances"; indeed, "in order that the newly acquired territory shall be saved from utter ruin and desolation," the Puerto Ricans protested that no one offered an answer to their most important questions: "Have we been invited to come under the sheltering roof, only to starve at the doorstep?"[69]

And on the island itself the natives were quite restless. Even the newspaper that most openly allied itself with U.S. interests—*El País*—could note, on March 22, 1900, that the Foraker Act offered no way to resolve the "incomprehensible" situation of the Puerto Rican people. "In no place in the world is it known what we are."[70]

Senators not only never recognized the Puerto Ricans complaints, they turned them upside down. Senator Perkins noted that "no territory of the United States has ever been treated in so liberal a manner as this Government proposes to treat Porto Rico." When Senator Foraker summed up the administration's position on April 30, 1900, he repeated a theme that he first voiced in early March: "Never in the history of this Government has there been such unexampled generosity and liberality in legislating for the people of any territory."[71]

A cynic might argue that these statements were pure hyperbole, nothing more than politicians announcing a public rationale for what they privately knew to be a moral and constitutional double standard.

With mathematical certainty there is no way to prove the cynics wrong. But as the years go by, the historical record will manifest generations of U.S. administrators who *sincerely* complain of the Puerto Ricans' lack of gratitude. These complaints are genuine because they are rooted in an assumption—what the United States touches she makes holy—that generally makes it impossible for Americans to put themselves "in the other person's moccasins." From the very beginning of U.S. involvement in the island, the Puerto Ricans were invisible because they were considered children, ungrateful when they had the audacity to reject the helping hand of their extremely generous Uncle Sam.

Ironically, the most liberal territorial legislation in U.S. history would ultimately be decided by politics of the worst sort. McKinley, who started the debates by emphasizing principle, would eventually concede that personal ambition was more important than a promise he made to Congress in his December 1899 State of the Union address: "Our plain duty is to abolish all customs tariffs between the United States and Puerto Rico and give her products free access to our markets."[72]

The president then believed that free trade was the only decent course to follow because "Puerto Rico had lost her free intercourse with Spain and Cuba without any compensating benefits in this market."[73] McKinley correctly perceived the islanders' terrible dilemma; what he neglected to consider was the Philippines and his own political party.

Free trade meant that Puerto Ricans were being treated like Americans. How could Congress assert its authority to do with the colonies whatever it pleased if the president failed to discriminate between us and them?

Equally important, the president had neglected to consider the "protectionist fraternity" central to his party and his reelection. In Louisiana sugar beet growers complained about the president's even-handed approach, and in Connecticut tobacco growers had no intention of competing equally with Puerto Rican produce.

Submitted in early January 1900, the Foraker legislation was quickly in deep trouble. Indeed, independently of one another and for very different reasons, Democratic and Republican opponents of the president believed that focusing on the trade issue was the best way to assert a principle or promote a policy. Thus, as if a boomerang, extraordinarily extensive—and often eloquent—debates always returned to the same point of origin: trade used as a tool to assert the powers and wishes of the U.S. Congress.

Legislators in the House were the first to abandon ship. In early February a bill that would make islanders pay 25 percent of the prevailing tariff duties was introduced as an alternative to McKinley and Foraker's proposal. The 25 percent rate was a compromise that proved that Congress could discriminate between the mainland and its colonies, while it also kept the tariff low enough to open Puerto Rican markets to those of the United States and close them to the Philippines if that was Congress's ultimate desire.[74]

The House bill suddenly made McKinley the issue. Open and widespread revolt in the ranks meant the president could accept a defeat on principle or reverse course to accept a victory rooted in contradiction. The president chose contradiction—the *Nation* would call him "Mr. Facing-both-ways"—because there was need of "party harmony in a subject even more important than the Philippines." That subject was the president's reelection, put in jeopardy by a large number of angry and motivated constituents.

To mask his about-face the president first tried ambiguity. Two congressmen who saw him in mid-February said he was still for free trade but he would nevertheless support the bill imposing tariffs. Because this was contradiction rather than ambiguity, the president planted an article in the *New York World*. He publicly admitted his conversion to the tariff cause, knowing full well that opponents would charge that he had abandoned his moral principles to vote for his own reelection. In the words of the then undersecretary of the navy, Theodore Roosevelt, "McKinley had a spine like a piece of chocolate cake."[75]

But despite the criticism, the president could still have his cake and eat it too if he could get Congress to pass the new revision of his proposals. Put together in a late February party caucus, the new bill put a 15 percent duty on Puerto Rican products, and in a compromise between those pushing for protection and those pushing for free trade, the imposition of duties would last only two years. Again, the real fear was the Philippines; the Puerto Ricans were simply a precedent-setting appetizer.

Senator Foraker had the difficult job of explaining the president's flip-flop. He did it by focusing on "the poverty, bankruptcy, and ruin that prevailed everywhere." Even if a new policy of taxation was introduced to the island, "it would require at least a year, and probably two years, to inaugurate one and secure returns from it." Meanwhile, the island desperately needed funds to maintain itself; so "casting about to see if we could find an easier way to raise it," Congress settled on the 15 percent tariff as a way to tide the Puerto Ricans over until better times prevailed.[76]

Foraker's opponents, recognizing pure balderdash when they heard it, jumped on his rationalizations. Senator Henry Teller of Colorado pointed to a precedent set by the thirteen colonies. "It may be that if we collect the tax for and pay it over to them there will be no injury to them, and yet I recollect that the fathers of the Revolution declined to allow Great Britain to collect taxes from us and then turn them over to us." The Founding Fathers had said, "So long as you claim the right to tax us without representation you cannot condone that wrong by giving to us the proceeds of your robbery."[77]

Following Senator Teller, Augustus Bacon of Georgia never charged robbery, but he was bothered by what he thought was a clear contradiction in Foraker's reasoning. If the United States levied a duty on Puerto Rican goods in New York harbor and also a duty on Puerto Rican goods in San Juan, how could Foraker argue that the Constitution did not apply in our new possession?[78]

Foraker responded by talking about power. Congress had it and our new possessions did not. Therefore normal reasoning did not apply when Puerto Rico was the topic. Bacon, for example, simply failed to recognize that "the duty that is imposed is not an export duty, but a duty paid for the privilege of entering that port (San Juan), which is not under the Constitution, and for which Congress has plenary and absolute power to legislate as it may see fit."[79]

An able opponent, Foraker bobbed and weaved his way through endless weeks of debate. Ultimately the charge of taxation without representation would be resolved in this manner: The 15 percent tariff was a two-year imposition, required by the exigencies of Puerto Rico's desperate economic situation. But opponents had to remember that during and after the two years of tariff, Puerto Rico kept all the excise taxes imposed on imports and exports. The United States, instead of exercising its plenary powers and keeping the tax money for itself, allowed islanders to use funds that actually belonged to the U.S. Treasury. Thus, Congress had favored "the Porto Ricans with the most liberal and generous provisions that have ever been made for anybody by our Government."[80]

To Foraker the claim of generosity erased the allegation of robbery. The truth is that the Senate's debates raised issues that have never been resolved.

In levying duties on exports and imports the United States closely followed the practice of the Spanish. They also taxed the islanders, and they too returned virtually all the collected revenue to the island's treasury.[81] If the Spanish were tyrants, what were the Americans? And how could the United States legitimate a practice that the Founding Fathers had declared robbery when the British did it, much less continue the practice into the 1990s?

Equally important, under the Spanish, islanders were always represented in the mainland legislature. Under the United States, senators actually refused to allow Puerto Rico's representative to be called a delegate to Congress. Senator Spooner of Wisconsin stressed that the term *delegate* "has always been considered a pledge of statehood."[82] So, Puerto Rico's official was called a resident commissioner, a status that not only provided no vote in Congress but stipulated that the resident commissioner was not allowed on the floor of the House. If the commissioner wanted to conduct business, he or she was literally confined to the halls of Congress.[83]

The Senate's refusal even to hint at statehood also helped to explain the island's exemption from federal taxation. Proponents of the measure cited Congress's beneficence when the actual explanation rested on two points that had nothing to do with generosity: To forever tax the Puerto Ricans without representation was a pill too many senators refused to swallow, and to impose a federal income tax on the island was to extend the Constitution to the possessions and therefore set a bad precedent for the Philippines.

The Foraker Act explicitly recognized that the internal revenue laws did not apply because of the 15 percent temporary tariff;[84] thus Foraker had underlined the point that Congress had plenary power in the possessions. Theoretically, the United States could do as it pleased in Puerto Rico, and once the Philippine insurgents were defeated, in those islands as well.

The one stumbling block was Congress. Would Foraker have in the Senate the same problems he and the president had encountered in the House of Representatives?

In that chamber the battle lines had hardened McKinley's men postponed a scheduled vote on the Puerto Rican legislation. During the two-day intermission McKinley personally called a number of representatives to his office, asking them to sacrifice principle for party. Nehimiah Sperry of Connecticut, Robert Morris of Minnesota, George Prince of Illinois, and James Watson of Indiana all walked to the White House to hear this line of reasoning from McKinley. Representative Watson explained, "I voted for the bill at the earnest solicitation of President McKinley and the leaders of the Republican party, simply as an emergency measure. . . . I subordinated my own personal views as to the expediency of the passage of such a bill and voted for it in the interest of party harmony and to sustain the Administration."[85]

Even with this kind of pressure, the president and his men still fell short of enough support for House passage of the Puerto Rican bill. An estimated six additional votes were then garnered by dragging in senators lying in sickbeds, and in a rare move indeed, McKinley had carriages rush to local hospitals where, rolled onto stretchers, two representatives were carried to the House floor. They helped McKinley gain the victory he sought. The final vote in the House had McKinley ahead by a healthy margin, 172 to 161.[86]

In the Senate the president tried to avoid emergency measures by making the compromises already discussed: Citizenship for the Puerto Ricans was eliminated, the tariff would last only two years, and the president could issue a proclamation of free trade whenever he felt like it. Simultaneously McKinley again sounded the trumpet of party unity married to a Republican victory in November. In a satirical tribute to the Republicans, Senator William Allen of Nebraska noted that "whatever the head of that party thinks, it makes no difference who he may be, every man rolls his own will in subordination to the wishes of the chief."[87]

Not quite. Despite intense pressure to stand up and be counted, eight Republicans still voted with the Democrats; nevertheless, given that fully sixteen senators failed to show, the president won easily. The final vote, taken on April 3, 1900, was 40 to 31.

Whether then or now, overall assessments of the Foraker legislation are politically charged. In 1900 Republicans patted themselves on the back for their unparalleled generosity while Democratic critics like Joseph Simon of Oregon said the legislation violated "every principle of justice, good faith, and common honesty."[88]

In 1950 the then governor of Puerto Rico Luis Muñoz Marín told Congress that "at all times the attitude of the United States Government has been one of helpfulness toward Puerto Rico.... I would say that not only has the attitude of the Federal Government been helpful but that by all modern definitions of what constitutes colonialism, it has not been a colonial policy in Puerto Rico."[89]

Yet in 1977 an internal assessment done for the Carter administration underlined the "shocking contrast" between the Spanish and U.S. systems of island government: "Puerto Rico under a supposedly decadent monarchy had voting representation in *both* chambers of parliament in Madrid, whereas Puerto Rico under the world's greatest democracy had no voting representation in either Chamber of Congress" (emphasis in original).[90]

Happily, there exists a contemporary analysis of the Foraker legislation written by a political scientist who also served as a key member of the island's government. William Willoughby was treasurer of Puerto Rico from 1901 to 1907 and president of the Executive Council from 1907 to 1909. He published a number of articles about Puerto Rico in the journals of the time, and in 1905 Willoughby completed *Territories and Dependencies of the United States: Their Government and Administration*. Like Senator Foraker and his colleagues, Willoughby naturally had his biases (e.g., he was a member of the government he wrote about), but his analysis nevertheless remains the clearest and most comprehensive assessment of what Willoughby called the United States' "first essay in the field of the government of a dependency partaking of the essential character of a colony."[91]

Willoughby explained that the primary goal of the United States had been to assure an efficient administration that simultaneously provided the largest possible degree of self-government. To achieve these goals alone would have been easy; together they presented a "vastly more complicated and delicate" task. On the one hand, the Americans could easily have furnished the efficiency on their own, but that would have eliminated self-government. On the other hand, Foraker and his colleagues could have provided a "liberal form of government," but that would have left the Puerto Ricans "free to work out their own destinies with all of the dangers of misrule and inefficiency that the experience of other Latin-American countries" so obviously demonstrated.[92]

Because it wanted to furnish both efficiency and self-government, the Foraker Act contained this organization of the island's political institutions. Positioned at the top of the executive branch was a governor appointed by the president of the United States with the advice and consent of the Senate. The governor had a four-year term of office; he was commander-in-chief of the island's militia; his approval was required before any legislation became law; and in the unlikely event that two-thirds of both Houses overrode his veto, the governor could simply take his complaints to the ultimate authorities in Washington.

At all times the laws enacted had to be reported to Congress, which "retained full power, not only to modify such legislation, but to take such further action in relation to the government and administration of the island as it may see fit."[93]

Willoughby argued that the island's upper house, or Executive Council, was, first, the "center or keystone of the whole system"[94] and, second, a U.S. innovation "entitled to take front rank among the interesting political institutions of our country."[95]

What the Foraker Act did was to virtually eliminate a system of checks and balances. The chiefs of the administrative departments (e.g., the attorney general, the treasurer, the commissioner of education) were simultaneously appointed members of the Executive Council. This "union of executive and legislative powers in the same persons" assured competency because all these men were appointed by the president of the United States.

Willoughby also stressed that since the heads of the executive departments had "unusual degrees of authority," that alone "to a large extent took the whole control over the manner in which the actual administration of affairs shall be exercised out of the hands of the people of the island itself."[96] But as members of the Executive Council, the department heads also "sat throughout the year as a quasi-legislative or general supervisory body." This made the Executive Council the "dominant one of the two houses" in most legislative and personnel matters, with the result that the Foraker Act entrusted to these six Americans "the actual work of the administration of the affairs of the island." For example, the Executive Council also had the authority to "grant all franchises, privileges, and concessions of a public or quasi-public character."[97]

The thirty-five-member House of Delegates was the elected branch of the Puerto Rican government. Its members held two-year terms of office, but since a delegate could be elected in a district in which he or she did not reside, "the result of this freedom of residence" could be a centralization of power in the hands of the political parties. However, "in view of the political character of the people this concentration of power would have taken place to a considerable degree under any system."[98]

To the extent the House had any real power under the Foraker Act, that power was as much negative as positive. House members could initiate legislation, but if blocked by the Executive Council, the House's bills died at once. If, however, the House refused to approve an upper-chamber bill, then the Executive Council's legislation also died a quick death. In Willoughby's words, the ability of each chamber to cancel out the work of the other "eliminated the danger, on the one hand that a people inexperienced in self government and legislative methods might enact injurious legislation; and, on the other hand, that legislation strongly disapproved of by the Porto Rican people would not be forced upon them without their consent."[99]

Turning to the power of the purse, the Executive Council had not only the right to hire all departmental personnel but also the power to decide salaries and to pay those salaries "out of the revenues of Porto Rico as the executive council shall, from time to time determine." In Willoughby's judgment, only the Executive Council had the right to appropriate government funds. However, he conceded that since the power of the purse made it clear "how largely power was centered in the hands of the American appointees,"[100] the Puerto Ricans might have to be granted at least the appearance of budgetary power; otherwise, "the house of delegates might refuse to exercise its functions."[101]

The judicial system was also Americanized. Boston became the seat of the island's federal district court; with the advice and consent of the Senate, the justices and marshall of the island's Supreme Court were appointed by the president; and the justices of the district courts were appointed by Puerto Rico's governor, "with the advice and consent of the Executive Council."[102]

Assessing the overall merits of the Foraker Act, Willoughby argued that as objective observers, it was not "within our province" to criticize the wisdom of the Senate's legislation. However, he did answer one question that "naturally arose" when considering Puerto Rico's government. What did the islanders think? Were they satisfied with the U.S. system?

Willoughby wrote that "to this there can be but one answer: They are not."[103] In fact, during the first four years of U.S. administration, the majority Puerto Rican party would resign from the government; the streets of San Juan would often be filled with "Las Turbas Republicanas" (the Republican disturbances); and the leader of the majority party would be threatened with assassination. He chose temporary exile in New York instead of death.

No one factor explains the islanders' antagonism toward U.S. colonial authority. But a political science colleague of Willoughby's nevertheless suggested one good starting point for any analysis was the first twenty years of U.S. rule. The opening line of L. S. Rowe's *United States and Puerto Rico* is this: "To the people of the United States the West Indies are hardly more than a name."[104]

And an incorrect one at that. The United States of America ruled "Porto" Rico. The multilayered island[105] of foreigners, slaves, *criollos* (the native born), and Indians was an island the Americans never visited. As the wives of many colonial administrators later boasted, they had been on the island for years and, except for servants, "no Puerto Ricans had ever set foot in their homes."[106]

NOTES

1. Stanley Karnow, *In Our Image* (New York: Random House, 1989), p. 108.

2. *Congressional Record*, 56th Congress, 1st session, March 8, 1900, p. 2642.

3. Ibid., p. 2649; 2645; and on March 2, p. 2475.

4. Ibid., April 30, 1900, p. 4855.

5. Ibid., March 8, 1900, p. 2653.

6. Ibid., April 30, 1900, p. 4857.

7. See Genevieve Tabouis, *The Life of Jules Cambon* (London: Johnathan Cape, 1938), esp. pp. 100–102.

8. See Carmelo Rosario Natal, *Puerto Rico y la Guerra Hispanoamericana* (Río Piedras: Edil, 1989) p. 259; Walter Millis, *The Martial Spirit* (New York: The Literary Guild, 1931), p. 338.

9. See *Documents on the Constitutional History of Puerto Rico* (Washington, D.C.: Commonwealth of Puerto Rico, 1964), p. 55.

10. See Margaret Leech, *In the Days of McKinley* (New York: Harper & Brothers, 1959), p. 283.

11. Rosario Natal, *Puerto Rico*, p. 262.

12. Tabouis, *The Life of Jules Cambon*, p. 104; also Leech, *In the Days of McKinley*, pp. 286–289.

13. See Ricardo Alegría, *Temas de la Historia de Puerto Rico* (San Juan: Centro de Estudios Avanzados, 1988), p. 187.

14. See, *Congressional Record*, Senate, 56th Congress, 1st session, February 26, 1900, p. 2231.

15. See the doctoral dissertation of Luis Antonio Velez Aquino, *Puerto Rican Press Reaction to the Shift from Spanish to United States Sovereignty*, Columbia University, 1969, p. 32.

16. See, e.g., Fernando Pico, 1898: *La Guerra después de la Guerra* (Río Piedras: Huracán, 1987); also María Dolores Luque de Sánchez, *La Ocupación Norteamericana y la Ley Foraker* (Río Piedras: Editorial de la Universidad de Puerto Rico, 1986), p. 28.

17. Rosario Natal, *Puerto Rico*, p. 263.

18. For a summary of this debate see Thomas G. Patterson, ed., *American Imperialism and Anti-Imperialism* (New York: Crowell, 1973).

19. See Edward Berbusse, *The United States in Puerto Rico* (Chapel Hill: University of North Carolina Press, 1966); also, Pedro A. Caban, "El Aparato Colonial y el Cambio Económico en Puerto Rico, 1898–1917," *Revista de Ciencias Sociales* 27 (1988): pp. 53–88.

20. Laird Bergad, "Agrarian History of Puerto Rico, 1870–1930," *Latin American Research Review* 13, no. 3 (1978): p. 74.

21. Ibid., p. 68.

22. See *Hearings before the Committee on Pacific Islands and Puerto Rico*, Senate, 56th Congress, 1st session, 1900, p. 34.

23. See, e.g., Governor Charles H. Allen, *Opportunities in the Colonies and Cuba* (New York: Lewis, Scribner, 1902), pp. 290–291.

24. See "Our New Possessions and the Diplomatic Processes through Which They Were Obtained," *The Tribune*, New York, 1899, pp. 32–34.

25. See William Dinwiddie, "Puerto Rico and Its Possibilities (New York: Harper, 1899), p. 216; for the estimate of seventy-five cents to the dollar see Bergad, "Agrarian History of Puerto Rico," p. 75; see too Albert Gardner Robinson, *The Porto Rico of Today: Pen Pictures of the People and the Country* (New York: Charles Scribner's, 1899), esp. pp. 163–179.

26. Dinwiddie, *Puerto Rico and Its Possibilities*, p. 216.

27. This is drawn directly from Bergad, "Agrarian History of Puerto Rico," p. 75; see also Andres A. Ramos Mattei, "Las Inversiones Norteamericanas en Puerto Rico y la Ley Foraker, 1898–1900," *Caribbean Studies* 14, no. 3 (1981): pp. 53–69, esp. p. 58; also Berbusse, *United States in Puerto Rico*, pp. 126–136.

28. Dinwiddie, *Puerto Rico and Its Possibilities*, p. 224.

29. See Bergad, "Agrarian History of Puerto Rico,"; also Ramos Mattei, "Las Inversiones Norteamericanas."

30. See Governor Allen, *Opportunities*.

31. See *Hearings*, 1900, p. 204. A. A. Ramos Mattei, "The Growth of the Puerto Rican Sugar Industry under North American Domination: 1899–1910," pp. 121–131, in B. Albert and A. Graves, eds., *Crisis and Change in the International Sugar Economy, 1860–1914* (Norfolk, U.K.: ISC Press, 1985).

32. *Congressional Record*, Senate, 55th Congress, 1st session, February 6, 1899, p. 1480.

33. See Elihu Root, *The Military and Colonial Policy of the United States* (Cambridge: Harvard University Press, 1916), p. 170.

34. *Congressional Record*, Senate, 55th Congress, 1st session, February 4, 1899, p. 1448.

35. See Leech, *In the Days of McKinley*, p. 357.

36. Ibid., pp. 357–358.

37. Millis, *The Martial Spirit*, p. 403.

38. See *The Tribune*, p. 83.

39. See *The Tribune*, pp. 87–88.

40. See, e.g., Anthony Lauria, Jr., "Respeto, Relajo, and Interpersonal Relations in Puerto Rico," *Anthropological Quarterly* 37 (1964): pp. 1–11.

41. See *Documents on Constitutional History*, p. 51.

42. See G. R. Jantscher, *Bread upon the Waters: Federal Aid to the Maritime Industries* (Washington, D.C.: Brookings, 1983), pp. 46–47.

43. *Congressional Record*, Senate, March 2, 1900, p. 2475.

44. See Víctor Rodríguez, *External and Internal Factors in the Organization of Production and Labor in the Sugar Industry of Puerto Rico, 1860–1934*, University of California, Irvine, 1987, p. 119.

45. *Congressional Record*, House, March 2, 1900, p. 2483.

46. See Velez Aquino, *Puerto Rican Press Reaction*, p. 41.

47. See Joseph Foraker, *Notes of a Busy Life*, Vol. 2, (Cincinnati: Stewart & Kidd, 1916), p. 85; also Everett Walters, *Joseph Benson Foraker: An Uncompromising Republican* (Columbus: Ohio History Press, 1948), pp. 162–163; *Congressional Record*, Senate, March 2, 1900, p. 2478; Root, *Military and Colonial Policy*, pp. 164–165; see also Whitney T. Perkins, *Denial of Empire* (Amsterdam: Sythoff, 1962), pp. 116–117.

48. *Congressional Record*, Senate, March 2, 1900, p. 2478; also Walters, *Joseph Benson Foraker*, p. 163.

49. Foraker, *Notes of a Busy Life*, Vol. 2, p. 85; for Roosevelt, see p. 83.

50. Lyman Gould, *La Ley Foraker*, (Río Piedras: University of Puerto Rico, 1969), p. 69. I have closely followed Gould's analysis.

51. *Congressional Record*, Senate, February 26, 1900, p. 2232.

52. Ibid., p. 2232.

53. *Congressional Record*, Senate, 56th Congress, 1st session, April 2, 1900, p. 3608; see also the remarks by Senator Benjamin Tillman on March 8, 1900, p. 2651.

54. Foraker, *Notes of a Busy Life*, Vol. 2, p. 85.

55. See José A. Cabranes, *Citizenship and the American Empire* (New Haven, Conn.: Yale University Press, 1979), p. 24; Carmen I. Raffucci de García, *El Gobierno Civil y la Ley Foraker* (Río Piedras: Editorial Universitaria, 1981).

56. *Congressional Record*, Senate, March 2, 1900, p. 2473.

57. *Congressional Record*, Senate, April 2, 1900, p. 3632.

58. See, e.g., ibid., p. 3617.

59. Michael Hunt, *Ideology and U.S. Foreign Policy* (New Haven, Conn.: Yale University Press, 1987), p. 49.

60. *Congressional Record*, Senate, April 2, 1900, p. 3619.

61. Hunt, *Ideology and U.S. Foreign Policy*, p. 58–59.

62. *Congressional Record*, Senate, April 2, 1900, p. 3638; for Senator Spooner's statement see p. 3632.

63. Ibid., p. 3635. See also Foraker, April 30, p. 4857; Depew, April 2, p. 3619.

64. Hunt, *Ideology and U.S. Foreign Policy*, pp. 61–62; the cartoon appears on p. 68.

65. See Pico, *La Guerra*, p. 190.

66. Robert Nisbet, *The Present Age* (New York: Harper, 1988), p. 29.

67. *Congressional Record*, Senate, April 2, 1900, p. 3638.

68. Merle Curti, *The Roots of American Loyalty* (New York: Columbia University Press, 1946); see, too, Hunt, *Ideology and U.S. Foreign Policy*, p. 19.

69. *Congressional Record*, Senate, February 26, p. 2231.

70. See Velez Aquino, *Puerto Rican Press Reaction*, p. 50.

71. *Congressional Record*, Senate, 56th Congress, 1st session, 1900, April 30, pp. 4850–4857, esp. p. 4856; the quote is from the March 8 debate, p. 2649; see also Foraker's comments on March 8, p. 2646; also his long speech, entitled *Porto Rico*, before the Union League of Philadelphia, April 21, 1900; Senator Perkins's statement appeared on April 2, p. 3639.

72. See Gould, *La Ley Foraker*, p. 208.

73. Ibid.

74. See *Congressional Record*, Senate, March 8, p. 2651.

75. See Gould, *La Ley Foraker*, pp. 84, 208–210; also Walters, *Joseph Benson Foraker*, pp. 163–165.

76. *Congressional Record*, Senate, March 8, 1990, p. 2647, also p. 2645; also the summary of Foraker's views presented on April 30, p. 4854.

77. *Congressional Record*, Senate, March 8, 1900, p. 2655.

78. Ibid., p. 2659.

79. Ibid., p. 2660.

80. *Congressional Record*, Senate, April 30, 1900, p. 4856.

81. *Congressional Record*, House, June 8, 1911, p. 7610.

82. *Congressional Record*, Senate, April 2, 1900, p. 3632.

83. See *Congressional Record*, House, 58th Congress, 1st session, June 28, 1902; p. 7608; also House, February 2, 1904, pp. 1523–1529, esp. p. 1525.

84. See *Documents on Constitutional History*; the Foraker Act is on pp. 64–80. The relevant parts of the legislation are Section 14 (p. 69) and Section 3 (pp. 64–65).

85. *Congressional Record*, House, April 11, 1900, p. 4058; see also Leech, *In the Days of McKinley*, pp. 490–491.

86. Gould, pp. 208–211; Walters, *Joseph Benson Foraker*, pp. 164–165.

87. See Leech, p. 495.

88. *Congressional Record*, Senate, April 2, 1900, p. 3642.

89. *Puerto Rico Constitution, Hearing before the Committee on Interior and Insular Affairs*, Senate, 81st Congress, 2nd session, 1950, p. 7.

90. William Tansill, Government Division, *Puerto Rico: Independence or Statehood* (Washington, D.C.: CRS, 1977), p. 8.

91. See William Franklin Willoughby, *Territories and Dependencies of the United States: Their Government and Administration* (New York: The Century Company, 1905), p. 81.

92. William Franklin Willoughby, "The Executive Council of Porto Rico," *American Political Science Review* 1 (1907): p. 561.

93. Ibid., p. 564; also, Willoughby, *Territories and Dependencies*, pp. 83–85.

94. Willoughby, *Territories and Dependencies*, p. 98.

95. Willoughby, "Executive Council of Porto Rico," p. 563.

96. Willoughby, *Territories and Dependencies*, p. 86.

97. Willoughby, "Executive council of Porto Rico," pp. 566, 573.

98. Willoughby, *Territories and Dependencies*, p. 93.

99. Willoughby, "Executive Council of Porto Rico," pp. 568–569.

100. Willoughby, *Territories and Dependencies*, p. 104.

101. Ibid., p. 105.

102. Ibid., p. 108.

103. Willoughby, *Territories and Dependencies*, p. 116.

104. L. S. Rowe, *The United States and Puerto Rico* (New York: Longmans, Green, and Company, 1904), p. 1.

105. See José Luis González, *El País de Cuatro Pisos* (Río Piedras: Huracán, 1983).

106. See Earl Parker Hanson, *Transformation: The Story of Modern Puerto Rico* (New York: Simon & Schuster, 1955), pp. 41–42.

Chapter 2

San Juan and Washington, Ponce and Boston

In this government all administrative powers were vested in a governor and these six heads of departments, all of whom were appointed by the President of the United States. It resulted from this that Puerto Rico had, from an administrative standpoint, an autocratic government.

William F. Willoughby, President of Puerto Rico's Executive Council[1]

To modern eyes it looks like a series of imaginatively arranged Lego building blocks: red on top of black on top of red on top of black until, on the roof, two octagonal watch towers provide a perfect spot for anxious firefighters to scan the city of Ponce. Built in 1802, Parque de Bombas (literally park of the pumps) is an elegant building that defies architectural classification. Victorian catches its eccentric spirit but the roof lines resemble those of a French mansard structure while the octagonal towers, one at either end of the building, call to mind a castle. However, instead of guns, these men carry the water that preserves "the moral capital of Puerto Rico."[2]

Ponce symbolizes the island, Puerto Rico separated from the city of San Juan. Even today, when two people walking in San Juan talk about a trip, they will travel "to the island." And when they return to San Juan, they have just come back "from the island."[3] Ponce, with its hundreds of delightfully colored stone buildings, covered in Spanish tile and surrounded by eye-catching configurations of wrought iron, was made by and for Puerto Ricans. San Juan was a walled city overflowing with soldiers and typified by El Morro, a fortification that eventually became one of the Caribbean's most famous historic monuments.

El Morro is a cold structure, a gigantic, empty mass of rock first constructed in 1539. The Spanish wanted to protect their interests in the Caribbean, and through a nasty accident of geography, Puerto Rico sat at the center of a chain of islands running in an arc from what is today Florida to the shoulder of South America.[4] To the estimated 30,000 Taino Indians who lived in a place called Boriquen, Puerto Rico was home; to Spanish soldiers it was a piece of turf bequeathed by the pope, a perfect spot to construct a fortress best symbolized by a tiny cell still secreted along one of the staircases leading to the sea. If you walked too fast, you missed this barred hole in the wall; if you stopped, you caught a snapshot glimpse of life in a military fortress.

El Morro meant discipline; troublesome soldiers died in damp, dark, concrete holes, and those who managed to escape fled "to the island." Called *cimarrones* (the wild ones) if they were black slaves, the resisters also included any of the soldiers, Indians, or laborers who also resisted military might. Indeed, in a give and take that lasted well into the nineteenth century, the Spanish used structures like El Morro to maintain control of the Caribbean, while "on the island" survivors tried to hide themselves and their way of life from the San Juan soldiers who never went home.

Some say that Spain neglected Puerto Rico; a truer statement is that as soon as Indians and slaves came out of the gold mines empty handed, Spain forgot about Puerto Rico. When the Dutch tried to capture San Juan, as in 1625, Spanish soldiers successfully defended the king's possessions. They maintained control of a devastated San Juan, and their king said thanks by sending money to maintain the presidio when and if he had the time. From 1651 to 1662 the king was so preoccupied with other matters that not a single ship came to Puerto Rico. The island had become a bastion in search of a ruler.[5]

Pirates, many operating with "licenses" from their country of origin, dominated Puerto Rico's economy. If Spain refused or forgot to send enough trading ships to the island, other nations happily obliged the commerce-starved islanders. From England, France, Portugal, and Holland contraband arrived in the form of clothes, wine, slaves, spices, and salt; ships docked full and left full—of cattle, leather, wood, tobacco, and cocoa.[6]

Governors, priests, soldiers, *hidalgos* (nobles): Everybody traded with pirates, and if an official tried to be honest, the citizens of Ponce knew how to deal with them. When a parish priest complained to the authorities about Ponce's affection for pirates, forty men kidnapped the priest, took him into the mountains, and almost killed him. Apparently the men were acting on advice from San Juan. "Poncenos knew how to kill cattle in the mountains and they also knew enough not to let a foul mouthed person live."[7]

Official change came in the form of an Irishman. Alejandro O'Reilly had done so well restoring the king's power in Louisiana that he was chosen by the reformist monarchy to examine the situation in Puerto Rico. In two months in 1765 O'Reilly prepared a report that requested radical social change.

Contraband was the island's only profitable enterprise, the one venture that kept islanders alive. But to legally and perpetually augment the king's returns from his Caribbean stronghold, O'Reilly argued that the Crown had to change its restrictive immigration policies. In the last sixty-five years, thanks to a high birth rate and an absence of devastating epidemics, the island's population had actually climbed to 45,000 people. Unfortunately, like their predecessors, the king's latest issue were also overwhelmingly poor and unskilled. O'Reilly, a soldier by profession and inclination, indicated that he could easily reorganize the island's defenses. But only the Crown could attract the men of capital and the skilled labor required for profitable sugar plantations.

So the King could act, or he could let O'Reilly's trainees efficiently oversee an economy of contraband and subsistence.[8] The Crown chose change. But it was change of a markedly conservative and selfish sort. In 1815 La Cedula de Gracias (literally the document of grace) greatly stimulated the migration of foreign men of capital to Puerto Rico. Promising white colonists with money 685 hectares (roughly 1,700 acres) of land for themselves, and 65 more for every negro slave they brought, the Spanish Crown successfully advertised its offer throughout Europe and America. Thousands of foreigners came to Puerto Rico, and even in Ponce they slowly began to supplant the established elite.[9]

In an economic sense the new money benefited the island; the foreigners quickly created the sugar plantations that profitably traded with Spain, and with newcomers like the United States as well. But the foreigners with money generally owed their political allegiance to Spain. Many accepted the Crown's offer of Spanish citizenship after five years of island residence, and none could fail to notice that economic change had nothing to do with political change.

On the contrary, when revolutionaries produced colonial problems in Venezuela, Spain often used Puerto Rico as a base of operations for its counterrevolutionary efforts. And when Spain finally lost its Caribbean and South American possessions, the most conservative of Spain's refugees were welcomed in Puerto Rico. Miguel de la Torre, the defeated Spanish commander-in-chief in Venezuela, not only received refuge in Puerto Rico but was made its captain general as partial reward for distinguished counterrevolutionary service.[10]

In order to attract capital and labor Spain had fractured the beginnings of Puerto Rican nationalism. Serious export commerce, instead of nourishing a native (*criollo*) class with a conjunction of economic and political interests, produced a situation in which many landowners were foreigners and many of the island's sparse credit facilities were in the hands of foreigners. Often these *peninsulares* (mainlanders) lived in castelike enclaves and spoke their own language whenever they had the chance. Many made their fortunes, returned to Europe, and, like the U.S. corporations that today dominate the island's economy, invested their earnings outside of Puerto Rico.[11]

Throughout the nineteenth century, for example, Puerto Rican sugar was consistently a troubled enterprise because, among other things, it lacked the funds required to modernize and mechanize. In Cuba the first railroads were operating in 1837; in Puerto Rico construction did not begin until 1878, and when the Americans conquered the island, they saw trains pulled by oxen. Nobody had the wherewithal to buy locomotives.[12]

Nor did enough landowners have the funds required for slaves. Plantations flourished when landowners had lots of bodies to exploit. Slaves, however, cost money; so despite flesh peddlers willing to provide "the product," foreign and native landowners in Puerto Rico had no way to increase a slave population that in 1846 totaled only 51,216 men, women, and children. Moreover, as the drive for abolition began to have some effect, the price of slaves rose as the ability of Puerto Ricans to solve their scarcity of labor problems declined. When, in April 1848, the French abolished slavery on the islands of Martinique and Guadalupe, Puerto Rico got another influx of conservative landowners in search of more repressive pastures.[13]

To provide labor to its colonists the Crown switched from slavery to a form of indentured servitude. In essence, a society unable to exploit slaves decided to exploit the roughly 80,000 free laborers—the *cimarrone* descendants of Indians, soldiers, and slaves—who had the audacity to live as they pleased.

In June 1848 the Spanish governor of Puerto Rico issued El Bando de Jornaleros (the laborer decree). Any free but poor Puerto Rican had to work in the plantations and farms and ranches of the island. Conscripted for this agrarian army were all males between sixteen and sixty years of age who lacked at least four *cuerdas* of land and/or a job that provided a meaningful income.[14]

To the government these men were the island's idle, parasites who refused to develop an export economy. To the laborers the government's oppression was best symbolized by their *libreta*, the notebook that all poor but now indentured islanders had to carry with them wherever they went. In these books the government listed the worker's name and number, the date he began work, his everyday behavior, and the debts he had contracted in the "company store." Thus, landowners literally branded these men because they would never find work elsewhere until and unless they had first repaid all debts to the foreigners *and* natives who were the authorized auditors of the men's *libretas*.[15]

Combined with slavery, the *libreta* system quickly institutionalized deep and bitter resentments against the owners of Puerto Rico's sugar, coffee, and tobacco enterprises. The poor people who might have been the natural allies of the native upper class became instead its natural enemies. Tragically, many *campesinos* (peasants) who were barred from political participation used alcohol to escape the miseries of everyday life; when the Americans invaded, many of those same *campesinos* used one hand to attack the homes and properties of their "betters" while, with the other, they extended a welcome handshake to their presumed liberators."[16]

Throughout the 1840s and 1850s the Spanish further weakened the native upper classes by continuing to stimulate immigration and by continuing to discriminate against native Puerto Ricans.[17] Spaniards perpetually received the positions of power in the government, in the church, in the military, and in commerce. Meanwhile, natives who tried to "improve" themselves by obtaining prestigious degrees abroad found that their *criollo* origins barred them from the positions that were "rightfully" theirs. In many locations tightened legal restrictions guaranteed that Spaniards were the only merchants in town; and even when foreigners returned home to spread the wealth abroad, new *peninsulares* quickly replaced their predecessors.[18]

On this wheel of fortune few birthright islanders got a chance to play, and even fewer the opportunity to succeed. Resentments simmered. And so too did the desire for revolutionary social change. Workers despised their *libretas*. Small farmers despised merchants who demanded 12 to 18 percent on their money. And doctors and lawyers despised a society with none of the political freedoms promised and gained by revolutionaries in South and North America.

On September 23, 1868, Puerto Rico witnessed El Grito de Lares (the shout of Lares). A group of roughly 500 rebels (almost 60 percent of them *jornaleros*, small farmers, and slaves) not only founded an independent nation but warned the Spaniards living in Puerto Rico that "they had three days to declare themselves in favor of the Republic, to leave for Spain, or to accept the punishment reserved for traitors."[19]

For a variety of practical reasons, such as insufficient funds to buy arms, the revolution died stillborn. But a telling sign of its institutionalized weakness was the reaction of the native property owners: Few wealthy *hacendados* joined the rebel cause. But they had no problem putting their lives on the line to protect the Spanish, who provided the coerced labor required for the natives' continued prosperity.[20]

Born under a colonial yoke, Puerto Rico was and remains a fundamentally subordinated society.[21] Outsiders made policy, and natives
responded in a variety of ways. At Lares, though many reacted with
indignation and courage, the majority nevertheless "accepted" their oppressors. Given more time and a chance to develop not only native
sources of wealth but native sources of self-esteem, islanders might have
united with their Cuban counterparts and defeated the Spanish long
before Teddy Roosevelt yelled "Charge!"

But in 1868, and in 1898, Puerto Rico still lacked a positive vision of
the nation that cut across class, ethnic, and color barriers.[22] For example,
from birth native elites used Spain as a positive frame of reference; given
that model as guide, they let the Spanish set and maintain the standards
for aspects of island life as different from each other as the oppression
of the *jornaleros* and the splendid architecture of Puerto Rico's soul, the
city of Ponce.

In a late-nineteenth-century painting called *El Velorio* (the wake) the
Puerto Rican artist Francisco Oller created a scene in which mourners
who represented his rich patrons surrounded the body of a dead *jíbaro*
(peasant) child. "All eyes avoided the cadaver." The mourners' lives
had barely been interrupted by the death of this young boy. To Oller
his duty as an artist was to point out the indifference of his patrons; his
dilemma, and Puerto Rico's, was that the rich supported the paintings
that were defined as real culture but remained indifferent to the culture
of "magnificent diversity" created over four centuries by the predecessors of that young *jíbaro* boy.[23]

The elite turned its eyes to Spain, which, after Lares, finally decided
to concede a measure of reform to its Caribbean bastion.

From the 1870s through the 1890s Spain played political Ping-Pong
with the Puerto Rican people. Welcomed changes (e.g., the abolition of
slavery in 1873 and of the *libreta* system in 1876) were linked to extraordinarily tight control of everyday political life. In response to the Spanish, island elites sought to achieve local rule by taking the path of least
resistance. Advocating a strategy of "extreme pragmatism," men like
Luis Muñoz Rivera argued that the Spanish would never permit a republican approach to politics in Madrid, much less in San Juan. Thus,
the Puerto Ricans should unite with whatever Spanish party offered
them a chance to achieve local autonomy under the umbrella of the
Spanish monarchy.[24]

As if using a machete, Muñoz's suggestion split the island's elite.
With countries like Canada as the model, autonomy was everyone's
moderate goal, but many islanders refused to embrace monarchy. To
men like Dr. José Celso Barbosa, ideals like equality and the will of the
people could not be married to parties that bowed at the throne of a

king. By all means, search for a way to achieve local rule, but do it without sacrificing the ideals that the vanguard—led by Barbosa and his followers—would make an institutionalized part of Puerto Rican life.[25]

Ultimately, pragmatism won out. Muñoz united with a conservative Spanish party, and for his support in the Spanish legislature he received the Autonomic Charter of 1897. Puerto Rico remained a Spanish colony but, despite the bitter criticism of his island opponents, Muñoz could legitimately claim a significant degree of success. The new insular parliament had "exclusive power" to frame the island's budget and expenditures; it also had the power to frame the tariff and fix both export and import duties; and, most important of all, "this new constitution could not be amended except by virtue of a law and *upon the petition of the insular parliament* [my emphasis]."[26]

War quickly eliminated the fruits of twenty years' labor. Soldiers sent from Washington crushed soldiers stationed in San Juan as businesspeople from Boston used Ponce as headquarters for their new banking and sugar enterprises.

Yet the fundamental allegiances of the island's elite never changed. Although the autonomists had split into two parties—called Republicans, led by Barbosa, and Federals, led by Muñoz—General George Davis assured the Congress considering the Foraker legislation that "as respects the principles of these two parties, no characteristic differences are stated. Each desires to control the insular government and considers the first elections as stepping stones to that end."[27]

Charles Allen, the first U.S. governor of Puerto Rico, echoed General Davis. He noted that both parties proudly announced "their unqualified loyalty to the United States of America." In fact, neither even mentioned independence in their platforms or discussions because each desired the statehood status that would produce results like free schools, universal suffrage, and free trade with the United States.[28]

Puerto Ricans wanted to be Americans. The only problem was a "malcontent" named Luis Muñoz Rivera. His vision of statehood included a desire for local autonomy; to Allen he and his Federal party were "obstructionists" because they wanted the city councils to have "large powers" to decide local issues.[29] The Republicans put no such roadblocks in America's way, and so Governor Allen tilted so far in their direction that he decisively changed the character of Puerto Rican politics.

Four hundred years of Spanish rule and no colonial government had ever managed to create a serious and widespread push for independence. But within fifteen years of taking over the island, Americans produced such a desire for independence that Congress gave the islanders U.S. citizenship to permanently eliminate their then ardent desire for a divorce.[30]

It's an interesting story, which begins with the attitudes and demeanor of America's first colonial administration.

Leo Rowe was a friend of the United States. In fact, in 1900 he served as a member of the commission to revise and compile the laws of Puerto Rico. In 1901 Professor Rowe became chairman of the commission that completely rewrote the island's judicial codes. Rowe enthusiastically applauded U.S. policy. What bothered him was the potentially disastrous inability of Americans to see things from a Puerto Rican point of view.

First came the attitudes displayed toward native institutions. "To the mass of Americans resident in the island—and this was particularly true of the lawyers—the entire system of law and government, of domestic and public institutions, was bad simply because it was different from our own. Everything that did not conform to our system was not only un-American but anti-American."[31] Haughty, condescending, and ethnocentric, the Americans met any complaint voiced by the islanders with the same refrain: In Rowe's words, "This is the way we do it in the States was regarded as an argument sufficient to bring conviction to the mind of every native."[32]

And if the natives had the temerity to reject U.S. opinions, if, in fact, they demanded to control their own affairs, Rowe noted that his colleagues refused to sacrifice administrative efficiency for democratic rights: "Almost every step taken to give the native population control over its own affairs met with the disapproval of the same element that had condemned all native institutions. This seeming contradiction was traceable to the same feeling of superiority which inspired contempt for the local law."[33] In essence, if the Puerto Ricans would listen, progress was possible. If not, islanders would move ahead despite their own recalcitrance.[34]

If Rowe's arguments received no additional support, they could easily be discounted. Perhaps Rowe wanted a government position he never received? However, the same arguments were also made by many other "objective" observers of the Puerto Rican scene. In a letter to Secretary of War Elihu Root, the journalist Richard Harding Davis complained "of the snobbishness of untrained administrators." To these men "the native no matter how well bred and educated he may be is a Speakitte and a Dago. . . . It is most unfortunate because Hunt's [the governor's] good work is often undone overnight by the impertinence of some foolish woman to a native's wife, or by the insolence of one of our own officers."[35]

In education officials pursued a policy of Americanization. Natives had to learn English even if it was taught by men who could not speak it! As the U.S. commissioner of education reported to Washington in

1901, "These American teachers at the outset were mostly young men who came to Porto Rico with the American Army. None of them knew Spanish and some of them knew little English."[36] Now, how Puerto Rican children could learn anything from teachers speaking neither Spanish nor English well was impossible to understand, unless, following Rowe's argument, anything brought by Americans was better than what the Puerto Ricans already possessed.

Rowe had zeroed in on the attitudes of superiority that made it impossible for U.S. officials to take the role of the other. Even a cursory glance at the last thirty years of Puerto Rican history would have shown an ardent desire for a moderate goal: local autonomy. Instead of perceiving this reality, Americans alienated the islanders with their everyday displays of condescension and, with another U.S. invention, gerrymandering.

To implement the Foraker legislation, Governor Allen and the Executive Council divided the island into seven electoral districts. This presented no theoretical problems until the Allen-sponsored Republicans,[37] trying to prevent another overwhelming victory by their Federal opponents (the Federal party had won 66 percent of the municipalities in the island's pre–Foraker law elections),[38] divided the island in an extremely creative fashion. For example, Aquadilla, at the west end of the island, was linked to Utuado, in the center of the island, and to Lajas, in the extreme southwest corner of the island.

In Governor Allen's words, "The two Federal members of the Executive Council were greatly disappointed"[39] with this Republican scheme, as well as with a companion proposal to assure neutrality in all electoral districts. Famous in Puerto Rico as the *dos por uno* (or two-for-one) deal, the idea was to have a three-person electoral college in each district. In law each college was to have one member of each island party and one neutral or independent; in fact, each college had its one Republican and one Federal, but in each and every district the neutral was also a Republican.[40] No wonder Governor Allen reported to the president that "the Republican party is firmly in favor of American methods and renders an honest and intelligent support to the Administration and its policies."[41]

The Federals, labeling the election scheme El Jorabado (the crooked election) resigned from the government. Aware that the Executive Council's 9-to-2 approval of the scheme had been engineered by the Republican party leader, José Barbosa,[42] the Federal members followed a custom with deep roots in the island's history. Instead of participating in a corrupt or despotic Spanish process, the custom in Puerto Rico was to "retire" from the political process. Thus, the two Federal members resigned from the Executive Council, the party refused to participate in the elections of 1900, and Governor Allen reported that in the Executive Council "matters moved on with much more harmony."[43]

Even with the Republicans, however, the harmony was short lived because the completely Republican legislature protested when it "fully appreciated" the autocratic implications of the Foraker Act. Specifically, at the very first session of the legislature representatives complained about the budgetary powers of the Executive Council. If the council had the power of the purse, then the legislators argued that there would be "little justification" for the existence of the lower chamber.

In response to this complaint the Americans essentially argued that (1), the Foraker Act gave them the power and (2) it "was impossible to deny that such an interpretation (that of the Republicans) would mean a very great limitation upon the powers of the Lower House and generally of self-government by the inhabitants of the island."[44]

Torn by the realities of the law and the fear that no Puerto Rican would participate in the government if the council obeyed the law, the Americans conceded rights they did not believe the Puerto Ricans had. As then treasurer of Puerto Rico William Willoughby put it, "To avoid the danger that the house of delegates might refuse to exercise its functions at all unless they included this right [the power of the purse] . . . it was decided that, after the heads of the departments had prepared and passed the budget, that it should be sent to the house for its approval."[45]

The Republicans imaginatively and immediately used the power they thought they had. From the first session of the colonial legislature, the lower house (the House of Delegates) refused to pass the budget until literally midnight on the final day of the legislative session. Sometimes the clock would be stopped, debate would proceed, and at "midnight" the House would finally give in to the pressures exerted by the Executive Council. As Willoughby noted in a memo marked confidential, "The House makes no secret of the fact that its reason for this practice is, that it is unwilling to make the session of the legislature a success—in the sense that at least necessary legislation is had—until it knows to what extent it has succeeded in having passed by the Executive Council bills in which it, the House, is interested."[46]

One bill the House pressed with genuine passion was a design for an agricultural bank. Devastated by war, the devaluation of the currency, tariff policies, *and* a brand-new (1901) property tax, large and small farmers all stood on a precipice overlooking ruin. The larger farmers at least had acreage to sell, but the small ones had no ready reserves of land. If they were forced to pay debts with the parcels they owned, they had to pick up a machete and look, at best, for seasonal employment on land they might have once owned.

Ironically, in the United States, the federal government actively sought to assist farmers in search of credit. Theodore Roosevelt argued that "the betterment which we seek must be accomplished, I believe, mainly through the national government." So the Republicans actively and successfully pushed for a variety of agricultural measures designed to assist farmers gouged by high interest rates, crop failures, or the giddy rise and fall of prices on national and world markets.[47]

In Puerto Rico the Executive Council pursued a policy of survival of the fittest. Indeed, even when Governor Taft set up a bank for the Filipinos, Puerto Rico's administrators refused to follow suit; instead, they took the tax money that was forcing foreclosures and invested it in New York with Seligman Brothers and the Royal Bank of Canada.[48] Islanders received 3 percent on the New York tax money while small as well as large farmers in search of credit paid 9 percent to 18 percent for the funds needed to survive another harvest.[49]

The House's sense of urgency was rooted in Governor Allen's redesign of the Puerto Rican taxation system. Allen argued for, and quickly achieved, "radical reform." Only the temporary 15 percent tariff on exports and imports provided the funds needed "to meet the most ordinary requirements of the government." But Puerto Rico had extraordinary requirements, including pay for the soldiers who filled civil positions, pay for the insular police required to maintain order, funds for a multiplication of the island's schools, and pay for the code commissioners that Congress had sent to redesign the island's judicial system.[50]

Allen stressed that he had only two alternatives: reduce expenses or increase revenues. Since he saw no way to reduce the expenses cited, he chose a tax policy that immediately aroused "a storm of protest." Farm owners claimed the rate of taxation would ruin them, and manufacturers and merchants threatened to close their factories and stores.[51]

Under the Spanish, taxes were essentially imposed on income earned by a farm or business. Under the Allen plan taxes were based on the assessed value of the land or factory. To Allen this seemed a logical way to proceed—it was, after all, standard practice in the United States— but in an economy ruined by the Spanish-American War, islanders had no income with which to pay the new taxes. Allen solved this problem by obtaining authority to confiscate and auction the properties of producers unable to earn enough or borrow enough to pay the new taxes.[52]

The failure to establish the agricultural bank helped transform an economy already turning to sugar as its main source of income and jobs. Farmers who once grew coffee turned to "safe" money crops like sugar and tobacco because that was the only way to obtain the funds needed to pay the taxes needed to retain their land. For those unable to pay the tax collectors who literally came knocking, the island's Treasury Department—headed until 1907 by William Willoughby—placed ads in the island's newspapers. On some days the colonial administration auctioned off as many as forty properties.[53]

Sugar became king. It ruled Puerto Rico for forty years, but any explanation of its dominance must be rooted in a variety of factors. However significant the tax policies, they were always accompanied by interests and forces that, all together, crowned sugar an anything but benevolent monarch.[54]

Many native sugar growers welcomed the Americans—simultaneously embracing the all-American Puerto Rican Republican party—because of their desire to gain a free market for their sugar, plus access to the technology that would make Puerto Rican produce competitive on world markets. In 1898 coffee was king, and sugar a poor relative exhausted by struggles with the beet sugar coming from Europe and the increased productivity coming from everywhere. So Puerto Ricans in search of profits said thank you to the Americans who would help them build the *centrales* (the sugar mills or factories) supposedly essential to profitable sugar production.

As men like Frank Dillingham (secretary of the South Porto Rico Sugar Company) and Lorenzo Armstrong (vice-president of the Fajardo Sugar Company) put it to Congress, to make money in sugar you had to own large tracts of land and you had to be willing to invest, "exclusive of any land," $1 million or more for a factory. Especially in a climate as warm as Puerto Rico's, the cane deteriorated rapidly. It had to be ground in twenty-four hours or the sun turned the juice into starch. Therefore, using the latest technology, owners built mills in the center of their sugar-growing properties. In this way produce from the surrounding areas was quickly fed into the *centrale*'s furnaces, which, far more productively than in the Spanish past, turned the cane stalks into greenbacks.[55]

You could make big profits in sugar, but the Americans argued that you had to own or control at least 3,000 acres of land. And that was against the law! The Foraker Act specifically mandated that "corporations organized for the purpose of engaging in agriculture should be restricted by their charters to the ownership of not more than 500 acres of land."[56] The intent of the restriction was to avoid the monopolies that would crush the small Puerto Rican farmer; even more importantly, its intent was to avoid causing too much competition to mainland and Hawaiian sugar producers.

The striking thing about this law was that no one ever enforced it. On the contrary, Governor Allen stressed the "conservative" nature of the island's governmental organization, boasting that "the corporate law which was passed was modeled on that of New Jersey, which was understood to be liberal toward corporate organizations."[57]

Granted, "gold will not be had for the picking"; but in a section of his book titled "Chances for the Colonist," Allen stressed that "there was a great opportunity for returns for the thrift and industry of the farmer." The climate was good, the living conditions advantageous, and "capitalists could be assured of protection to their property and investments, guaranteed in the form of government, in the tax laws, and in the reorganization of the courts." Capital, in Allen's assessment, "was pretty sure to take care of itself."[58]

And that, after all, was Puerto Rico's problem. Capital, by definition, is dynamic; it is wealth in search of more wealth. If profits fall, or the investment opportunities are weak, or in the worst case nonexistent, capital packs up its bags and seeks profits elsewhere. That is the harsh nature of the system, well understood by its boosters as well as its critics.[59]

What Allen and his associates had done was to expose the island's economy to the harsh vulnerabilities not only of capitalism but also of virtually a one-crop economy. Certainly, under a government its own administrators labeled autocratic, only the Americans had the power to enforce the law or to nurture alternatives (e.g., coffee or the agricultural bank) or to say no to industries that would make it impossible for islanders to weather the "inescapable exposure"[60] of each capitalist to the profit-making efforts of others.

In saying yes to sugar, for example, Allen and his supporters tied the economy not only to one crop but to one part of one crop. In the United States, tariffs for refined sugar were much higher than for raw sugar because U.S. manufacturers wanted to maintain their control of the refining industry.[61] Thus, from the outset sugar was a dead-end crop in the hands of absentee owners. Where, after all, was the incentive to invest in the refining factories or in the related industries that would have provided jobs for Puerto Rico's fast-growing population?

In forgetting, or not caring, that the island's economic future depended on the *political* will of outsiders, Allen and his supporters assured perpetual dependency rooted in perpetual inequality. Quotas, tariffs, refining, shipping, machinery: Everything depended on the desires and needs of well-organized mainlanders, who in getting Foraker to pass the law had served notice that they knew how to deal with the inescapable exposure of one capitalist to another. Puerto Rico, for example, did not even have one vote in the legislature that decided its fate.

Theoretically the Puerto Ricans could have said no. In reality a society without political, economic, and military power saw no viable way to seriously resist the policies and proposals of Governor Allen and his colleagues. In fact, instead of violence directed at the Americans, what Puerto Rico witnessed was islanders attacking fellow islanders. Called Las Turbas Republicanas (the Republican disturbances) in Puerto Rican history, the four-year run of mob violence was silently sanctioned by the U.S. colonial administrators, who saw in the island's class divisions a way to foster support for the authority of the United States.[62]

His name was José Mauleón y Castillo. He had blue eyes, a body full of scars earned in fights, and although a cigar maker by trade, after 1900 he earned a living ridiculing and intimidating anyone who opposed the Puerto Rican Republican party. As the acknowledged head of Las Turbas—officially known as the Committee for the Defense of the Republican Party—Mauleón orchestrated demonstrations that moved from the ridiculous to the dangerous. In a February 1901 political parade he rode through the streets of San Juan dressed as *una loca* (a crazy person); his followers shouted "long live the people's rights" and "down with despots" as Mauleón proudly displayed a sign on his back: He was the "crazy man of Caguas," none other than Luis Muñoz Rivera, the head of the island's majority or Federal party.[63]

Muñoz was *the* Republican target. When he used his newspaper to editorialize about issues like gerrymandering or lack of local control, a Mauleón-led crowd of 100 citizens went on September 14, 1900, to the paper's offices, "broke the furniture, destroyed the presses, and threw the fragments into the streets."[64] A week later, the leader of the Republican party, José Barbosa, announced that "if Muñoz does not stop publishing his rude attacks against the people of Puerto Rico, HIS LIFE WILL BE IN CONSTANT DANGER. It will not be the Republican party that is responsible. We are unable to forever contain the spirit of the people [emphasis in original]."[65]

Barbosa knew what he was talking about because the next day Muñoz was assaulted while walking near the docks. He escaped with a wound to the head, but a crowd soon appeared at his house. No one was killed, although some 300 shots were fired, with the municipal police also joining in the assault. Thankfully they only fired into the air, but Muñoz obviously got the point. How could he avoid it, when mobs acting in the name of the people soon suggested that any Federal party member who continued to struggle with the Republicans should "have his throat cut."[66]

When, after the assault on his home, Muñoz was accused of instigating the violence, the leader of the majority party chose life over death. He tried to lead the Federal party from a self-imposed exile in New York; meanwhile, at home Mauleón and his men paraded through the streets of San Juan with a band, two dancing policemen, and a group of marchers proudly carrying a picture of President Theodore Roosevelt. In the words of one commentator, "Las Turbas never ignored the fact it was under the Northamerican government that they were able to play the leading role in Puerto Rican politics."[67]

In public documents Governor Allen blamed the violence on an alliance between local "malcontents" and the Federal party. However, in private Republicans not only applauded the governor's partiality but happily admitted that "the sympathy and friendship demonstrated by Governor Allen and his men to the Republican Party manifested itself in a variety of ways."[68] For example, in the attack on Muñoz's house U.S. soldiers had intervened to stop the violence; the next day Governor Allen wanted to know who had authorized the soldiers to act. In the future they were not to intervene in purely local matters.

And when José Mauleón was wounded in a San Juan mob activity, the Republican mayor of San Juan noted that Governor Allen took an interest in Mauleón's injury; he "constantly" asked Doctor Barbosa about the progress of Mauleón's recuperation because "Allen knew that Mauleón was a popular leader of the Republican party."[69]

In the name of democracy, U.S. officials let Mauleón, and the men who directed him, eliminate or intimidate or defraud any opposition to the government established by the Foraker Act.[70] When, in 1902, the Federal party reversed course and participated in the island's elections, the Republicans maintained control of the lower house by using the *dos por uno* power given them by the Executive Council. Instead of stuffing ballot boxes, as in the United States, what they did in Puerto Rico was disenfranchise members of the majority party. In more than 50 percent of the electoral districts Federals found that they had no right to vote. They had been "shut out" by the Republicans.[71]

Although personality, greed, and ambition certainly played a part in the battles between the two island parties, serious ideological issues also separated the two groups. For example, when the Code Commission headed by Prof. Leo Rowe asked for suggestions from the Puerto Rican people, the commission "was answered with a deluge of petitions, requesting that local autonomy be assured and that local officials be relieved from all central control. There was general unanimity of opinion that until this was done no progress toward the Americanization of the island could be made."[72]

Both parties only wanted autonomy, but they differed on the means to achieve their goal. That difference in tactics (e.g., to embrace the Americans or to resist them) was rooted in the battles that dated back to Spanish rule. To the Republicans the Federals represented the Old World, the one dominated by lordly owners who had no problem subordinating the illiterate masses. The United States supposedly equaled change in the form of new opportunities for wealth, a rise in political freedom, and a hoped for lessening discrimination against black Puerto Ricans.

Why a nation then openly lynching black Americans promised freedom was, of course, a good question. But given their decades-old distrust of the Federals, the Republicans chose to link up with the Americans, even to the point of accepting the forced imposition of the English language.[73]

The Federals resisted the Americans because the Foraker Act did, in fact, establish an autocracy, controlled by and for the United States. However, in addition to their resentment at the canyon that separated the Constitution and the Foraker law, the Federals wanted to maintain their newly established (in 1897) chance of controlling island life. Sugar mills financed and dominated by outsiders threatened their antiquated *haciendas* (farms). Americanization devalued four centuries of Spanish heritage and to seriously consider increasing the rights of the masses was to possibly eliminate the cheap labor that was the foundation of many Federal landowners' profits.[74]

Ironically, because Las Turbas Republicanas also persecuted the head of the island's labor movement, in 1902 the Federals found themselves in league with the just-born Free Federation of Puerto Rican Workers. But their alliance was short lived because the Federal party had no intention of seriously helping labor and because the Federation argued that the status debate was a smokescreen intended to divert attention from the terrible economic conditions of the overwhelming majority of the Puerto Rican people.[75]

In another moderate approach to change, labor became a Caribbean subsidiary of Samuel Gompers's American Federation of Labor. The masses were represented by men who argued that "the fundamental preoccupation" of the worker should be the struggle for better salaries and more humane working conditions. Meanwhile, the transformation of the economy into sugar and tobacco—crops that offered at best five or six months of work a year—guaranteed that generations of Puerto Ricans would never need a union because they would never have a job. They were born marginal.[76]

In Washington complaints from a variety of sources (e.g., Americans worried about the years of mob violence in San Juan) forced the War Department's colonial office[77] to take a more even-handed approach to island politics. When, in 1904, the Republicans proposed a particular candidate for resident commissioner, the new governor of the island, Beekman Winthrop, invited the Republican leadership to an official reception where they were told to change candidates. The designated fellow was simply unacceptable to the governor, who would, of course, inform President Roosevelt unless the islanders did as they were told.[78]

To avoid trouble on the island, Americans eventually began to tilt toward the majority party. But in Congress insults continued at such a fast pace that they quickly undid any good achieved by the new political tilt. For example, when the House passed a bill authorizing a delegate (instead of a resident commissioner) for Puerto Rico, the Senate agreed, but only if the Puerto Ricans agreed "to make a careful investigation into property titles and claims of the Holy Roman Catholic Church" and if it agreed to empower the secretary of war "to authorize the construction or extension of any wharf, pier, dolphin, boom, weir, breakwater, sea wall, bulkhead, jetty, or other structure on any lands belonging to the United States."[79]

When the island's lower house sent a petition to Congress requesting greater autonomy, Congress never even mentioned receipt of the document. And when, in February 1904, Puerto Rico's resident commissioner finally received the right to speak on the floor of the House, it was only through parliamentary sleight of hand that the right was granted. Even then the House underscored Puerto Rico's second-class status by noting that the commissioner from Puerto Rico was not entitled (but the delegate from Hawaii was entitled) to a secretary or to the right to receive mileage.[80]

Through a policy of indifference and insult the Americans managed to transform island politics: On February 19, 1904, the Federals united with many dissident Republicans to form the Union party—a party that would totally dominate island politics for the next twenty years.

Citing their obligation to peacefully resist the "wave of enslavement from the North,"[81] Union party members represented the majority of the island that vacillated between disillusionment and anger over the actions and attitudes of U.S. officials. However, although the Union party was in fact united in its desire to adamantly oppose the Foraker Act, the fragile coalition of Federals and Republicans fell apart when discussion turned to the issue of ultimate political status.

In debate over which future to choose, many members were willing to sacrifice a degree of political autonomy for economic assistance. Others wanted statehood, while still others adamantly opposed the inclusion of the statehood ideal in any Union platform; to paraphrase one protester, the United States was able to deny Puerto Rico both statehood and self-government. That was its right. "But it was not able to deny the island its independence because that was a right of the Puerto Rican people."[82]

In politics eloquence often makes way for compromise. In this case Article 5 of the Union party's platform indicated that all three statuses were acceptable to the Puerto Rican people. They were willing to consider any reasonable proposal, but the Union party and its supporters meant to be heard because Puerto Ricans were no longer willing to accept laws that obligated them "to pledge allegiance to the Constitution and to be outside the Constitution."[83]

When the Union party overwhelmingly triumphed in the 1904 elections (it won twenty-five of thirty-five House seats), it immediately assumed that it had a mandate from the people. So in 1905 the House sent another "memorial" to Washington. It was called a memorial because the Executive Council refused to approve any critical resolutions coming from the House. As a result, to get their message to Washington island legislators resorted to memorials as a roundabout way of expressing the desires of the only body that "represented the will of the Puerto Rican people."[84]

Written by José De Diego, a leader of the Union party, the memorial passionately criticized those aspects of the Foraker Act that men like Treasurer William Willoughby praised. The Executive Council's union of legislative and executive authority seemed especially unfair, as was the denial to islanders of the right to administer the treasury that housed their tax monies. De Diego pleaded with Congress to change "an Act that by artificial means created an imaginary people unknown in international law, without a fundamental juridical tie which would unite it to the people who are the arbiters of its destiny, without precedent in your political system of state and territories, with neither solidarity nor any political communication with the peoples of the universe."[85]

Congress never responded to the memorial. Nor did it respond to another equally critical plea in 1906. So islanders used the November elections in the following manner: They gave all thirty-five seats in the House to members of the Union party, who, armed with this absolute mandate, prepared another "memorial" for an especially welcome visitor: President Theodore Roosevelt.

The president landed in Ponce on November 21, 1906. Although he stayed for only two days, he thought the island's scenery "was wonderfully beautiful, especially among the mountains of the interior, which constituted a veritable tropic Switzerland." But Roosevelt complained about San Juan. Because the harbor had not been dredged out, he was unable to dock his battleship in the island's capital: "I do not think this creditable to us as a nation and I earnestly hope that immediate provision will be made for dredging San Juan Harbor."[86]

Islanders also had hopes, but theirs had nothing to do with battleships. Instead, when the president toured the island, House leaders arranged for him to be greeted by a multitude of people who, as they acclaimed his arrival, asked the president to walk through "triumphal arches" bearing this inscription: "We desire self government."[87]

The president's visit was the islanders' best chance for change, an opportunity to lobby first-hand "the apostle of justice in the world." Therefore as they saluted him with U.S. flags at each stage of his journey, islanders tried to impress upon the president "the cruel injustice committed against the Puerto Ricans in declaring them to be unfit for self government."[88]

Roosevelt's response was quick and to the point. He wrote Senator Foraker to tell him that "the law for the government of the island was one of the best bits of legislation ever put on our statue books."[89] And to the people of Puerto Rico Theodore Roosevelt sent this message: Not only had "no injustice of any kind resulted from it [the American government]" but "under the wise administration of the present governor and council, marked progress has been made in the difficult matter of granting to the people of the island the largest measure of self government that can with safety be given at the present time." Indeed, "it would have been a very serious mistake to have gone any faster than we have already gone in this direction."[90]

Despite this prompt and public rebuff, islanders still hoped to somehow influence U.S. policymakers. On a day U.S. authorities had made a legal holiday—July 25th—islanders refused to participate in ceremonies marking the ninth anniversary of the U.S. invasion; right after this symbolic protest, the islander legislators had the speaker of their House go to the president's house. On August 12, 1907, José De Diego stopped at Oyster Bay to once again plead for more self-government. The end result of this trip was a note from the president's secretary to the secretary of the interior: "This [the petition] was delivered to the President at Sagamore Hill on the occasion of the call of the Speaker of the Porto Rican House of Delegates."[91]

When the petition was duly filed and, like the memorials sent to Congress, never heard from again, islanders struggled to find some way to get Washington's attention. Representative Matienzo Cintron argued that "to say we are not prepared is humiliating for Puerto Ricans and has tones of the arrogance our [Spanish] forefathers showed in the sixteenth century when they believed they were the owners of the world."[92]

When even Luis Muñoz Rivera wrote that "a dignified people is not resigned, it rises up and vibrates," it was clear that islanders were ready for a dramatic confrontation. Force, however, was never seriously considered because a large majority were opposed to its use and because U.S. intervention in Cuba in 1907 suggested that U.S. officials had no compunction about initiating another invasion of the island. Roosevelt himself had told De Diego, "Do not ask for too much. There you have Cuba's example where we proceeded with too much haste."[93]

De Diego took the president at his word, for he asked his colleagues to "struggle without pause" but to do it "within the regime, to hurt it from close up because outside of the regime our claims will be lost in emptiness, and our rights in violence."[94]

Ironically, the crucial confrontation occurred under the governorship of Regis Post, a former member of the New York State House of Representatives and a protégé of Theodore Roosevelt. In a report to the president, Post noted that during the summer and fall of 1908 island politicians had objected more strenuously than ever to the present system of government "and some of the more hot-headed orators even advocated petitioning for independence." Things had reached such an impasse that in its September 1908 political convention, "many of the more conservative members of the house of delegates failed of renomination and several extremists were nominated in their places."[95]

What Post also reported was that these "extremists" had the support of the Puerto Rican electorate. He told the president, "The results of the elections were a complete sweep of all seven districts of the Island for the Unionist party, and for a second time the house of delegates was composed entirely of Unionists."[96]

Sparks flew on the very first day of the new legislative session— January 12, 1909—because all members of the House met with the Central Committee of the Unionist party to discuss the following resolution: The House should refuse to enact any legislation or pass any bills coming to it from the Executive Council as a protest against the existing political system of the island.[97]

Only nine of the thirty-five Unionists voted to accept this resolution, but Governor Post and President of the Executive Council Willoughby both argued that just proposing the resolution made it clear that "there was a strong disposition on the part of the House to do all in its power to make the session of the Legislature a failure."[98] To Willoughby the negative, "intolerant attitude" of the Puerto Ricans was yet another manifestation of their inability to govern. For example, they had actually called the Federal court system "repugnant" when it "had always enjoyed the highest respect in the Island of Puerto Rico and there was no ground for complaint against the court other than that it was distinctly an American institution."[99]

That, of course, was the Puerto Ricans' point. But as if wearing a pair of blinders, Willoughby and his colleagues focused only on the willingness of the Puerto Ricans to threaten "recklessly . . . ten years of patient effort." Caught between a rock and hard place, the Unionists could submit to a government they labeled tyrannical—and so be labeled docile—or in resisting it further alienate the officials who genuinely believed that the islanders should be grateful for U.S. colonial administration.[100]

Willoughby, for example, became incensed when the Unionists resorted to "vicious and immoral tactics." What the Unionists had done was introduce and pass in the House a variety of bills they considered especially important. One bill took the power to shape educational policy out of U.S. hands. Another reestablished the practice of cock fighting, and a third abolished property assessments by the "corps" of people attached to the Treasury Department. To the islanders control of assessments was a way to stop the wholesale land auctions still channeling Puerto Rican farms into the hands of U.S. sugar and tobacco corporations. To Willoughby, "it needed no comment to make clear the viciousness of the system proposed, and that, if adopted, the grossest injustice in assessments would result that have ever been seen anywhere in the world."[101]

In passing these bills, the Unionists wanted to engage in a bit of horse trading. If the Executive Council approved its legislation, the House would pass the budget. If not, the House would use the only power it had, and by refusing to approve a budget for the next year, it would deliberately and hopefully paralyze the island's government.

The Unionists sought somehow to catch the attention of Congress. What they caught instead was a bit of hell from Governor Post. To the House's demand, he issued one of his own. In a special session called by Post, the House could either pass the budget or Post would ask President Taft to use his March 15 address to Congress as a vehicle to silence the Puerto Ricans.[102]

Nobody backed down, so Willoughby, in one last try at conciliation, told Muñoz Rivera that

it was highly improper for him to seek to have the Council purchase the passage of the appropriation bill by voting against its convictions; that not only were the bills of House sought to have enacted vicious bills but that the principle insisted upon by the House of trading legislation by purchasing the passage of one bill by another so thoroughly bad that, if adopted, nothing but disaster could follow.[103]

When the Unionists immediately refused this compromise, the government was in fact paralyzed. Post retaliated by shutting off the lights and water in the insular library—where, after all, was the budget to pay for necessities?—while, on the very same ship, Willoughby and two associates, accompanied by Muñoz Rivera, and two associates, sailed for Washington. The Unionists had finally gotten their way. President Taft himself had agreed to listen to each side present its case.

In the brief filed by the Puerto Ricans, legislators tried to focus the president's attention on U.S. constitutional precedents. Citing everything from Oliver Wendell Holmes's *Annals* to Sir William Blackstone's *Commentaries*, from Chief Justice John Marshall on colonies to Justice Joseph Story on the Constitution, they demonstrated their knowledge of democratic process, linked to their total unwillingness to back down on an essential point: "Taxes are donations from the people on whom they are imposed and must be levied by the *immediate* representatives of the people."[104]

When they left the president's office, the islanders believed they had achieved a measure of success: William Howard Taft would send a commission in June to discuss the island's problems. But after meeting with the Unionists, Taft also met with Willoughby and his associates. They suggested that Congress amend the Foraker Act so that if and when the Puerto Ricans refused to pass a budget, there would be an automatic appropriation of last year's budget to meet the next year's expenditures. There was precedent for such a proposal in the organic law of the Philippines. Thus the U.S. officials simply suggested that the president once again use the Pacific colony as a standard for the Atlantic possession.[105]

Taft announced his decision in a May 10, 1909, message to Congress. He noted, "The facts demonstrate the willingness of the representatives of the people in the House of Delegates to subvert the government in order to secure the passage of certain legislation." This was bad enough, but the Puerto Ricans had also forgotten that they were "the favored daughter of the United States." Schools, 172 miles of "macadamized roads," medicine, and free trade—these were America's gifts to the Puerto Ricans since the United States had "assumed guardianship over them and the guidance of their destinies."[106]

But instead of gratitude, all the Puerto Ricans could do was complain. Of course, "this should not be an occasion for surprise," continued Taft, since "we must have been conscious that a people that enjoyed so little opportunity for education could not be expected safely for themselves to exercise the full power of self government; and the present development is only an indication that we have gone somewhat too fast in the extension of political power to them for their own good."[107]

Taft suggested that Congress immediately take away from the Puerto Ricans the absolute power of appropriation they had "shown themselves too irresponsible to enjoy."[108] As Willoughby stressed in his book, that would mean there was now "little justification for the existence of [a] House of Delegates,"[109] but Taft and Willoughby had to consider the welfare of the Puerto Rican people. The president told Congress at the conclusion of his message, "There is not the slightest evidence that there has been on the part of the governor or any member of the executive council a disposition to usurp authority, or to withhold approval of such legislation as was for the best interests of the island, or a lack of sympathy with the best aspirations of the Puerto Rican people."[110]

Taft and Willoughby honestly believed what they said. If these men were conscious hypocrites, or simply dictatorial, the Puerto Ricans might have had some success with their arguments. It is, after all, possible to reach a person who is aware of his contradictions; and a dictator is at least sometimes aware of the realities that threaten his power.

But a close reading of the documentary material "proves" that neither of the U.S. principals recognized the obvious facts that would undermine his arguments. For example, in his confidential memo to the president Willoughby called the desire to trade legislative approvals a "vicious and immoral act." Ironically enough, that was exactly the tactic used by

President McKinley to pass not only the Treaty of Paris but also the legislation that gave Willoughby and the Executive Council their autocratic powers.

And to cite the immorality of voting against a person's convictions was to forget the point made by Representative James Watson when he explained his vote in favor of the Foraker Act: "I subordinated my own personal views as to the expediency of the passage of such a bill and voted for it in the interest of party harmony and to sustain the Administration."[111]

Willoughby and Taft and Post were true believers: They actually thought that whatever the United States touched she made holy. They were therefore genuinely angered by the "ingratitude" of the Puerto Ricans, who despite one failure after another still believed they had no choice but peaceful protest and intelligent dialogue.

To some islanders the Cuban example meant that petitioning Congress was the lesser of two evils. Others, still eyeing statehood and autonomy, thought they could somehow convince senators and representatives to act on the facts overlooked by the president. And still others, making money from sugar, simply wanted no interruption in the profits earned in a free market closed by tariff to unwelcome competition.

In any event the Puerto Ricans decided to take their case to Congress, even if they had to do it under the president's suggested replacement for the exhausted Governor Post: William Willoughby.[112]

NOTES

1. William F. Willoughby, *The Government of Modern States* (New York: D. Appleton-Century Company, 1932), p. 106.

2. Angel G. Quintero Rivera, *Patricios y Plebeyos* (Río Piedras: Huracán, 1988), p. 69.

3. Ibid., p. 27.

4. See *Report on the Progress of Puerto Rico*, House, 78th Congress, 1st session, Document no. 304, 1943, p. 2.

5. See Arturo Morales Carrión, *Puerto Rico: A Political and Cultural History* (New York: Norton, 1983), p. 37; also his *Puerto Rico and the Non-Hispanic Caribbean* (Río Piedras: University of Puerto Rico, 1971), pp. 32–34.

6. See Fernando Pico, *Historia General de Puerto Rico* (Río Piedras: Huracán, 1988), pp. 94–97.

7. Ibid., p. 96; see also Morales Carrión, *Non-Hispanic Caribbean*, pp. 35–57.

8. See Carlos Hernán Padilla, *Political Economy in Nineteenth Century Puerto Rico*, University of Connecticut, 1989, pp. 19–24; Pico, *Historia General de Puerto Rico*, pp. 104–106.

9. See Francisco A. Scarano, "Inmigración y Estructura de Clases: Los Hacendados de Ponce, 1815–1845," in Scarano, ed., *Inmigración y Clases Sociales* (Río Piedras: Huracán, 1985), p. 23.

10. Morales Carrión, *Puerto Rico*, pp. 73–77.

11. José Luis González, *El País de Cuatro Pisos y Otros Ensayos* (Río Piedras: Huracán, 1985), p. 24; also Scarano, "Inmigración y Estructura de Clases," pp. 150–154.

12. Laird W. Bergad, "Agrarian History of Puerto Rico, 1870–1930," *Latin American Research Review* 13, no. 3 (1978): p. 66.

13. See Ricardo Alegría, *Temas de la Historia de Puerto Rico* (San Juan: Centro de Estudios Avanzados, 1988), p. 143.

14. James L. Dietz, *Economic History of Puerto Rico: Institutional Change and Capitalist Development* (Princeton, N.J.: Princeton University Press, 1986), pp. 42–51; also Alegría, *Temas*, pp. 147–148.

15. Alegría, *Temas*, p. 147.

16. See, for example, Fernando Pico, *Libertad y Servidumbre en el Puerto Rico del Siglo XIX* (Río Piedras: Huracán, 1983), p. 112; also Pico's *La Guerra después de la Guerra* (Río Piedras: Huracán, 1987).

17. See, for example, Pedro San Miguel, *El Mundo Que Creó el Azucar: Las Haciendas en Vega Baja* (Río Piedras: Huracán, 1989), p. 40.

18. Olga Jiménez de Wagenheim, *Puerto Rico's Revolt for Independence: El Grito de Lares* (Boulder, Colo.: Westview Press, 1985), pp. 39–40; Dietz, *Economic History of Puerto Rico*, pp. 54–56.

19. Jiménez, *Revolt for Independence*, p. 87.

20. Ibid., p. 115.

21. See Juan M. García Passalacqua, *Puerto Rico: Equality and Freedom at Issue* (New York: Praeger, 1978), p. 2.

22. See, González, *El País de Cuatro Pisos*, p. 26.

23. See Pico, *Historia General*, p. 220; the issue of magnificent diversity is drawn from José Luis González; see especially his *La Luna No Era de Queso* (Río Piedras: Editorial Cultural, 1988).

24. On extreme pragmatism see German Delgado Pasapera, *Puerto Rico: Sus Luchas Emancipadoras* (Río Piedras: Editorial Cultural, 1984), pp. 419–420; also Alegría, *Temas*, p. 181.

25. See Mariano Negrón Portillo, *Las Turbas Republicanas, 1900–1904* (Río Piedras: Huracán, 1990), p. 26; see, too, Aaron Gamaliel Ramos, ed., *Las Ideas Anexionists en Puerto Rico Bajo la Dominación Norteamericana* (Río Piedras: Huracán, 1987), pp. 73–80.

26. See *Documents on the Constitutional History of Puerto Rico* (Washington, D.C.: Commonwealth of Puerto Rico, 1964), pp. 37, 38, 45.

27. See *Report of Brigadier General George W. Davis on Civil Affairs of Puerto Rico* (Washington, D.C.: GPO, 1899), p. 535.

28. See *First Annual Report of Charles H. Allen*, Senate, 57th Congress, 1st session, Document no. 79, 1901, p. 45.

29. Ibid., p. 45 and, on the malcontent charge, pp. 48 and 49.

30. See, e.g., *Hearings before the Committee on Insular Affairs*, House, 63rd Congress, 2nd session, 1914, p. 13.

31. See L. S. Rowe, *The United States and Porto Rico* (New York: Longmans, 1904), p. 15.

32. Ibid., p. 15.

33. Ibid., p. 16.

34. Charles Allen, "How Civil Government Was Established in Porto Rico," *North American Review* 174 (February 1902): pp. 159–174.

35. Wilfrid Hardy Callcott, *The Caribbean Policy of the United States, 1890–1920* (Baltimore: Johns Hopkins Press, 1942), p. 170.

36. See *Report of the Commissioner of Education for Porto Rico* (Washington, D.C.: GPO, 1901), p. 498.

37. See Roberto Todd, *Desfile de Gobernadores de Puerto Rico* (San Juan, 1942), pp. 16–17.

38. See Negrón Portillo, *Las Turbas Republicanas*, p. 71.

39. Allen, "Civil Government," p. 165.

40. See Alegría, *Temas*, p. 215; also Todd, *Desfile de Gobernadores*, p. 29.

41. See *First Annual Report of Charles H. Allen*, p. 49.

42. See, Todd, *Desfile de Gobernadores*, p. 16.

43. Allen, "Civil Government," p. 165.

44. William F. Willoughby, "The Executive Council of Porto Rico," *American Political Science Review* 1 (1907): p. 572.

45. William F. Willoughby, *Territories and Dependencies of the United States: Their Government and Administration* (New York: The Century Company, 1905), p. 105.

46. The memo is dated March 29, 1909. National Archives, Washington, D.C., Record Group 126, File 9–8–48, Pt. 1, p. 2.

47. Theodore Roosevelt, *The New Nationalism* (Englewood Cliffs, N.J.: Prentice Hall, 1961), p. 36.

48. See House Committee on Insular Affairs, *A Civil Government for Porto Rico*, 63rd Congress, 2nd session, 1914, p. 65.

49. See *Congressional Record*, House, 61st Congress, 2nd session, June 8, 1910, pp. 7609–7610.

50. See Charles Allen, ed., "Opportunities in Porto Rico," in *Opportunities in the Colonies and Cuba* (New York: Lewis, Scribner, 1902), pp. 275–369, esp. p. 340.

51. See Rowe, *United States and Porto Rico*, p. 195; also Pedro Caban, "El Aparato Colonial y el Cambio Económico en Puerto Rico: 1898–1917," *Revista de Ciencias Sociales*, 27 (March-June 1988): pp. 89–102.

52. See, for example, Caban, "El Aparato Colonial," p. 71.

53. See *Congressional Record*, House, June 8, 1910, p. 7609.

54. See, for example, Arthur Gayer, Paul T. Homan, and Earle K. James, *The Sugar Economy of Puerto Rico* (New York: Columbia, 1938).

55. See *Civil Government for Porto Rico*, Senate, January 10, 1911, pp. 7–15, esp. p. 12; on the technology see Christian Schnakenbourg, "From Sugar Estate to Central Factory: The Industrial Revolution in the Caribbean (1840–1905)," in B. Albert and A. Graves, eds., *Crisis and Change in the International Sugar Economy, 1860–1914* (Norfalk, U.K.: ISC Press, 1985), pp. 83–91.

56. See *Congressional Record*, Senate, 56th Congress, 1st session, April 30, 1900, p. 4852.

57. Allen, *Opportunities*, p. 358.

58. Ibid., p. 366.

59. See, for example, Robert Heilbroner, *The Nature and Logic of Capitalism* (New York: W. W. Norton, 1985), esp. pp. 33–52.

60. Ibid., p. 57.

61. See John E. Dalton, *Sugar: A Case Study in Government Control* (New York: Macmillan, 1937), esp. chap. 15.

62. See Negrón Portillo, *Las Turbas Republicanas*.

63. Ibid., see esp. pp. 88–89, 97.

64. See *First Annual Report of Charles H. Allen*, p. 46.

65. Ibid., p. 114.

66. Ibid., p. 115; see also p. 46.

67. Ibid., p. 98; see, too, Alegría, *Temas*, pp. 215–216.

68. See Todd, *Desfile de Gobernadores*, p. 17; *First Annual Report of Charles H. Allen*, p. 49.

69. Todd, *Desfile de Gobernadores*, pp. 17–18.

70. See, especially, Negrón Portillo, *Las Turbas Republicanas*, pp. 204–205.

71. See Michael Sam Hornik, *Nationalist Sentiment in Puerto Rico from the American Invasion until the Foundation of the Partido Nacionalista, 1898–1922* (Buffalo: University of Buffalo, 1972), p. 56.

72. Rowe, *United States and Porto Rico*, p. 154.

73. See the introductory essay in Gamaliel Ramos, *Ideas Anexienistas*, pp. 28–29; also Negrón Portillo, *Las Turbas Republicanas*, esp. Chap. 1.

74. See A. G. Quintero Rivera, *Conflictos de Clase y Política en Puerto Rico* (Río Piedras: Huracán, 1977).

75. See Gervasio L. García y A. G. Quintero Rivera, *Desafío y Solidaridad* (Río Piedras: Huracán, 1982), esp. p. 34.

76. See Quintero Rivera, *Patricios y Plebeyos*, p. 125.

77. See Earl S. Pomeroy, "The American Colonial Office," *Mississippi Valley Historical Review* 30 (1944): pp. 521–532; also Major General Frank McIntyre, "American Territorial Administration," *Foreign Affairs* 10 (January 1932): pp. 293–303.

78. See, Todd, *Desfile de Gobernadores*, pp. 27–29.

79. See *Congressional Record*, House, February 2, 1904, p. 1526.

80. Ibid., p. 1527.

81. See Alegría, *Temas*, p. 219.

82. See Hornik, *Nationalist Sentiment*, pp. 58–59; also see Alegría, *Temas*, p. 219.

83. See Delma S. Arrigoitia, "José De Diego: A Legislator in Times of Political Transition" (Ph.D. diss., Fordham University, 1985), p. 103.

84. Ibid., p. 102.

85. Ibid., pp. 104–106.

86. See *Message from the President of the United States Relative to His Recent Visit to the Island of Porto Rico*, Senate, 59th Congress, 2nd session, Document no. 135, 1906, p. 3.

87. See the letter sent by the House of Delegates to President Theodore Roosevelt, March 14, 1907. National Archives, Puerto Rico, 9–82.

88. Ibid., p. 6 in my copy of the House's memo to the president. The actual document is not paginated.

89. Joseph Foraker, *Notes of a Busy Life*, Vol. 2, (Cincinnati: Stewart & Kidd Company, 1916), p. 83.

90. *Message from the President*, p. 5.

91. National Archives, Puerto Rico, 9–82, the letter from the president's secretary is the cover document on the petition of the island's House; on the protest see Hornik, *Nationalist Sentiment*, p. 61.

92. See Arrigoitia, "José De Diego," p. 113.

93. Ibid., p. 123; and for the comment of Muñoz Rivera, see p. 125.

94. Ibid., pp. 128–129.

95. See War Department, Annual Reports, 1909, *Report of the Governor of Porto Rico*, Washington, D.C., 1909, p. 25.

96. Ibid., p. 25.

97. Memo of William F. Willoughby, marked confidential, in the National Archives, Puerto Rico, 9–8–20, p. 3.

98. Ibid., p. 3.

99. Ibid., p. 8.

100. Ibid., for Willoughby see pp. 13–15; for the tyranny comment see a letter of Muñoz's cited by Willoughby on p. 4.

101. Ibid., p. 12.

102. See Truman Clark, "President Taft and the Puerto Rican Appropriation Crisis of 1909," *The Americas* 26 (October 1969): p. 158; also relevant is Clark's "Educating the Natives in Self-Government: Puerto Rico and the United States, 1900–1933," *Pacific Historical Review* 42 (May 1973): pp. 220–233.

103. Willoughby memo, p. 15.

104. See *Brief of the Commission of the House of Delegates to the Federal Government about the Present Legislative Difficulties in the Island*, in the National Archives, Puerto Rico, 9–8–48; the document is dated March 29, 1909, and the comments cited appear on pp. 10–11.

105. See Clark, *Appropriations Crisis*, p. 161.

106. See *Affairs in Porto Rico, Message from the President*, Senate, 61st Congress, Document no. 40, 1909, pp. 4–6.

107. Ibid., p. 6.

108. Ibid., pp. 5–6.

109. See Willoughby, *Territories and Dependencies*, p. 104.

110. *Affairs in Porto Rico*, p. 6.

111. *Congressional Record*, House, April 11, 1900, p. 4058.

112. See Clark, *Appropriations Crisis*, p. 161.

Chapter 3

Puerto Rico:
The Permanent Possession

We are the southerners of the twentieth century.
Luis Muñoz Rivera, House Speech, May 5, 1916

We welcome the new citizen, not as a stranger but as one
entering his father's house.
President Woodrow Wilson, April 1, 1917[1]

Decoration was a problem. To learn children needed stimulation, the
effervescence that came from delightful surroundings. Unfortunately,
quickly constructed island schools had as much zest as an orange crate.
Thus, to give students their first picture of mainland life teachers anx-
iously searched for symbols that personified the United States of America. They wanted the best, but through the first decade of the twentieth
century teachers often settled for art that was "not of the highest aes-
thetic order." Indeed, on the walls of their new schools many Puerto
Rican youngsters could gaze only at a con man selling elixirs and a
brewer hawking beer. For their first glimpse of American life students
eyed the posters taken from breweries and patent medicine companies.[2]

Beginning with the military occupation, English was the mandated
medium of instruction; however, none of the children, and few of their
native teachers, understood English. So like the biblical Tower of Babel,
education in Puerto Rican schoolhouses confused everyone in the room.
Even in 1991 only 20 percent of islanders spoke English;[3] in the first
decades of the twentieth century the tiny portion of islanders who spoke

the language was a sure guarantee that few students would ever garner even basic educational skills.

Understanding this, native teachers often disregarded the rules. They spoke in Spanish but they had to watch out for the U.S. monitors, who demanded that teachers also be treated like children. To keep a job, the Puerto Rican instructors had to attend English-language classes and, presumably, provide a satisfactory explanation if they failed to show up at school. In a circular given to his U.S. employees, the commissioner stressed that "teachers of English are required to keep an exact record of the attendance of every teacher and forward to the Superintendent each month a report of absences."[4]

Mirroring the movement then active on the mainland, U.S. officials sought to Americanize the immigrant who, in Puerto Rico, was not an immigrant.[5] Moreover, island educators seemed to be using the metaphor of an assembly line instead of a melting pot. By changing the names of schools to Washington, Lincoln, and Jefferson; by eliminating holidays celebrated for centuries (e.g., the Epiphany or in Puerto Rico, Three Kings Day); and by asking students to begin their schoolday mornings with the pledge of allegiance, the "Star Spangled Banner," and "America the Beautiful," teachers hoped to instill the love of country that would make islanders 100 percent Americans.

It never worked. As early as 1907 the U.S. commissioner of education admitted that it would be "useless" to expect the attendance of students on that day (January 6, Three Kings Day);[6] and he also provided this short summary of a decade of Americanization: "That there is any deep-seated affection for us among them would be absurd to assert and probably most foolish to expect. . . . A mutual respect which bears fruit in mutual forbearance is the limit to which the relations of the two races can be expected to go."[7]

For Congress that forbearance reached its limits as soon as the Puerto Rican legislature refused to pass the 1909 budget. Citing the "joy ride" enjoyed by the Puerto Rican people, Representative Marlin Olmstead of Pennsylvania prepared his colleagues and the nation for a debate that included not only the budget suggestions of the president but also an analysis of the entire Puerto Rican political and educational system.[8]

Living in Texas, Representative James Slayden thought he knew why Puerto Rico was saddled with "chronic troubles": "They and we are of different races. . . . We are mainly Anglo-Saxon, while they are a composite structure, with liberal contributions to their blood from Europe, Asia and Africa. They are largely mongrels now." And those mongrels threatened to destroy the United States of America. Because Slayden believed that a future historian seeking to explain the nation's demise would "unavoidably reach the conclusion that the downfall began with the Spanish-American War . . . when we abandoned homogeneity and harmony for race complexity and discord."[9]

Slayden wanted to throw the dogs out. But when the House did it, Slayden declared, representatives should also confess their blunders and contradictions. Although race differences inevitably guaranteed a failure in Puerto Rico, he said, "we put on them a government without consultation and we should not be surprised that it does not work smoothly nor to the satisfaction of those who are its subjects."[10]

Representative Atterson Rucker of Colorado lacked Slayden's compassion. He argued that "the question in its acute form is whether this Congress will allow the government we have established there, and by which so many Americans with their capital have found permanent footing, to be subverted." Congress had to remember that "money was the biggest coward in the world." Indeed, just because it dashed away from any and all signs of political instability, it was Congress's solemn obligation to rewrite the Foraker Act in a fashion that would significantly increase the powers of colonial administrators.[11]

For Rucker politics did not stop at the water's edge. It started there because of the character of the Puerto Rican people. "The riffraff, adventurers and pirates of Spain" cohabited with slaves and Indians; and then "the French and English and Santo Dominicans and Venezuelans furnished their quota in turn." The end result was "admixture after admixture, cross after cross, far beyond the multiplication table" so that Puerto Rico now had "an unreadable genealogical tree."[12]

Rucker, however, read the tree to say subjugation. A race as mixed as the Puerto Rican was doomed to inferiority, a fact proved by Rucker with evidence like this: "The production of children, especially of the dark color, is largely on the increase. The country ones are naked until they reach the age of 10 or 12 years, and thereafter they are but little better clad. Their food consists mainly of the windfall of fruit and refuse, if they beat the dog or the hog to it."[13]

The *Congressional Record* indicates that Rucker's comments met with this reaction from his colleagues: "laughter."[14] Racism was still an official joke at this stage of U.S. history so, with Puerto Rico's resident commissioner listening to each and every statement, representatives first blasted the Puerto Rican people and then explained why Puerto Rico had to forever remain a possession of the United States.

Representative Henry Cooper of Wisconsin thought the United States should use the entire island as a naval base. When his colleagues literally applauded this idea, Cooper explained his reasoning: "We want Porto Rico to help us make the Gulf of Mexico an American lake. We want it for purposes of self defense."[15] The problem was that congressional carping alienated a people we needed to use: "I know of no more unwise method of attempting to awaken the gratitude of a people than to speak bitterly about the 'ingratitude' of the people of Porto Rico."[16]

Cooper's suggestion was to offer a form of citizenship without rights. Let them become sort of Americans and don't worry about the issue of statehood. For example, "Arizona and other Territories came to us under an act which practically pledged that they should be made States and we have kept them out of statehood upward of sixty years." Promise them anything but stop creating problems "in a land forever to be retained by this Republic."[17]

Cooper's suggestion was an idea in search of support. In 1909 Congress had no intention of granting Puerto Ricans even a second-class citizenship. But in underlining the island's strategic importance, Cooper cited *the* principal reason Puerto Rico had to be a permanent possession of the United States.

For example, a war board study of 1898 focused on the geography of the Caribbean in relation to defense of the Panama Canal. Because the Caribbean was virtually landlocked, "one cork alone was necessary for this body."[18] Right up to World War II the cork in question was Cuba, the point of access to the Caribbean's Windward Passage. But suppose sailors needed another cork? Or something happened to the base at Guantanamo? Then Puerto Rico might assume great importance. Thus despite the skeleton forces remaining on the main island into the late 1930s, and on the "baby" islands of Vieques and Culebra, the United States had to retain Puerto Rico.[19]

In the words of Major General Frank McIntyre, head of the War Department bureau that governed Puerto Rico until 1934, "There should be full recognition of the fact that in assigning small islands for supervision it is proper to keep in view the specific object for which they were acquired." Indeed, "an island or a small group of islands acquired primarily for naval purposes does not differ greatly from a war vessel or fleet at anchor."[20]

People on boats, islands or cannons—they all looked the same to sailors and to the successive Congresses that underlined Puerto Rico's strategic significance in America's largest salt water lake, the Caribbean.

Right after Representative Cooper asked his colleagues to stop criticizing the Puerto Ricans, James Kennedy of Ohio made this remark: "The great mistake we made was in assuming that the Porto Ricans had any capacity for self government whatever. . . . Had we considered history we would have learned that the Spaniard, of all civilized races, had the least capacity for self government.[21]

In 1909 representatives like Kennedy were simply too angry to do anything but reject all memorials and proposals coming from the Puerto Rican legislators and their constituents. Instead, on July 15, 1909, Congress quickly and overwhelmingly passed the law requested by President William Howard Taft. Now, should the Puerto Ricans refuse to approve another budget, last year's appropriations immediately went into effect.

On the island the Unionists were naturally disappointed. Instead of their nonviolent tactics leading to greater autonomy, they had lost the one power they had. Moreover, a commission established by President Taft actually wanted to expand substantially the powers of an already autocratic government.

As usual islanders had no one solution to offer. But to many, independence seemed the only viable alternative. How else gain control of an economy that after only ten years exported 88.5 percent of its goods to the United States and received, in return 84.5 percent of its goods from the United States? (The figures for 1897 were 21 percent and 15.2 percent respectively.)[22]

However revealing and necessary, statistics forever miss the everyday impact of the U.S. occupation. A nation as powerful and eager as the United States set off ripples of change in every direction, extending into areas as different as the meaning of life and the manufacture of cigarettes.

Protestant ministers followed U.S. soldiers into Puerto Rico as soon as the invasion succeeded. Solemn and methodical, these ministers brought a message of hope and spiritual regeneration, linked to an often outright rejection of the island's overwhelmingly dominant religion, Roman Catholicism. One minister noted that Protestants sought a communion between the individual and his or her god; what Catholics sought was a confession between one person and a snoop. Convert to Protestantism because it is the pathway to heaven, he preached, and while waiting for death islanders should also remember that Roman Catholicism is an obstacle to democracy: "Freedoms will come if God wills it but they will in spite of the never changing Catholic church."[23]

On the sidewalks of San Juan and the back roads of the mountainous Jayuya, citizens dressed in black produced the religious converts who soon had a political impact. Politicians trying to unite the people by stressing their long links to Spain and Catholicism suddenly discovered that island Protestants had been immunized. Their god looked to Washington, not Madrid, and used as a metaphor for the coming of the Americans Jesus' efforts in Jerusalem.[24]

In Spanish the words are *habichuelas con arroz*; in English, rice and beans; and in any language they translate into the food staples of island life. Until the U.S. invasion islanders would complement the staples with codfish (*bacalao*), but as living conditions deteriorated, fish consumption fell. Discussing the first decades of the twentieth century, one scholar suggests a situation as bad as the Irish potato famine.[25] Whatever characterization we use, the certainty is that islanders tried to survive by significantly increasing their consumption, not only of rice, but of rice from a particular location: the United States.

Between 1900 and 1902 rice imports increased by 1,500 percent. This extraordinary rise eventually leveled off at 300 percent, yet islanders soon bought so many U.S. products—cars and meat and furniture for the rich, rice and beans for the poor—that Puerto Rico quickly became one of the most important trading partners of the United States. Indeed, throughout the twentieth century Puerto Rico has consistently ranked first or near first in per capita purchases from the United States, and as late as February 1991 the island's yearly purchases exceeded the combined sales of U.S. products to Argentina, Colombia, and Brazil.[26]

So many imports had a variety of effects: an increase in the cost of living, a marked tendency to devalue native products, and the creation of business interests whose well-being depended on close ties to the United States. Historically, importers traded with Spain; the occupation opened up opportunities for newcomers with a fluency in English and the ambition to establish commercial ties in cities like Baltimore, New York, and Philadelphia. As in sugar and tobacco, the shipping companies were owned by Americans—the New York and Porto Rico Steamship Company, for example, was incorporated in Maine—and the cabotage laws protected U.S. interests far better than any tariff.

Still, in a poor country totally dependent on sea traffic, shipping and related industries always provided a guaranteed source of income.[27] Importers and dock workers, warehouse owners and truckers, tourist facilities and service staff, all became part of a lifeline that linked their well-being to that of trade with the United States. Often natives resented the attitudes and actions of the federal government, yet like most of us, if it came to a choice between survival and political ideals, they would probably refuse to bite the hand that fed them, especially since they were literally at sea.

Good things sometimes have unforeseen consequences. In Puerto Rico U.S. administrators tried to significantly improve the medical and sanitation facilities available to the masses of the island's population. Proceeding from the premise that Latin people were "not quite rigid and conscientious" about health and sanitation,[28] U.S. colonial administrators instructed doctors and their associates to make significant improvements in a variety of areas immediately. Under the directive many thousands of men, women, and children received vaccinations against smallpox free of charge and by 1909 fully a quarter of the population had already received treatment for a form of "tropical anemia" that hacked its way through and across the island.[29]

Americans could be justly proud of their accomplishments in health and sanitation. The problem, common to colonial governments, was that the Americans had initiated only the first phase in the demographic transition: The death rates quickly fell.[30] But with birth rates as high as ever, no one tried to check population growth or, more probable in the early twentieth century, plan an economic future for Puerto Rico's burgeoning population.

The terrible irony was that administrators who lobbied for improvements in health and sanitation also welcomed the sugar and tobacco producers, who at best provided part-time labor for a population that would increase by almost 200,000 during the first ten years of U.S. rule and by another 200,000 during the second decade of the U.S. occupation.[31]

During the Victorian era, and in a predominantly Catholic country at that, help for Puerto Rico's population would have to come from economic and political sources. Unfortunately, the two groups who might have, together, pressured the United States for change were still divided as to the means necessary to obtain change.

Labor was angry, so angry that it soon adopted the *jacho* (or torch) as the symbol of its struggle. In the sugar fields workers singed pieces of cane before they were cut and processed; however, the burned cane now had to be cut in a very short period of time or the stalks would be useless. Thus workers "torched" the cane but refused to cut and move it unless labor negotiations went their way. Meanwhile, anger with, and distrust of, the American Tobacco Company produced no less than sixteen strikes between 1911 and 1913. The supposedly docile labor force meant to be heard, although in general they still refrained from active participation in the island's political processes.[32]

Labor's rejection of politics was not rooted in rejection of the colonial government. On the contrary, labor still distrusted many Unionist leaders every bit as much as it distrusted the U.S. plantation owners. In the eyes of many labor leaders, Unionists wasted their time in futile efforts at political change and, equally important, supported the economic interests that were exploiting the masses. José De Diego, a Unionist leader, was in fact an attorney for the U.S. sugar interests; and one of his colleagues made this remark about Santiago Iglesias, head of the labor movement: "I assure you that if Puerto Rico was free and in control of its own destiny . . . I would deport him for perniciousness, for corrupting the public conscience."[33]

Rejecting cooperation with island politicians, simultaneously labeling the corporations "as the capitalist tigers that devoured the country," labor had only one resource left: the authorities in Washington. Why labor thought the politicians who had put the corporations in power would change the behavior of those corporations was, of course, a good question. A part of the answer lay in the still-lingering lure of the U.S.

Constitution. Men like Iglesias believed in the promise of America;[34] they thought that the authorities in Washington would unite ideals and reality. And so in letter after letter Iglesias complained to the president. Samuel Gompers even acted as a sponsor when Iglesias voiced his concerns.

President Woodrow Wilson received and read the letters. He passed them on to his secretary of war, who even as late as 1918 offered this advice about Iglesias's desire to have a commission investigate labor conditions in Puerto Rico. Secretary of War Newton Baker told the president:

Such a commission would find the condition of the great mass of the laborers in Puerto Rico, if anything, worse than it is reported by Mr. Iglesias. The commission would find that even the poorly paid laborers in the sugar fields were in fact among the most fortunate of the agricultural laborers. The commission would find that the question of the day's wage would be relatively unimportant, in view of the fact that so many people in Porto Rico cannot get a day's work at any wage, except occasionally. This condition is unfortunately chronic.... From no official source has it been brought in question. As to agricultural conditions the commission would, therefore, have no divergent views to compose.[35]

So much for Washington, which, as it heard from labor, was also besieged by complaints from the Unionist party. President Taft's humiliating rebuke was followed by congressional legislation that promised to be far worse than anything imagined by the island politicians. The Executive Council was to be expanded from eight to thirteen members, but instead of granting more autonomy, the new plan stipulated that eight of the thirteen members would be appointed by the president and none of the eight had to reside in the districts they represented. The vote was to be taken away from a substantial portion of the population—islanders would now be able to vote only if they met literacy and property qualifications—and, most frightening of all, Puerto Ricans would be forced to be citizens of a country that absolutely refused to consider statehood as an island option.[36]

Congress's idea was to make the Puerto Ricans citizens collectively in spite of themselves. They would have a specified period of time to decide whether they wanted to accept citizenship, but once that time was up, only Americans could participate in the Puerto Rican government. However, even those Americans had to understand that citizenship had nothing to do with ultimate political status. As Taft told the nation shortly before his term of office expired, "It is a happy sign of the realization of what should be the most fitting political aspiration of the island, as well as a recognition of the public opinion of the United States, that in the minds of neither people is the grant of citizenship associated with any thought of statehood."[37]

Alternating between humiliation and anger, islanders searched for a way to avoid citizenship without statehood. One splinter group actually formed the Puerto Rican Independence party, but the Unionists nevertheless managed to create a consensus around the following ideals. Because statehood was a denied option, the Unionists removed it from their 1913 platform, substituting instead the goal of a republic under the protection of the United States. As De Diego put it, "If the Cubans, who in three wars sacrificed thousands of lives for their independence, were compelled to submit to the right of intervention, what could we Puerto Ricans do against what is imposed by unavoidable, irresistible circumstances in our weakness and helplessness?"[38]

De Diego understood the realities of Washington's Latin American policy.[39] His hope was that by offering guarantees to the United States, he could persuade the Progressive President Wilson to point his country toward ultimate independence. For example, in the 1913 proposal De Diego stipulated that, as in Cuba, the United States could intervene civilly or militarily in the event of disturbances that worried Washington.[40]

Congress was fit to be tied. Eliminating the statehood option from the Unionist's platform angered representatives who yet again failed to comprehend the Puerto Ricans' ingratitude. And the idea of independence—whatever the U.S. rights of intervention—was another insult to the American people. The Puerto Ricans had to understand they had no rights, except those given by Congress. So in a remarkably frank set of 1914 hearings, Congress explicitly told the Puerto Ricans what their final destiny would be.

Arthur Yager was the first witness to appear before the House Committee on Insular Affairs. Appointed governor of Puerto Rico only three months before these February 1914 hearings took place, Yager nevertheless had decided opinions about the best way to maintain peace and progress in Puerto Rico. He agreed that islanders had to be made citizens, but Yager argued that citizenship should be granted to the Puerto Ricans in this way: "that we give them simply an opportunity to become citizens without any cost or delay or any conditions of any sort—just offer it to them and let them have an opportunity to take it or leave it."[41]

Asked why he favored a voluntary approach to citizenship, Yager explained, "The advantage is this: It is purely the condition of things that exist in Porto Rico." Islanders had complained about the Foraker Act for so many years that the citizenship question was now a major issue of island politics. Yager believed that "they will all come into the fold if given an opportunity, or at least the great bulk of them. But if Congress attempts to force them in they will feel embarrassed and troubled and one party will use it as a hammer or club."[42]

Yager wanted to avoid trouble, so much so that he was even willing, as Congress was not, to let islanders who chose to remain Puerto Ricans participate in their own government. Congress sought to exclude anyone who rejected U.S. citizenship, but Yager, agreeing that "we have never had the slightest idea of renouncing it [Puerto Rico] or giving it up," nonetheless stressed that Congress must realize that "there is a large section of one of the political parties that in sheer desperation, after the matter of citizenship has been postponed time and again, turned away from that idea and proposes now to develop and cherish what Congress has heretofore given them, namely, the citizenship of Porto Rico."[43]

Try not to "irritate" them, suggested Yager, because humiliation was never the best way to foster allegiance to the stars and stripes. In Yager's words, "My objection to the whole thing is that I would rather lead a horse to water, than drive him."[44]

Chairman William Jones understood Yager's argument. But he still wasn't sure what to do. After all, "if we were to put such a provision [i.e., Yager's voluntary citizenship] in the law it would be regarded as notice to the people of Porto Rico, especially to those who favor independence, . . . that the U.S. has not determined the future political status of the Porto Ricans, and they were therefore at liberty to go ahead and clamor for independence." But the American people were "practically unanimous" that the island would remain forever a part of the United States, so "is it not best to remove this question from Porto Rican politics?"[45]

Representing the Wilson administration, Secretary of War Lindsay Garrison had this answer to Jones's question: "As I understand the situation . . . there is no suggestion that it [Puerto Rico] should not be connected with the United States for all time, and that we should not in the fullest measure be responsible for it as we are for any other thing that is under our flag."[46]

But lurking in the wings of Jones's collective grant of citizenship was the same problem Foraker confronted in 1900:

if every one there by this act was declared to be a citizen of the United States, and the Territory, the actual physical soil was unmistakably real estate belonging to the United States, you might have a situation in which all the laws enacted by Congress would ex proprio vigore apply to the land and people and things there.[47]

Thus Puerto Ricans might be Americans to whom the Constitution applied. Congress could no longer discriminate between incorporated and unincorporated territories.

This "undesirable" prospect frightened the Wilson administration so much—"if you say everyone in Porto Rico is a citizen of the United

States you make it a territory of the United States with a capital 'T' "[48]— that Garrison offered this solution to the potential Constitutional dilemma: "Fix a time sufficiently long in advance to enable acquiescence, and easy and free, and to say after that time there should be no elector and no elected that was not a citizen of the United States." In this way Congress never said that all Puerto Ricans were Americans; the exceptions proved the rule, the rule that America would be free to legislate for the islanders outside the limits set by the Constitution for those people who were really 100 percent Americans.[49]

What happened to the islanders who wanted to remain Puerto Ricans? What would we call them? Garrison said, "I would call them denizens." But the important point was to avoid the possible constitutional problems created by a blanket grant of citizenship. "We say you are under our flag; if you want to participate in this Government, you must become citizens. If you do not, if you wish to remain outside, that is no concern of ours; and we have done all that justice and equity requires us to do."[50]

On other issues concerning the Puerto Ricans—for example, franchises and sanitation—the Wilson administration believed the essential thing was to "safeguard" U.S. interests. Garrison, for example, not only had never been to the island but openly admitted he knew "very little" about it.[51] Thus, this legislation was an "experiment"; indeed, "it may be that this is slightly premature, and perhaps we will find the thing will sag in some places, and it may bend; but it represents the best thought of those who have given it their attention. That is why I have approved it."[52]

Luis Muñoz Rivera, Puerto Rico's resident commissioner, was the committee's next witness. Arguing that he represented both the Union and Republican parties, Muñoz opened with a salvo about representative government. He spoke for the 99 percent of his people who wanted nothing to do with either Yager's or the president's suggestions. In fact, if Congress actually wanted to hear from the Puerto Rican people, their sentiments could easily be condensed in this fashion: "If you wish to make us citizens of an inferior class; . . . if we cannot be one of your States; if we cannot constitute a country of our own then we will have to be perpetually a colony, a dependency of the United States. Is that the kind of citizenship you offer us? Then, that is the citizenship we refuse."[53]

Chairman Jones asked Muñoz if he did not "recognize the fact that there is no sentiment in the United States in favor of granting independence to the Porto Ricans?"[54]

Of course Muñoz understood that; it was in fact, he said, "the very reason my party advocates that the question be left open." Perhaps

Congress would find out more about Puerto Rico and therefore change its mind?

Chairman Jones thought not.

For one I think the chance that there will be any change of sentiment upon this subject is too remote to be seriously considered now. This bill is framed upon the idea that Porto Rico is to remain a permanent possession of the United States. It proposes to settle this question and thus remove it from Porto Rican politics. What do you say about that Mr. Rivera?[55]

Muñoz Rivera tried to walk a tightrope, but Chairman Jones pushed him off. "This talk of independence is an idle dream on the part of the Unionist Party and it would be much better to have the matter settled now, better for the Port Ricans themselves."[56] After fourteen years the political bickering would cease and, as American citizens, islanders could at least avoid the Catch–22 experienced by Puerto Ricans who recently tried to become naturalized: They were told they were not aliens so they could not be citizens. They were denizens, a sort of invisible people.[57]

To the Puerto Ricans even no status was better than that of second-class American. In yet another memorial to Congress, dated March 27, 1914, the Puerto Rican legislature unanimously approved a resolution that stipulated, "While rendering just and sincere homage to your citizenship, we firmly and loyally maintain our opposition to being declared, in defiance of our express wish or without our express consent, citizens of any country whatsoever other than our own beloved soil that God has given us as an inalienable gift and incoercible right."[58]

Congress dutifully printed the memorial, ignored it, and then postponed action on Representative Jones's legislation. Among other things, fear of the constitutional implications of citizenship outweighed the consensus established in the 1914 (and earlier) debates.[59] Perhaps if the president took a personal hand in the Puerto Rican legislation? Or if the islanders turned from peaceful to violent protest? Perhaps, at that point, Congress would move on the already-established consensus?

Whatever the case, in 1914 Congress's attitude was best expressed by a bit of everyday American wisdom: If it's not broken, don't fix it. The Puerto Ricans could continue to live in limbo because they were a patient people without any support in the United States. For example, after Puerto Rico's fifteen years in the American family, some educated Americans still wanted to know how to drive to Puerto Rico, and others sent the governor letters addressed to "San Juan, Porto Rico, Philippine Islands, U.S.A."[60]

Puerto Rico was a dot in the Pacific or an extension of the Florida coastline. At best it was a peripheral topic to Americans of all political persuasions until, yet again, the Philippines played a decisive role in determining Puerto Rico's future.

As chair of the House Committee on Insular Affairs, Representative Jones had responsibility not only for Puerto Rico but for the Philippines as well. So when President Wilson expressed public support for Philippine independence only weeks after his election, and then reiterated that support in his 1913 State of the Union address,[61] Jones prepared legislation with this startling preamble: "Whereas it is, as it always has been, the purpose of the people of the United States to withdraw their sovereignty over the Philippine Islands and to recognize their independence as soon as a stable government can be established therein."[62] The United States agreed to free the Philippines as soon as they established a government acceptable to the United States.

Jones easily got this bill through the House of Representatives in October 1914. The stumbling block—and this was a large block—came in the form of ex-President Taft. A former governor of the Philippines, Taft was determined to prevent the loss of any U.S. colony. He established a blue-ribbon committee to derail any plan for Philippine independence. He believed the Filipinos unfit for self-government; they needed more tutelage from the Americans, who barred natives from social clubs and, unless a servant, refused to allow a Filipino in the Army and Navy Club, "whose lovely garden of bougainvillea, palms and flame trees faced Manila Bay."[63]

Taft was both consistent and successful. He, as well as a variety of other interests, managed to defeat the Philippine bill in 1914 primarily because of an amendment that promised full U.S. withdrawal in not less than two nor more than four years. Such a speedy departure scared Congress. But in 1916 supporters of the Philippine bill seemed willing to erase the time limit clause. If they did that, passage of the Philippine legislation might force Congress's hand on Puerto Rico; it would, after all, be very difficult to pass legislation for one colony yet disregard another equally unhappy member of the U.S. empire.[64]

On January 4, 1916, nine months after they first received it, Congress published another memorial from the Puerto Rican legislature;[65] representatives were still protesting their island's "intolerable" political situation when Representative Jones reintroduced his 1914 bill, which was, in fact, very similar to the legislation first introduced in 1910. However, to underline the difference between one colony and another, the preamble to the Puerto Rico bill contained the following clause: "that the provisions of this Act shall apply to the island of Puerto Rico and to the adjacent islands belonging to the United States."[66]

Whatever happened in the Pacific or in Congress, Puerto Rico belonged to the United States. Nobody planned to give up this possession, and that infuriated Resident Commissioner Luis Muñoz Rivera.

Sick, and sensing that this time something might actually happen, Muñoz made an extended plea to Congress on May 5, 1916. "For sixteen years we have endured this system of government, protesting and struggling against it, with energy and without result." To Muñoz there was simply no reason to deny self-government to any Puerto Rican and even less justice in the provision of the bill that took the vote away from so many islanders. "Is illiteracy the reason? Because if in Puerto Rico 60% of the electorate cannot read, in the United States in the early days of the Republic 80% of the population were unable to read; and even today there are twenty Republics and twenty monarchies which acknowledge a higher percentage of illiteracy than Puerto Rico."[67]

Muñoz could fathom only one reason for Congress's behavior: Puerto Ricans "were the Southerners of the twentieth century." Or as the federal judge in Puerto Rico Peter Hamilton put it in a letter to President Wilson:

The real difficulty here, as I take it, is not unlike that down South. The claim of the employers is that the laborers as a rule have no ambition and aim to make only enough to live on, with the result that they will work two or three days and be idle the rest of the week. I am afraid there is a good degree of truth in this, if I can judge from domestic servants. It is in the climate.[68]

As Judge Hamilton's remarks suggest, Muñoz knew what he was talking about. His problem was the island's perceived helplessness in the face of Congress's will and U.S. military power. To Muñoz Puerto Rico was "poor, isolated and defenseless." Thus his principal idea was to suggest a plebiscite because "it would be strange if, having refused it [citizenship] so long as the majority asked for it, you should decide to impose it by force now that the majority of the people decline it."[69]

Congress politely listened to Muñoz's long and detailed speech. It was an eloquent message that had absolutely no impact on Congress. Representative Clarence Miller of Minnesota stressed that "the agitation for independence in Porto Rico must come to a decided and a permanent end." Puerto Rico was "necessary to the United States as a key to the defense of the whole American continent against aggression from Europe." Thus, "if there is anything that you and I must be agreed upon it is this: That Porto Rico will never go out from under the shadow of the Stars and Stripes [applause from Congress]."[70]

To assure America's rights, the Jones Bill planned to take away the vote from the masses of the Puerto Rican people. To Representative Meyer London of New York this "assassinated the rights of the Porto Ricans" but Representative William Green, representing the views of a large majority of his colleagues, summed up the debate in this manner: "We are going to give them citizenship. Ten years from now they are going to rise up and call us blessed. But we are not going to give everyone the right to vote; and they are all going to rise up and bless us for doing that too."[71]

In truth only time would tell who would bless whom. In the meantime Chairman Jones still had to get his bill through Congress. With the time limit for independence no longer an issue, the Philippine Jones Bill passed Congress in August 1916. But for passage of the Puerto Rican legislation Jones still needed help from three additional sources: the president, the Great War, and the disgruntled Puerto Rican people.[72]

To many Americans the island seemed to be coming apart at the seams. Strikes on the docks, 50,000 workers protesting conditions in the tobacco fields, and then, in 1916, the biggest sugar strike in the nation's history. For five and a half months over 40,000 workers in some thirty-two separate municipalities tried to close down the sugar industry. They failed. But many workers did obtain better conditions, and far more significant for the Americans, labor alerted the authorities to the potential power of the Puerto Rican masses. What if politicians started to preach that independence would forever rid the island of its parasitic absentee owners?[73]

Led by José De Diego, many Unionists spent 1916 expressing great dissatisfaction with the proposed legislation. To the island's activists Jones's idea of giving the governor an absolute veto over all legislation defeated the purpose of an elected Senate. What power did the people's representatives actually have if the governor could do as he pleased? And what about the new powers Jones gave to the commissioner of education and to the island's (sure to be U.S.) auditor? These representatives of the American people actually had greater powers than those given by Foraker and his colleagues. The auditor, for example, was the safeguard suggested by Congress, an administrator who had fiscal jurisdiction over the municipal governments, over the municipal courts, and even over the local school boards. Writing to his people in a series of newspaper critiques, De Diego noted, "it seems to me that in Rome, during the first period of monarchy, there were officers like this one [the auditor]."[74]

In Washington the president heard from a variety of his island administrators. General McIntyre, head of the War Department's Bureau of Insular Affairs, warned of the "formidable dimensions" achieved by the island's independence advocates. To quell those forces the War Department informed Congress that if it could not pass the Jones Bill in October, General McIntyre wanted to postpone the island's elections. On September 2, 1916, Congress did just that, based on Colorado's

Senator John Shafroth's plea that the War Department was "very anxious" to have any elections held only after the new Jones legislation was in place.[75]

On November 23 Puerto Rico's Governor Yager wrote the president thus: "I beg of you to make mention in your forthcoming message to Congress of the Porto Rican bill as one of the most urgent items of unfinished legislation." To Yager Puerto Ricans would rightly think they had been discriminated against if Congress passed the Philippine legislation but yet again neglected Puerto Rico.

More importantly the death of Muñoz Rivera on November 15, 1916 "made still more urgent the prompt passage of the Porto Rican bill." Despite his criticisms, Muñoz was always willing to compromise. Now "the remnants of the anti-American party in the island have seized upon the occasion to renew their agitation for independence and to try to prevent the passage of the new bill, to which they are naturally opposed."[76] Yager stressed that it was of "urgent importance" to pass the legislation promptly at this session; in no other way could he assure U.S. ability "to allay all political discontent and place the Island in a condition of peace and progress."[77]

The president did as he was asked. Only four days after receiving Yager's letter he told the governor, "I fully appreciate the importance of the Porto Rican Bill and have embodied a strong recommendation of its passage which I shall make to Congress now in a few days." Moreover, the president assured Yager, "I shall try to interest myself continuously in the matter until something is accomplished."[78]

Woodrow Wilson kept his word because his administration's policy, as early as 1914, was to silence the independence movement and because, quite by accident, Puerto Rico had become a part of the president's plans for possible U.S. involvement in World War I. To preclude German action, Wilson had pressured the Danish government to sell the Danish West Indies to the United States. At first the Danes resisted, but Wilson gave them a choice between Germany and the United States. In essence, the Danes could watch the Germans take the islands and then watch the Americans seize what the Germans had seized. Or the Danes could take cash for land and people.

The Danes chose cash, but before accepting it, they set this condition for final transfer of the islands and their people: The United States had to make the islanders U.S. citizens. Secretary of State Robert Lansing balked. How could the United States admit Danish colonials as Americans without first changing the status of the Puerto Ricans? The deal was off—until President Wilson, worried about potential military problems in the Caribbean, overruled his secretary of state and immediately made the Danish islanders U.S. citizens.[79]

Despite the president's action, Congress still refused to act on Chairman Jones's legislation. Representatives did see the citizenship contradictions of U.S. policy; they understood the German threat; and they definitely wanted to "guarantee" the loyalty of a population that might be willing to do anything to achieve independence. For example, in a refrain that would be heard again and again in international forums (e.g., the United Nations in the 1950s and 1960s), the secretary of war told an attentive Congress that the "moral" dominance of the United States in the U.S. Caribbean was intertwined with the nation's treatment of the Puerto Ricans: As an example of our commitment to democratic principles, the United States had to welcome the islanders into the American family.[80]

But the Puerto Ricans drank rum, lots of it. Islanders apparently had such an affection for liquor that it threatened to undermine a people who already had racial deficiencies. To Senator Asle Gronna of New Jersey the citizenship bill could pass only if his colleagues attached an amendment to extend prohibition to the islands even before the United States went dry. Wilson and Yager tried to explain that nobody in Puerto Rico wanted prohibition, and the island's Treasury Department received substantial tax revenues from the sale of rum: Couldn't Senator Gronna forget his amendment?

Never. Armed with letters from "hundreds of patriotic [American] women" who had investigated the liquor-loving islanders, Senator Gronna attached his amendment to the Jones Bill. A mixture of rum, racism, and self-righteousness had apparently brought down the Puerto Rican people until, ever the savvy politician Senator Henry Cabot Lodge got Gronna to agree to a compromise: The amendment would stand with the proviso attached that the Puerto Ricans would hold a referendum on prohibition. In true democratic fashion they could decide for themselves whether they wanted to continue producing and drinking the devil's potion.[81]

Congress finally approved the Puerto Rican version of the Jones Bill in late February, and on March 2, 1917, the president formally signed the legislation. He welcomed Puerto Ricans into their "father's house"[82] while, on the island, José De Diego refused the invitation. The newly elected representatives of the people (the postponed elections were held on July 16, 1917) echoed the preferences of their predecessors. Days after taking office, they allocated $25,000 of their own money to hold a plebiscite. Puerto Ricans would tell the world what they wanted in a 1920 status referendum; meanwhile, the United States should understand that islanders despised the harsh and oppressive political conditions created by the latest colonial legislation. To a large majority of the islanders a few improvements could never mask the realities of a law that, repeating the precedents set by Foraker, centralized all meaningful power in the hands of U.S. colonial administrators.[83]

By making the Puerto Rican Senate an elective body, the Jones Act eliminated the powers of the Executive Council. After March 1917, administrative and legislative authority were no longer housed in an official appointed by the president of the Senate. But to "safeguard" the islanders, to explicitly underline that this was, in Secretary Lindley Garrison's phrase, "an experiment," the Jones Act engaged in legislative sleight of hand. If you looked at what Congress did with the Senate, you missed what it did with the powers of the president, the governor and a variety of other appointed executives.

Under the Jones Act the governor—who held his office "at the pleasure of the President"—had a number of new and significant powers. He alone submitted the budget at the opening of each legislative session because his estimates were the only lawful starting point for all island appropriations. Moreover, the governor now had a line item veto over any appropriations coming from the island's elective bodies. He could "object to one or more of such items, or any part or parts, portion or portions thereof."

The governor also now had veto power over all legislation, and if two-thirds of the Senate and House passed a bill over the governor's veto, the legislation then bypassed San Juan and went straight to Washington, where, if the President failed to approve it, "he shall return it to the Governor, and it shall not become a law."[84]

In the event a controversial bill got by the governor and the president, all legislation still had to be reported to Congress, which in Section 23 of the Jones Act reserved "the power and authority to annul" any and all Puerto Rican laws.

Congress also reserved to itself the last word on appropriations by maintaining the hated Olmsted provision of 1909; if the Puerto Ricans refused to pass the governor's budget, last year's appropriations immediately went into effect.

The federal courts were still controlled by U.S. judges, who, as secretary Garrison stressed, "have the idea that they are the protectors of American citizens in Porto Rico."[85] And as a final assertion of U.S. authority, the Jones Act gave substantial powers to two presidential appointees: the commissioner of education and the auditor of Puerto Rico.

The auditor was "the watchdog of the Treasury."[86] Representatives who would soon call Warren Harding president distrusted the ability of the islanders to avoid waste and corruption in the administration of their own affairs. The auditor's job was thus "to examine, adjust, decide, audit, and settle all accounts and claims pertaining to the revenues and receipts from whatever source of the government of Puerto Rico."[87] The law mandated that the auditor's jurisdiction over these accounts "shall be exclusive," and it also stipulated that his decisions "shall be final."

To fulfill his responsibilities the auditor always had the power "to summon witnesses, administer oaths, take evidence," and issue subpoenas "to compel witnesses to produce books, letters, documents, powers, records, and all other articles deemed essential" to any resolution of wrongdoing.[88]

The power of the auditor angered many Puerto Ricans. The power of the commissioner of education infuriated them. Islanders understood that the commissioner sought to influence the hearts and minds of Puerto Rico's children. While the Jones Act quickly silenced calls for independence, the commissioner of education would slowly mold a generation who learned the American language by saluting the U.S. flag. Only the commissioner prepared "all courses of study" and only he had the statutory authority to prepare rules governing not only the selection of teachers but the appointment of those teachers by local school boards.

As with the powers of the president, the governor, and the auditor, the power of the commissioner of education proved to islanders that under the Jones Act ultimate as well as everyday authority remained in the hands of U.S. officials.

By calling for a plebiscite, islanders hoped to overrule the Jones Act. But only Congress could approve such a plebiscite, and to even approach Congress, islanders had to be Americans to once again become Puerto Ricans! Following the suggestion first made by Jones in 1910, citizenship was extended in a collective fashion. One day a person was Puerto Rican, the next American. Islanders could remain Puerto Rican only by taking an oath that made them aliens in their country and, simultaneously, people very unlikely to find meaningful work. Thus, in a population of more than 1.2 million people, only 288 Puerto Ricans refused to give up their "god given identity."

Puerto Ricans became Americans in spite of themselves. And if they persisted with their pleas for independence, islanders should remember the brand-new powers deliberately given to the U.S. governor in the Jones legislation. The governor could, at his discretion, use U.S. military and naval forces "to prevent or suppress lawless violence, invasion, insurrection, or rebellion, and he may, in case of rebellion or invasion, or imminent danger thereof, when the public safety requires it," suspend the right of habeas corpus "or place the island or any part thereof, under martial law."[89]

The Americans meant business. The Puerto Ricans, now Americans, understood that if the Jones Act failed to silence them, soldiers—like the ones Wilson stationed in Haiti and Santo Domingo—certainly would.

While island politicians contemplated their future, labor leaders like Santiago Iglesias focused on the here and now. Despite rebuffs from

Secretary of War Baker, Iglesias continually tried to pester the Wilson administration into conducting a serious investigation of the sugar and tobacco industries. Absentee U.S. owners had turned the island into a "trading post operated by underfed and barefoot laborers."[90] Why didn't anyone care? Why didn't someone act?

Eventually someone did. In late 1918 the U.S. Labor Department sent a "special agent" to investigate the truth of Iglesias charges. Joseph Marcus traveled from one end of the island to the other. After two months of extensive interviews, he wrote a study full of empathy for the workers he met and questions for the owners of mills like the one located at Guanica, Puerto Rico.

Through the centuries Guanica had always housed a variety of welcome and unwelcome guests. Its harbor, linked to its remote location, made the small southwestern city a perfect point of entry for pirates in search of contraband or soldiers in search of a strategic beachfront. United States troops, for example, used Guanica as their port of entry in 1898, but like the pirates, soldiers left as fast as they came. Nobody tried to transform Guanica until a lawyer from New York used the town to house the largest sugar central in Puerto Rico.

Frank Dillingham came to Guanica soon after the war ended. He bought some land; he incorporated South Porto Rico Sugar in New Jersey in 1900; and as he and his colleagues slowly acquired more and more land—as of 1918 they owned or controlled 24,000 acres in Puerto Rico—Dillingham needed some way to process the produce derived from his company's extensive holdings. A man of ambition Dillingham built at Guanica the second largest sugar central in the world. It was so big that it processed all of South Porto Sugar's island crop and another 200,000 or so tons from Dillingham's 38,000 acre farm in Santo Domingo. What Dillingham told Congress was that he had excess processing capacity at Guanica so he brought the sugar in from Santo Domingo to keep his smoke stacks active and his pockets full. Reluctantly, Dillingham admitted to an angry Senate committee that the profits were bigger from Santo Domingo because after paying the small duty for entry into Puerto Rico, the sugar then entered the U.S. market duty free.[91]

South Porto kept an interesting set of books. Moody's *Manual of Industrial Corporations*, for example, published the accounts of a number of the Puerto Rican sugar companies. It was easy to grasp that Central Aguirre (the Boston company that owned or controlled 39,000 acres of land) earned in 1918 net profits of more than $2 million, a return of 33 percent figures as a percentage of sales and a return of nearly 100 percent figured as a percentage of net worth. And at the New York–based Fajardo Sugar Company (which owned or controlled 27,000 acres of land) the corporation netted $1 million, a 25 percent return figured on sales, and a roughly 70 percent return figured as a percentage of net worth.[92]

South Porto's statements showed no record of net earnings. It seemed that the company earned $2.7 million in 1918 (roughly 25 percent as a percentage of sales and 150 percent as a percentage of net worth), but the company never showed a bottom-line figure. The $2.7 million guesstimate was derived by subtracting "expenses, taxes, etc." from "gross receipts"; but a close analysis of the 1917 figures showed over $3 million unaccounted for. In 1917 the company had $3.9 million in accounts receivable; the figure for 1918 was $737,000 while the company's consolidated statements provided no explanation of what happened to the $3 million received in 1918.[93]

Confusion disappeared when the subject turned to what Iglesias called "the exportation of the wealth produced by Puerto Rican workers."[94] All three companies continually paid healthy dividends to their mainland investors—for example, at Central Aguirre roughly 70 percent of net profits were returned as dividends—but the war years produced such a rise in the price of sugar that South Porto Rico paid one and Central Aguirre seven extra monthly dividends between March 1917 and August 1918.[95]

When asked by special agent Marcus if they shared the war wealth, one employer explained that Puerto Rico provided no incentive to bring wages in line with the company's admittedly "enormous profits." Dramatically high rates of unemployment meant that employers could always find people willing to break even the most serious strike. Thus, "as long as there are laborers standing at the door of the mill or near the cane fields looking for a chance to get work, awaiting the time when some laborer will drop out of his task, and the overseer will call another to take his place, it is hardly to be expected that wages will rise of their own volition."[96]

Living conditions varied. At Guanica the entrance to the settlement contained spacious, modern homes; one reporter wrote that although a few of the houses were "quite pretentious," the overall atmosphere was softened by the addition of tennis and squash courts located in a branch of the YMCA. Moving in to the settlement, and toward the central smoke stack, a visitor spotted a small church, near houses that "while less roomy and less attractive, were still bright and clean."[97] Finally, after the streets and sidewalks disappeared, a visitor saw in and around the smokestack the homes of the field and factory workers. Pictures in the labor department study, said to be typical, show a series of square wooden boxes, measuring perhaps ten by twelve feet. None contained windows—pieces of wood covered the openings—and few had any furniture inside.

However, to avoid any feelings of relative deprivation, the owners at

Guanica and the other centrals had a strict rule: "No Porto Rican, however high his position, or however proud his family, or, for that matter,
however white his color, may venture here [into the U.S. settlement]
for any social life."[98]

The modern conditions prevailing at Guanica deteriorated as a visitor
moved from factory to field. A central processed only what the plantations produced, so as Marcus moved across the island he found houses
characteristically made of tin gasoline cans, soap boxes, and any pieces
of wood that laborers could somehow unite. Few of the houses contained
any furniture; in many instances workers ate but once a day, and even
then they had to purchase their food at the company store, since they
lived on land owned or controlled by the Americans and Spanish and
French, who effectively controlled the island's sugar industry.

Marcus described "the evils of the credit system." Somehow he managed to obtain an account of purchases and charges made by what he
called a "representative" worker. On the fellow's bill was a charge for
"rice and things," another for "beans and things," and a third just for
"things." Nobody knew what these "things" were, least of all the workers who often could not read and write. In any event, "the worker was
at the mercy of his employer," and in the many instances where such
a credit system prevailed, "the laborer very seldom found himself out
of debt at the end of the week's work."[99]

When workers complained about the practices of the company store,
"one of the largest sugar mills in Puerto Rico" (Marcus does not say
which one) developed a unique way to establish better labor relations.
The central assumed responsibility for the company store, and it maintained such scrupulous accounts that with the profits earned from the
workers' purchases, it paid the laborers a bonus for their efforts in the
fields.[100]

That was American ingenuity—which Marcus claims the owners
understood to be outright exploitation. For example, "a wealthy American citizen," a fellow who had lived on the island since the occupation
began and who presently employed "thousands of laborers," made this
anonymous statement to Marcus: "The peon is just living from day to
day without any hope or preparation for the future. . . . He cannot move
away because he cannot get land to buy and if there were land he would
not have the money with which to pay for it."[101]

To remedy the peon's problems the American suggested that "land
must be procured and sold to the peon on easy payments." But how
this could be accomplished was a problem, for as the American stressed
about himself, "I am not on the side of labor. I am on the side of
capital."[102]

That left the government or revolution as the workers' only options.
Since the island's Labor movement ardently advocated statehood, how-

ever, workers never challenged the prevailing economic or political systems. They worked from week to week. Marcus advised his superiors to open labor department offices in Puerto Rico, and as partial remedy for the misery he found—"Porto Rico is on the one hand an island of wealthy land proprietors and on the other hand of landless workers"[103]— Marcus made a suggestion that would be repeated again and again and again throughout the twentieth century: Puerto Ricans should migrate.

Perhaps forgetting that companies like South Porto Rico Sugar owned the land, Marcus suggested a migration to Santo Domingo. Cuba was another possibility, the United States a third, and even Hawaii had its advocates. After all, in 1903 Hawaiian sugar recruiters had managed to put 1,000 Puerto Ricans on a boat by promising high, year-round wages.[104] Any destination would do because neither U.S. nor Puerto Rican leaders offered the comprehensive strategy suggested by the wealthy American: redistribution of the land so that people had some opportunity to sow the seeds of their own future.

In 1918 that future contained no promises of change, no hope of eliminating a system based on company stores. Responsibility for the island's misery undoubtedly rested on many native as well as foreign shoulders; but before and after passage of the Jones law, the U.S. government had to accept primary responsibility for Puerto Rico's economic and political conditions. In 1924, for example, the island's U.S. governor still proudly assured Congress that "the United States still has absolute control, because in its legislation Congress can do anything it wants to. . . . We are the governing power."[105]

In 1921 that power would exempt all island-based U.S. corporations from all federal income taxes. And as if icing on the corporation's cake, Congress appointed a governor who called himself "the ruler" of Puerto Rico.

NOTES

1. See *Congressional Record*, House, 64th Congress, 2nd session, May 5, 1916, p. 7471; also see Arthur S. Link, ed., *The Papers of Woodrow Wilson*, Vol. 41, (Princeton, N.J.: Princeton University Press, 1983), pp. 515–516.

2. See *The Report of the Governor of Porto Rico*, Senate, 59th Congress, 1st session, Document no. 135, 1906, p. 145.

3. See *Testimony of Governor Rafael Hernández Colón before the Energy and Natural Resources Committee*, January 30, 1991, p. 7.

4. See Aida Negron de Montilla, *Americanization in Puerto Rico and the Public School System* (Río Piedras: Editorial Edil, 1970), p. 101.

5. For a superb summary of these efforts see John Higham, *Strangers in the Land* (New York: Atheneum, 1971).

6. Negron de Montilla, *Americanization in Puerto Rico*, p. 121.

7. See Roland Falkner, "Commissioner of Education in Puerto Rico (1904–1907)," *The Forum* 16, no. 3 (1909): p. 206.

8. See *Congressional Record*, House, 61st Congress, 1st session, June 7, 1909, p. 2919.

9. Ibid., p. 2921.

10. Ibid., p. 2922.

11. Ibid., p. 2923.

12. Ibid.

13. Ibid.

14. Ibid.

15. Ibid., p. 2926.

16. Ibid.

17. Ibid.

18. Richard D. Challener, *Admirals, Generals, and American Foreign Policy, 1898–1914* (Princeton, N.J.: Princeton University Press, 1973), pp. 87–88.

19. See María Eugenia Estades Font, *La Presencia Militar de Estados Unidos en Puerto Rico, 1898–1918* (Río Piedras: Huracán, 1988).

20. See Major General Frank McIntyre, "American Territorial Administration," *Foreign Affairs* 10 (January 1932): p. 300.

21. *Congressional Record*, House, June 7, 1909, p. 2929.

22. James L. Dietz, *Economic History of Puerto Rico* (Princeton, N.J.: Princeton University Press, 1986).

23. Emilio Pantojas García, "La Iglesia Protestante y la Americanizacion de Puerto Rico: 1898–1917," *Revista de Ciencias Sociales* 18 (March-June 1974), pp. 99–121, esp. p. 111.

24. Ibid., p. 110; on the link to politics see Fernando Pico, *Historia General de Puerto Rico* (Río Piedras: Huracán, 1988), p. 252.

25. See Dietz, *Economic History of Puerto Rico*, p. 123.

26. See *Testimony of Governor Rafael Hernández Colón*, p. 3; also see Frank Bonilla and Ricardo Campos, "A Wealth of Poor: Puerto Ricans in the New Economic Order," *Daedalus* 50 (Spring 1979): pp. 133–176.

27. Bailey Diffie and Justine Diffie, *Porto Rico: A Broken Pledge* (New York: Vanguard Press, 1932), pp. 119–120; A. G. Quintero Rivera, *Conflictos de Clase y Política en Puerto Rico* (Río Piedras: Huracán, 1984), pp. 127–128.

28. See *A Civil Government for Porto Rico, Hearings Before the Committee on Insular Affairs*, House, 63rd Congress, 2nd session, February 26, 1914, p. 48.

29. See *Affairs in Porto Rico, Message from the President of the United States*, Senate, 61st Congress, 2nd session, Document no. 40, p. 4.

30. Barry Commoner, *Making Peace with the Planet* (New York: Pantheon, 1990), p. 160.

31. *Historical Statistics of the United States* (Washington, D.C.: GPO, 1961), p. 7; see, too, Truman Clark, "The Imperial Perspective," *Revista Interamericana* 4, no. 4 (1975): pp. 505–517.

32. Gervasio L. García and A. G. Quintero Rivera, *Desafío y Solidaridad* (Río Piedras: Huracán, 1986), pp. 90–91.

33. Ibid., p. 92; also see Felix Mejias, *Condiciones de Vida de las Clase Jornaleras de Puerto Rico* (Río Piedras: University of Puerto Rico Press, 1946), chap. 5.

34. See, for example, Clarence Senior, *Santiago Iglesias: Labor Crusader* (Hato Rey: Interamerican University Press, 1972).

35. See Arthur S. Link, ed., *The Public Papers of Woodrow Wilson*, Vol. 48 (Princeton, N.J.: Princeton University Press, 1985), p. 15; a sample of Iglesia's complaints can be found in Vol. 40, pp. 146–153.

36. See *Conditions in Porto Rico, Message from the President Transmitting a Report Made by the Secretary of War upon Conditions Existing in Porto Rico*, House, 62nd Congress, 2nd session, 1912, Document no. 615.

37. The Taft letter appears in the *Congressional Record*, House, 74th Congress, 1st session, May 19, 1936, p. 7520.

38. See Delma S. Arrigoitia, "José De Diego: A Legislator in Times of Political Transition (Ph.D. diss., Fordham University, 1985), p. 188.

39. Walter La Faber, *Inevitable Revolutions* (New York: W. W. Norton, 1983).

40. Ibid., pp. 191–193.

41. *Hearings*, February 26, 1914, p. 5; see also José A. Cabranes, *Citizenship and the American Empire* (New Haven, Conn.: Yale, 1979).

42. Ibid., pp. 6–7.

43. Ibid., p. 8.

44. Ibid., p. 15.

45. Ibid., p. 14.

46. Ibid., p. 31.

47. Ibid., p. 32.

48. Ibid., p. 32.

49. Ibid., p. 33.

50. Ibid., p. 35.

51. Ibid., p. 51.

52. Ibid., p. 49.

53. Ibid., p. 54.

54. Ibid., p. 56.

55. Ibid., p. 58.

56. Ibid., p. 59.

57. Ibid., p. 72.

58. See *Congressional Record*, Senate, 63rd Congress, 2nd session, April 15, 1914, p. 6718; the entire memorial extends from p. 6718 to p. 6720.

59. See, especially, the House debates in June of 1910. *Congressional Record*, House, 61st Congress, 2nd session, June 8, 1910, pp. 7603–7629.

60. See Mary White Ovington, "The United States in Porto Rico," *New Republic*, July 8, 1916, p. 244.

61. See Grayson L. Kirk, *Philippine Independence* (New York: Farrar & Rinehart, 1936), p. 45.

62. See Maximo M. Kalaw, "Why the Filipinos Expect Independence," *Foreign Affairs* 10 (January 1932): pp. 304–315, esp. p. 305.

63. Stanley Karnow, *In Our Image: America's Empire in the Philippines* (New York: Random House, 1989), p. 213.

64. See Kirk, *Philippine Independence*, pp. 46–48.

65. See *Congressional Record*, Senate, 64th Congress, 2nd session, January 4, 1916, p. 443.

66. See *Documents on the Constitutional History of Puerto Rico*, Commonwealth of Puerto Rico, 1964, 2d ed., p. 81.

67. See *Congressional Record*, House, 64th Congress, 2nd session, May 5, 1916, p. 7471.

68. See Link, *Papers of Woodrow Wilson*, Vol. 48, p. 48.

69. *Congressional Record*, House, May 5, 1916, p. 7472.

70. Ibid., p. 7473.

71. Ibid., pp. 7475 and 7474 respectively.

72. In assessing the factors that allowed the Jones Bill to pass, I have relied on Truman Clark, "Educating the Natives in Self Government: Puerto Rico and the United States, 1900–1933," *Pacific Historical Review* 42 (May 1973): pp. 220–233.

73. See García and Quintero Rivera, *Desafío y Solidaridad*, pp. 60–61.

74. See Arrigoitia, "José De Diego," p. 208.

75. *Congressional Record*, Senate, 64th Congress, 2nd session, September 2, 1916, p. 13666; also see Arturo Morales Carrión, *Puerto Rico: A Political and Cultural History* (New York: W. W. Norton, 1983), pp. 196–197.

76. Link, *Papers of Woodrow Wilson*, Vol. 40, p. 57.

77. Ibid., p. 58.

78. Ibid., pp. 90–91.

79. Morales Carrión, *Puerto Rico*, pp. 195–196.

80. Ibid., pp. 198–199.

81. See Truman Clark, *Puerto Rico and the United States, 1917–1933* (Pittsburgh: University of Pittsburgh Press, 1975), pp. 24–25.

82. See Link, *Papers of Woodrow Wilson*, Vol. 41, p. 516.

83. See Arrigoitia, "José De Diego," pp. 209–210.

84. *Documents on Constitutional History*, p. 99.

85. Clark, "Educating the Natives," p. 227.

86. See Charles T. Goodsell, *Administration of a Revolution* (Cambridge: Harvard University Press, 1965), p. 117.

87. *Documents on Constitutional History*, p. 93.

88. Ibid., p. 94.

89. Ibid., p. 90.

90. See Link, *Papers of Woodrow Wilson*, Vol. 40, p. 151.

91. See *Hearings before a Subcommittee of the Committee on Finance*, Senate, 71st Congress, 1st session, 1929, esp. pp. 280–285.

92. See Moody's *Manual of Industrial Corporations* for 1919. Central Aguirre's accounts appear on pp. 151–152; Fajardo's are on pp. 271–272; and those of South Porto Rico Sugar appear on pp. 704–705.

93. See Ibid., p. 705.

94. See, Link, *Wilson Papers of Woodrow*, Vol. 40, p. 151.

95. See Moody's, *Manual*, pp. 705 and 151.

96. See Joseph Marcus, Department of Labor, *Labor Conditions in Porto Rico* (Washington, D.C.: GPO, 1919), p. 29.

97. See Ovington, "United States in Porto Rico," pp. 271–273.

98. Ibid., p. 271.

99. Marcus, *Labor Conditions*, p. 18.

100. Ibid., pp. 29–30.

101. Ibid., p. 34.

102. Ibid., p. 34.

103. Ibid., p. 13.

104. See Luis Nieves Falcon, *Maleta'nd Go: Puerto Rican Seasonal Migration*, New York, 1970, p. 2. This is the English version of a study Professor Nieves Falcon did in 1970. It was later published in Spanish as *El Inmigrante Puertoriqueno*.

105. See *The Civil Government of Porto Rico, Hearings Before the Committee on Territories and Insular Possessions*, Senate, 68th Congress, 1st session, 1924, p. 6.

Chapter 4

King Monty

We think we are better than other people. Anyone who does
things in different fashion from us is either comic or stupid.
We regard being a foreigner in the nature of a defective moral
attribute.... Naturally this does not make us popular.
Governor Theodore Roosevelt, Jr.,
Colonial Policies of the U.S.[1]

Tax law is a foreign language. You diligently read the regulation; you
diligently read the regulation; and then, with Job's wife, you curse the
tax collector, accepting death as a welcome relief from the hell called tax
law.

Take, for example, this time from the U.S.–Puerto Rican tax codes:
"For Federal income tax purposes a citizen of a possession of the United
States who is not otherwise a citizen of the United States is a citizen of
the possession of the United States who has not become a citizen of the
United States by naturalization."[2]

This regulation, initially understood by no one, had great significance
for Puerto Rico and for the U.S. corporations who established operations
on the island. Before Congress issued the above regulation in 1918,
Puerto Ricans theoretically had to pay federal taxes. However, since the
island was an unincorporated territory, and since Congress did not want
to tax a people who had no voting representation in Congress, taxes
collected from islanders were returned to their own, island, treasury.

Things got confusing when the subject turned to real Americans. Did
a citizen born on the continent, say Frank Dillingham of South Porto

Rico Sugar, have to pay federal taxes on his Puerto Rican income? And what about South Porto Rico itself? Did it owe money to Uncle Sam?

Up to 1913 no tax was imposed only on income derived from U.S. sources. But from 1913 to 1917 U.S. citizens and U.S. corporations were taxed on worldwide income. And then when Congress again changed the rules in 1918, the Internal Revenue Service's (IRS's) everyday interpretation of the regulation cited above was that Americans born on the mainland suddenly had to pay double taxes. After 1918 a man like Dillingham, and his New Jersey–based corporation, owed money to the Puerto Rican government and to Washington because unlike the Puerto Ricans, who were citizens by statute (i.e., the Jones Act of 1917), the Americans were citizens by birth. They got penalized for being real Americans and they were angry.[3]

One way birthright Americans got even with Uncle Sam was never to pay their taxes. In the Philippines—subject to the same tax laws as Puerto Rico—Congress estimated that 95 percent of the U.S. businesspeople simply disregarded the law. However, these same Americans were so angry with Uncle Sam that they asked to be relieved of the taxes they never paid.[4]

In fact, with no push from their colleagues in Puerto Rico, Americans in the Philippines carried the banner of tax relief to Washington. What they did was this: They convinced the new governor of the Philippines, General Leonard Wood, to send an urgent cablegram to Washington asking Congress "to let them off from their taxes." In congressional debate Senator Robert La Follette of Wisconsin wanted to hear some facts. When the U.S. Treasury Department experts appeared in committee hearings, they offered no definite information about what taxes Philippine businesspeople had and had not paid. All La Follette knew was that the Treasury Department admitted that these men refused to comply with the law; and Congress, instead of penalizing them, was rewarding them for thumbing their noses at the government.[5]

While La Follette waited for his facts, the debate turned, not to the Philippines—or the rarely mentioned Puerto Rico—but to China. The British threatened our share of the "inviting and gigantic opportunities" offered in the land of opium and open doors. In essence, the argument went, forget the Philippines because China is the ultimate mass market potentially denied to enterprising Americans. As Senator Reed Smoot of Utah noted, "China is one of our great fields for exportation and for business. I say now that where the American corporation doing business in China is compelled to pay a double tax as against the British . . . the American cannot compete successfully."[6]

Opponents never found the double tax. But so what? The government gave exemptions to Puerto Rico based on complaints made from the Philippines in a debate that revolved around China. Senators who pointed out that the exemption was unfair—U.S. businesses, after all, paid double taxes when they made out checks to state and federal governments—were ignored. And no one answered Senator Robert Broussard when he asked this question:

If we are put to great expense [i.e., employing the U.S. Navy] in order to maintain and to protect domestic concerns doing business in foreign countries, what justification is there for relieving them entirely of the taxes which are paid by other people living and doing business within the borders of the United States who employ home labor and pay taxes to the United States and their subdivisions?[7]

Perhaps because there was no good answer to this question, U.S. interests in Puerto Rico let others carry their tax ball. When it passed the legislation, Congress simply lumped one possession in with another, and for lobbying on the sidelines men like Frank Dillingham and corporations like South Porto Rico Sugar got this reward: No federal taxes for as long as the eye could see. More specifically, after 1921 a U.S. citizen or a U.S. corporation qualified for tax exclusion on income from a foreign source or a possession if they derived 80 percent or more of their gross income for the three-year period immediately preceding the close of the taxable year from sources within a possession of the United States (e.g., Puerto Rico or Guam) and if at least 50 percent of gross income was derived from the active conduct of a trade or business within a possession of the United States—the so-called gross-active business test.[8]

Again tax law is a foreign language, which in this case was not Spanish. For the tax exemption granted to possessions corporations neither the federal government, nor the Puerto Rican economy, nor the Puerto Rican masses living in shacks, received any discernible benefits. In the 1940s there was at least the appearance of a quid pro quo; for taxes avoided, the country industrialized. But 1921 marked the beginning of a decade in which Warren Harding promised a return to "normalcy" and Calvin Coolidge said "the business of America is business."

Into the 1920s sugar and tobacco profits swelled. Accountants found ways to avoid taxes on dividends (e.g., put stock in a wife or child's name, and she or he met the income requirements of the new law). Warren Harding appointed as governor of Puerto Rico a man with a singular achievement: E. Montgomery Reilly made the nation's first speech suggesting that Warren Harding be president.

Reilly's speech is the first item in the one box of the governor's private papers. Reilly was quite proud that he had, as early as mid–1919, told his fellow Republicans that Senator Harding would make a great president: "He was the really big man of the entire list," and hailing from Ohio, he was "not too far West to upset the traditions of the effete East, nor too far East to be unsatisfactory to the sturdy West."

Flattered, Harding nevertheless asked Reilly in a pleasant but formal letter to cease his activities. The senator didn't feel he had "the elements of leadership" necessary for victory. Thanks but no thanks.[9]

When Harding became president, he apparently felt compelled to say thank you to Reilly for his inaugural and other campaign efforts. Unfortunately Reilly lacked any familiarity with the Caribbean in general or Puerto Rico in particular. He had lived most of his life in Kansas City, serving in 1902 as its assistant postmaster; and shortly before leaving for the island, Reilly earned a living as a mortgage broker. He was however, a man who knew a good opportunity when he saw one. As he told the Kansas City Lions Club shortly before he left for Puerto Rico, "The governorship is the best political appointment President Harding has to give, and the salary and perquisites would amount to $54,000 a year."[10]

A good living in 1991, $54,000 a year was a fortune in 1921. The problem was that the governor's salary was only $10,000 a year. Where Reilly meant to get the "perquisites" was an issue that worried many Puerto Rican politicians. The former mayor of San Juan, Roberto Todd, when warned by a Kansas City reported that Reilly was thoroughly incompetent, camped out at the governor's hotel, eager to see for himself whether Reilly was a "damn fool."

He wasn't. He had a great many intelligent questions for Todd: How much money did the governor get for his household expenses? How much for a secretary? And what about secret stashes? Did the governor have any of those?[11]

Todd left a disappointed man. A governor who asked not one question about political and economic affairs was sure to have an adverse impact on the island, especially when more people than ever before openly clamored for America's nemesis, independence at once.

Instead of silencing the islanders, the Jones Act moved them to search for new and original ways to achieve political change. José De Diego tried to get every Spanish-speaking person on earth to support Puerto Rico's struggle against U.S. colonialism. In his eyes the United States was the child of Spain, which had founded the New World and, despite cruelty against the Indians and exploitation of the colonists, also had the "providential mission" of discovering North and South America, plus bringing Christianity to their shores.

Moreover, by intermingling with the natives, Spain had helped to found an indestructible race, a people who could claim great achievements, except for "the shadow hindering the true and complete unity and harmony of the Hispanic races." That shadow was Puerto Rico. Light would once again shine on the Spanish race only when "all Hispanics, from Europe to the Andes, united in the common cause of the Puerto Rican people . . . an issue which is a common danger, a common matter of dignity, of life or death, for all men of the Hispanic race."[12]

Today we would call De Diegos plea for a search for his "roots." To unite his people, to create the pride that would lead to change, he sought to emphasize the ethnic ties that theoretically bound all Puerto Ricans. And in seeking support from Hispanics in Europe and the New World, De Diego tried to defeat one colossus by appealing to another.

On a political level, the Unionists, flying the banner of independence, achieved in 1920 one of the greatest political victories in island history. They won back districts lost in 1917 and for the first time ever achieved success in San Juan, the stronghold of statehood sentiment. At a banquet celebrating the party's success, Unionist leader Antonio Barcelo felt so strongly about the enthusiasm of his followers that he asked for permission to take a trip to Washington: Barcelo wanted to demand immediate independence for Puerto Rico.[13]

Barcelo never took the trip. Cooler heads prevailed, if only because a new administration now controlled the White House. The Unionists would patiently bide their time, but no one could deny that in a democratic fashion, islanders had expressed their true sentiments. Puerto Ricans wanted change and they wanted it so badly that their children showed open "contempt" for the United States and its blessings. Just six weeks before Governor Reilly made his inaugural address, a student in the graduating class of Central High School proudly waved the Puerto Rican flag during the exercises, loudly shouting "independence for Puerto Rico" as he waved the flag. The commissioner of education, Paul Miller, immediately asked police to remove "the enemy flag from the place," and students responded by telling Miller that if he removed the flag, the exercises were over: Puerto Rican students would follow the Puerto Rican flag.[14]

In 1921 Puerto Rico needed a diplomat as governor. It got E. Montgomery Reilly, a man who for all his faults accurately represented the will of the U.S. government. Reilly's inaugural address, for example, not only had been cleared by the president, it had been corrected by the president. Where Reilly had written "ruler" of Puerto Rico, Harding changed it to "executive"; and when Reilly spoke of the island "over which I may rule," the president penciled in "administer."[15]

Harding never wanted Reilly to wear a crown, but he nonetheless allowed his appointee to make a speech that allowed Reilly to mention "our matchless President, a President of all the peoples over whom he [Harding] rules." Reilly stressed that the president cared for Puerto Rico but islanders nevertheless had to understand that "there is no sympathy or possible hope in the United States for independence for Puerto Rico from any individual, or from any political party."[16]

To make sure the audience got his point Reilly (and Harding) ended with an appeal to statehood—sometime in the future. "If the majority of the people of these islands desire a change in their Government, I would suggest that they advocate Statehood. Plan to place yourselves in the same condition and situation that obtains today in New York, Missouri and California and trust the American people for a perpetual square deal."[17]

On the podium beside Reilly, none of the Unionists clapped. The governor went on anyway. He told his people that he had invited the Hardings to visit the island—"they love folks, not for what they have but for what they are"—and until they arrived, Puerto Ricans should rest assured—this was the speech's last line—that "all, all are welcome to come to me at any time, that I may be able to lift any burden or assuage any sorrow."[18]

A month after this speech Reilly told the president how islanders had reacted: "I received a number of letters threatening my life, others telling me that if I did not leave the island in 48 hours I would be killed, and that if I drove through the streets I would be murdered."[19] Reilly assured the president that he "would not show the white feather." The day after he received his initial death threat, he "drove through the streets and around the plaza." The people had to know who was boss and Harding had to know who was behind the push for independence: Outside agitators! Two hundred and eighty-eight very fertile Spaniards!

Reilly gave the president a "little sidelight" on independence in a letter dated September 17, 1921. The facts were these: When the United States "took over" the islands in 1898, all Puerto Ricans "renounced Spain," except for 288 recalcitrants. "These 288 refused American citizenship, and have remained loyal to Spain and at the same time have advocated independence all these years." And not only that, the 288 produced so many children that the movement has now "grown into quite an army of what might be called unbelievers. They have devoted months and years to this propagation and it seems that no one has ever tried to stop it until I came . . . so, when I struck as hard as I did, it naturally caused a commotion."[20]

Did Reilly believe this nonsense? Since this was a letter to the president of the United States, and Reilly certainly had no conscious desire to show the president how little he knew, I am inclined to think that Reilly did believe his theory of the 288 hot-blooded Spaniards. His letters demonstrate no understanding of the previous twenty-two years of U.S.–Puerto Rican relations; and the 288 figure was the number of Puerto Ricans who in 1917 refused U.S. citizenship. Reilly apparently took a number he saw floating about and used it to construct a theory explaining the independence movement.

Of course, Reilly might have been lying to the president. Or he might have thought that this was Harding's explanation of the Puerto Rican "army" seeking independence. Whatever the actual explanation, the letter is a terrible manifestation of the utter poverty of U.S. policy. Blinded by enthnocentrism, Reilly could never understand the Puerto Rican people's all-American desire to chart their own destiny. He never grasped the legitimacy of the islanders complaints and neither did those Americans who commented on Reilly's troublesome tenure as governor.

In a January 1922 article in *Current History*, H. P. Krippene spoke of "Porto Rico's playful politics"; despite a relationship "in which few nations have done more for any one of their possessions than the U.S. has done for Porto Rico," the islanders still "constantly" demanded independence. The explanation: "petty politics"; greedy and devious Puerto Ricans.[21]

And in the *New Republic* Luis Muñoz Marín first ridiculed Reilly for his ignorance and insensitivity, and he then argued that a principal reason the speech was a bomb was because the "unionist leaders never expected to be taken seriously." They didn't want to be free; on the contrary, they only "used independence as a bait to catch the votes of that vast majority who have a natural and obscure prejudice in favor of the land where they were born and for which they pay rent."[22]

But the bait worked! The Unionists had, after all, won an overwhelming victory on a platform that advocated independence as the national ideal. Unquestionably the Unionists leaders were reformers rather than revolutionaries; but those reformers nevertheless spoke to a real desire of their people, a desire that the Americans, as well as commentators like Muñoz Marín, refused to take seriously.

Reilly and Barcelo clashed less than two weeks after "the speech." To fill a vacant position in the insular government Barcelo followed a custom of many years' standing: He handed Reilly a list of three names—called a *yerna*—asking the governor to select one for the open spot. Now Reilly rightly understood that this was the Union's party's way of dispensing patronage, controlling appointments, and, to the extent possible, exerting authority over local affairs. Reilly's recent predecessors had never tried to rock this island boat; they let the majority party have its way as long as crucial appointments and real power stayed in their's and Washington's hands.[23]

Reilly broke with custom. In a letter that Barcelo immediately had published, he told the Union leader "that the old order has changed and will return no more." Reilly would never capitulate to the islander's demands—in a world-class display of irony he explained to Harding that "I cannot operate a successful administration founded on corruption"—but they must acquiesce in his. Either "Barcelo severed his connection with the independence party and became a loyal Porto Rican American or we cannot have any friendly political relations."[24]

After this confrontation the situation turned ugly. In local newspapers the letters-to-the-editor column contained correspondence headed "Darling Caesar" and "Letters to the Emperor." In old San Juan the governor's chief of police "amused himself" by tearing up Puerto Rican flags while Reilly explained to the president how he had used the U.S. flag to help the local economy:

A check has been made by the merchants on the island as to how many American flags have been sold before I came and since. The last three years of Governor Yager's administration 1300 American flags were sold in the island. Since I came to the island four months ago, 16,000 American flags have been purchased by the natives. . . . I think this in itself demonstrates the hold that your administration has on these people.[25]

Harding told Reilly that "the Porto Rican matter has been one of considerable anxious consideration of late." Harding would meet with the secretary of war that very day (November 11, 1921). Even though he wanted to settle the matter peacefully, Harding assured the governor that "we would not wish to bring it [tranquility] about by a surrender to those who have made the paths of government so difficult."[26]

Reilly took the president at his word. He kept squeezing the Unionists, who in February 1922 supposedly yelled uncle. At an islandwide assembly of the party they removed the independence plank from their platform and endorsed instead a January proposal made by Senator Philip Campbell: Puerto Rico was to become a free associated state.

The Unionists made this about-face for many reasons. First, they were willing to wait for eventual independence. Campbell promised changes now (e.g., an elected governor), changes no Congress would give if the Puerto Ricans continued to espouse independence. Second, the Unionists could always say one thing and do another. Almost a year after they "relinquished" the independence goal, Reilly angrily complained to Harding that wherever Barcelo and his followers "have held meetings they have spoken under one star flags and have indicated that Puerto Rico should control its own affairs."[27]

Third, the Unionists wanted to control patronage. Using the Jones Act as a legal tool, the governor could eliminate the few powers the locals had. So it was easier to say what was needed, work Congress for Reilly's dismissal,[28] and keep control of the jobs that helped keep the Unionists in power.

Finally, the Unionists were reformers not revolutionaries. Years later the United States would be challenged by a serious revolutionary force, Pedro Albizu Campos and the Nationalist party. But the Unionists harbored so many contradictions that their right hand always stopped their left hand. The same men who ardently defended the Spanish language and bitterly complained about Reilly's imperialism also discriminated against "dark" Puerto Ricans and often sided with the sugar and tobacco interests that produced places like the central at Guanica.

Commentators rightly talked about the "kaleidoscope" of Puerto Rican politics. A patriot on the island was an archconservative elsewhere. Indeed, except for local control and independence—but not necessarily independence today—the Unionists displayed a marked absence of clear and precise political parameters. They genuinely wanted political change but not if that meant serious social change; so from the outset the Unionists were limited by their own contradictions.[29] They complained, but fundamentally they would never engage in the kind of revolutionary behavior suggested by Reilly: When informed that the resident commissioner would visit the president, he told Harding that "every Porto Rican professional politician carries a pistol and I do not think you should see Cordova unless your Secretary or someone else is present."[30]

Reilly "won," but he quickly turned victory into defeat by adding to his political prejudices, prejudices against the Puerto Rican people. He told Harding that "Porto Ricans, as all Continentals say, are children and change their attitudes almost daily." He explained that he could not use Robert Todd as a consultant because the man was "a half blooded Negro"; and even if he consulted with the white islanders, it did no good because

these people are so unlike North Americans it is impossible to make any comparison. They make agreements one day and break them the next; they stand for certain principles one day and reverse them the next. This applies to the Republicans on the Island as well as the Unionists. It appears to me that they are all about the same.[31]

E. Montgomery Reilly made few friends in Puerto Rico. In March 1923 he finally gave in to pressures from every side and resigned the governorship. Thankful to the governor for "bringing an end to the warfare which has been made upon yours and mine," Harding congratulated Reilly for "the splendid work you have done." The president hoped that after such an ordeal Reilly would enjoy a "complete restoration" of his very weakened physical condition.[32]

William Howard Taft led a remarkable life. First president and then chief justice of the Supreme Court, Taft was the only man in U.S. history to lead both the executive and judicial branches of the federal government. However, whether as president or chief justice, Taft's stand on the colonies never changed: they were ours, to do with as we pleased.

Taft's consistency was clearly expressed in a 1922 Supreme Court decision. In *Balzac v. People of Puerto Rico*, Taft not only upheld a selective application of the Constitution but also managed to once again remind the Puerto Ricans they were still unfit for statehood.

Jesús Balzac edited an island paper called *El Baluarte* (the bulwark). In two 1918 articles he criticized a local citizen with such vehemence that the fellow had Balzac prosecuted for criminal libel. When Balzac went to court, he demanded a jury trial; in Puerto Rico a jury was not granted in misdemeanor cases, but citing the Sixth Amendment, Balzac said he was entitled to a jury of his peers. The local courts said no, the Supreme Court of Puerto Rico said no, and then William Howard Taft explained why he said no.

Taft wrote that "when Porto Ricans passed from under the government of Spain, they lost the protection of that government . . . and they had a right to expect, in passing under the dominion of the United States, a status entitling them to the protection of their new sovereign." This they got as citizens of Puerto Rico. But this was "an anomalous status"; so responding to the yearning of the islanders, the United States gave them the "boon" of citizenship.[33]

The question before the Court was, "What additional rights did it [citizenship] give them?" Taft's answer was that it all depended on where the Puerto Rican citizen was standing when a constitutional issue arose. In the United States citizenship meant full constitutional guarantees; on the island it meant that citizens could be denied any number of judicial rights. In the words of the chief justice: "It is locality that is determinative of the application of the Constitution, in such matters as judicial procedure, and not the status of the people who live in it."[34]

Taft had neatly defined second-class citizenship. Because Puerto Rico was an unincorporated territory, the courts could legitimately deny the Bill of Rights to U.S. citizens.

Puerto Rico belonged to the United States. Nobody ever said it was part of the United States. Nor did anyone ever suggest that it would be part of the United States. Repeating what President Taft had said in 1912, Chief Justice Taft reminded all Americans that "incorporation has always been a step, and an important one, leading to statehood . . . it is reasonable to assume that when such a step is taken, it will be begun and taken by Congress deliberately and with a clear declaration of purpose, and not left a matter of mere inference or construction."[35]

As of 1922 Congress had taken no such step. Thus Jesús Balzac lost his right to a jury trial and all Puerto Ricans lost elemental constitutional guarantees because "we [the Supreme Court justices] find no features in the Organic Act of Porto Rico of 1917 [i.e., the Jones law] from which we can infer the purpose of Congress to incorporate Puerto Rico into the United States with the consequences which would follow."[36]

Given the actions of E. Montgomery Reilly, and the opinions of William Howard Taft, Puerto Ricans had few viable alternatives. They couldn't leave the Union, and they weren't allowed in it; so in 1924 (and 1950, 1952, 1959, 1963, 1975, 1986, and 1991) they tried to establish and perfect a political original: the free associated state.

The men were hopeful. Harding had died and Reilly's replacement—the former member of the House Committee on Insular Affairs, Horace Towner—had actually accompanied them to Washington to seek changes in the Jones Act. Horace Towner knew how Congress worked. He also knew what moved and what upset particular personalities. Perhaps this time real change would occur?

First stop was a visit to the office of President Calvin Coolidge. More a courtesy call than a working meeting, the Puerto Ricans nevertheless received this message from the not-so-silent president. He advised them to cooperate, "to work together for the common welfare." They could and should harmonize all difficulties that might arise because "your island is prosperous, it is making great progress . . . your living conditions are better, and your whole atmosphere is one of prosperity and ought to be one of contentment."[37]

Armed with this advice, Towner and the Puerto Ricans testified before the House and Senate. Their main goal was permission to begin electing the governor in 1928, their main weapon a politeness bordering on obsequiousness. Towner assured his former colleagues that they "would not lose any of the control or the sovereignty over the country by the adoption of this proposition."[38]

The Puerto Ricans were honest. President of the Senate Barcelo told the House that despite representing different political parties, there was "complete unanimity" between members of the delegation. They sought "a larger degree of self government," differing "only in regard to our future political status which is as uncertain to us as it is to you."[39]

Speaker of the House Miguel Guerra-Mondragon assured Congress that "Porto Rico will make good; that we will govern Porto Rico in such a way that it will be an honor to the United States and an honor to Porto Rico."[40] When asked why he chose 1928 as the first time islanders would elect their own governor, Guerra said, "We want to show you that we are not demanding things. We are not so exacting. We are American citizens who have come to our fellow citizens of the North to talk over these facts. It shows the reasonableness of our position."[41]

Statehooders were represented by José Tous Soto. He told Congress that "the most potent reason for granting us now the power to elect our governor is because this is a step toward statehood, because if we do well . . . we will be justified, after a while, to come to you asking for statehood." Tous Soto agreed that statehood was still a distant goal, but

after a quarter of a century of American rule we are entitled to know what the Nation has in store for us. We ought to know if on account of race or geographical position insurmountable difficulties existing to our admission as a State. And that is precisely the main purpose of the joint resolution [i.e., the right to elect the governor] of our local legislature.[42]

Congress gave Puerto Ricans a speedy reply to their request. In March 1924 a House report suggested approval of the proposal as long as it included these amendments: The elected governor could be removed "at any time" and for "any cause" by the president of the United States; the power to appoint everyone from the chief justice of the island's Supreme Court to the island's postmasters would remain in U.S. hands; and Congress would reserve the explicit right to "annul or modify" all franchises, rights and privileges granted by the Public Service Commission of Porto Rico.[43]

The Senate lacked the House's spirit of compromise after it too included a provision to remove the governor for any cause and at any time, the Senate felt obliged to give the Puerto Ricans a history lesson. Using General Frank McIntyre, head of the War Department's Bureau of Insular Affairs as teacher, the Senate report indicated that "this bill is in line with the recommendations of President Roosevelt. It carries into effect the recommendations of President Taft. It does not provide statehood. It does not promise statehood. It does not incorporate Porto Rico into the United States." It only gave the islanders a chance to elect their own governor in 1932, according to the Senate bill, and that was good policy because it would prevent "the spasmodic talk, on the one hand, of independence, and, on the other hand, of an incorporated Territory and statehood—requests which could not be seriously considered."[44]

Another request that could not be seriously considered was the elective-governor bill itself. It died long before both houses of Congress had a chance to approve it, so in Puerto Rico islanders rearranged the political landscape.

Disgruntled Unionists and Republicans formed an alliance (La Alianza) dedicated to obtaining the free associated state Congress had just refused.

Statehooders formed a coalition (La Coalición) joining former Republicans and the island's moderate labor organization, the Socialist party. The Coalition was devoted to achieving the statehood status that Congress continually indicated was out of the question.

The third group was the Independence party. Formed in 1922, it began to achieve prominence in 1924 because of the attitudes and actions of one man, Pedro Albizu Campos. Like his island opposition Albizu was dedicated to a goal—independence—Congress refused to grant; in sharp contrast to any of his island opponents, Albizu preached revolution. Because the Americans refused to listen, "Puerto Rico had to create a grave crisis for the colonial administration in order to be able to get it to attend to the island's demands."[45]

The Americans who discussed Albizu always came back to the same point of origin: This dark-skinned man had personal problems. In a letter President Roosevelt called "extraordinarily good," Albizu's politics are explained in this manner: "He became imbued with a deep hatred of the United States due, chiefly, to his being assigned during the World War to a colored officer's training camp."[46] Or it was Albizu's experiences at Harvard (particularly from 19016 to 1918) that fueled his hatred of the United States. "He relentlessly attacked the United States on the race issue" because of prejudice he experienced in Boston.[47] Or, finally, perhaps because he was "illegitimate," it was shame that explained the "venomous bitterness" of Albizu's political career.[48]

The one factor that unites all these comments is a single-minded focus on personality. Living in a colony apparently had no effect on Albizu's politics. For example, when U.S. officials like Ernest Gruening told Congress that U.S. policy "is the establishment of Old World colonialism, under the Stars and Stripes, something which should be repugnant and repulsive to our ideas of democracy,"[49] this repulsive policy was not used to explain Albizu's politics. The man was simply a paranoid.

Equally important, when U.S. commentators explain Albizu's politics on the basis of his experiences in the United States, they disregard the first twenty-one years of his life. Albizu never needed to go to Boston to experience U.S. racial prejudice; all he had to do was take a short trip from his Ponce birthplace to the sugar central at Guancia. And his anti-Americanism certainly had something to do with coming to political maturity in a period when Congress constantly complained of the anti-U.S. sentiment that fueled Puerto Rican politics. Born in 1891, Albizu grew up with the 1909 budget struggle, the Olmstead Act, and the comments of President William Howard Taft as the political focus of his entrance into adult life. When he left for college in the United States, Albizu was twenty-one years old, a man influenced, not by his experiences in the United States, but by his experiences in the moral capital of Puerto Rico, Ponce.

Like any politician, personal factors certainly played a part in Albizu's political ideology. But it is fruitless to blame Harvard or the U.S. Army. His close friends agree that he came out of the U.S. Army proud of his military service; and Henry Epstein, then the solicitor general of the State of New York, wrote to President Roosevelt about "Pedro," his school chum at Harvard. The Pedro Epstein knew "was generally deemed to be a normal, high minded and idealistic human being."[50]

Paraphrasing the historian Truman Clark, by blaming Harvard or the U.S. Army, U.S. officials "could successfully deny to themselves that their nation was an imperial power."[51] By focusing on Albizu's fanaticism, U.S. officials could also avoid these questions: After twenty-six years of repeated refusals to grant self-government, why was a resort to revolution either surprising or unjust? What, after all, would the U.S. colonists have done in Albizu's and Puerto Rico's position?

After obtaining his law degree at Harvard, Albizu[52] returned to Puerto Rico in 1921. He settled in Ponce. When the Nationalist party was formed in 1922, Albizu never joined. Instead, his first public participation in the island's political life was to affiliate himself with members of the Unionist party. As Albizu later told a reporter, "[Governor] Reilly provoked a general rebellion in the country. I believed that it was then possible to organize a group disposed to openly combat the colonial regime."[53] So for two years, supposedly consumed with hate for Americans, Albizu made suggestions like these:

May 31, 1923: "We ought to look for legal means and the sanction of Congress if it is necessary to unite us in a Constituent Congress, that writes the Constitution that creates dignity for our people."[54]

October 12, 1923: Again seeking a constitutional Congress he writes that "the [U.S.] Congress would never deny our adopting a lawful project of this temper because the procedure derives from the Northamerican constitution."[55]

April 24, 1924: He scolds his fellow Unionists for not inviting the Socialist party to join their efforts; he seeks "to consolidate the nation in a beautiful unity" by urging "a formal compromise among all the political parties so that our legislature approves a resolution soliciting the United States Congress to convoke a Constituent Constitutional Convention for the Puerto Rican people."[56]

Pedro Albizu Campos *became* a revolutionary. His earliest position papers indicate a desire to work with everyone—including the Americans—to peacefully achieve the constitutional convention that would place all political power in the hands of the Puerto Rican people. But right after the Unionists returned from their (in Albizu's eyes) humiliating efforts to achieve the free associated state, Albizu made a statement that is a key to understanding his political evolution. On May 12, 1924, he wrote:

We offer a most exceptional spectacle: The people are the action, their leaders, the reaction; the people, the vanguard, their leaders, the impediment. All the force of our leaders seems to limit itself to organize armies that after they are organized, they become fearful, and the result is to deliver themselves, with their army, in order not to incur the ill will of the enemy.[57]

Albizu resigned from the Unionist party right after he made this statement. He resigned because the party had formally eliminated independence from its list of political goals, and because Albizu saw no way to create among the Unionist leadership what then became the principal object of his political life. As Albizu put it to a reporter, "Our program, its general thesis, is to bring the Puerto Rican people back to the moral position in which they found themselves in 1868."[58]

In essence Albizu agreed with men like Ernest Gruening: U.S. policy was "repulsive." His problem was how to create in the Puerto Rican people the sense of repulsion that fueled his politics.

On May 18, 1924, Albizu was elected vice-president of the Puerto Rican Nationalist party. He struggled to create a program that would appeal to the masses, and he struggled with the members of his party. Created in 1922, the Nationalist party sought independence but lacked a program, and from Albizu's point of view, the will to victory as well. Lawyers, doctors, and professionals joined the party; although they genuinely revered native culture and the Spanish language, their political posture was "essentially defensive," their tactics those of "respect" for and courtesy to all political opponents.[59]

In this party Albizu was *una rafaga*, a violent gust of tropical wind. At a San Juan political rally celebrating the birth of José De Diego—on April 16, 1925—Albizu stood in front of a podium that contained the Puerto Rican flag waving above the platform and, positioned on the handrail, a series of U.S. flags. When a speaker glancing at the stars and stripes suggested that if the United States really stood for freedom, it was time to free Puerto Rico, Albizu jumped on the podium and grabbed each and every one of the U.S. flags. He stuffed them into his pockets and then proceeded to explain that a U.S. flag had no place at a rally celebrating José De Deigo. On the contrary, "if it was true that the American flag represented freedom and democracy in the world, here in Puerto Rico it represented colonialism and plunder."[60]

The Nationalists had no idea what to do with Albizu. He frightened the party hierarchy because of his disrespect for U.S. authority *and* because of the color of his skin. Many of the Nationalists were prejudiced; they could not envision a dark-skinned man as their president; so rather than split the party wide open, Albizu and his colleagues decided on this alternative: Following the suggestion first made by De Diego, Albizu would travel through the Hispanic world trying to generate support for Puerto Rican independence. It would be his job to arouse the international repugnance that would finally convince the Americans to relinquish their hold on Puerto Rico and its people.[61]

Albizu spent a year and a half raising the money required to travel the Hispanic world. He left Puerto Rico in June 1927 and did not return until January 1930. If U.S. policy had changed while Albizu traveled abroad, his revolutionary pleas would have fallen on deaf ears. As it was, a 1928 visit from Charles Lindbergh helped lay the groundwork for the most violent decade in Puerto Rican history.

On February 3, 1928, the Puerto Rican people proudly welcomed "the worthy son of the American Eagle," Charles Lindbergh. In a San Juan ceremony that theoretically had nothing to do with politics, island dignitaries happily celebrated Lindbergh's daring exploits as they simultaneously tried to use him to air mail a message to Washington. President Calvin Coolidge should know that islanders understood Patrick Henry's historical cry, Give me liberty or give me death. Granted the times were different—Puerto Ricans had no intention of fielding an army—yet all Puerto Ricans wanted Coolidge to get this message: "Grant us the freedom that you enjoy, for which you struggled, which you worship, which we deserve and you have promised us."[62]

If only because these words reflected a concurrent resolution of both houses of the Puerto Rican legislature, President Coolidge quickly responded to the islanders' latest memorial. The president was offended, so offended that he decided to give the Puerto Ricans a history lesson.

Island politicians "completely misunderstood" the facts. The Treaty of Paris, for example, "contained no promise to the people of Puerto Rico." But despite the absence of any obligation or promise, the United States had happily given Puerto Ricans a government "with a greater degree of sovereignty over its internal affairs than does the Government of any State or Territory." Agreed, the island was presently experiencing "a grave economical situation," but this was "exclusively the result of the exercise by the elected representatives of the people of Porto Rico of an authority granted by the present very liberal organic law."[63]

Puerto Ricans wanted to stop being a "mere subjected colony." Coolidge thought this was a nice idea and a laudable goal, but the president nonetheless failed to see the islanders' point: "Certainly giving Porto Rico greater liberty than it has ever enjoyed and powers of government for which its people are barely prepared cannot, with propriety, be said to be established therein 'a mere subjected colony.' "[64]

The islanders totally forgot "the condition in which we found Porto Rico": Poor, underfed, people living in shacks subjected to a "state of social degradation." The Americans had come in, and if after thirty years the people were still barely prepared for self-government, and still living, underfed, in shacks, it was their own fault. To Coolidge, "it is not desired to leave the impression that all progress in Porto Rico was due to continental Americans. Without the cooperation and assistance of Porto

Ricans progress would indeed have been negligible but the cooperation is largely due to the encouragement of American assistance, American methods, and an increase in the reward of efforts made."[65]

This angry summary of thirty years of colonial history reflected the president's sincere analysis of the Puerto Rican situation. For Coolidge facts—such as Governor Towner's statement that "the U.S. still has absolute control"[66]—had nothing to do with Washington's appraisal of Puerto Rican realities. Cultural biases blinded the president to anything but U.S. benevolence. In closing his letter to the Puerto Rican people, Coolidge warned them not to try his patience. "There was no disposition in America and certainly not on my part, to discourage any reasonable aspiration of the people of Porto Rico." But to justify "high hopes for the future," Puerto Ricans had to "limit their petitions to those things which may be granted without a denial of such hope. . . . Is it unreasonable to suggest that the people of Porto Rico, who are a part of the people of the United States, will progress with the people of the United States rather than be isolated from the source from which they have received practically their only hope of progress."[67]

As soon as his letter was published, Coolidge received a variety of laudatory comments. James Bliss Coombs, of Wall Street, told the president that "the economic wisdom of this message will make a real contribution to our state papers. . . . I am grateful in having my interests so impartially and well protected." And another New Yorker, James R. Sheffield, advised the president that "the Latin mind may attempt to distort the picture, but it cannot escape the facts as you have presented them."[68]

In Puerto Rico the indignation expressed by many politicians never hid reality: Meaningful political change was now out of the question. President Coolidge had faithfully expressed a point of view no passage of time seemed to alter or even soften. Indeed, while Americans forever claimed they had a heart, Puerto Ricans often failed to find it. After thirty years the island was still a U.S. colony, and after thirty years Congress still refused to provide hurricane relief without asking not only for interest on funds expended but for third mortgages on lands just destroyed by what Senator Hinam Bingham called, on December 10, 1928, "a hurricane of greater intensity than was ever before reached in any West Indian hurricane we know about."[69]

San Felipe hit the island on September 13, 1928. Rain fell with such astonishing intensity that scientists refused to believe their instruments: It was difficult to accept that in less than two days the central mountain region tried to absorb thirty inches of rain, the heaviest ever recorded in Puerto Rico during the past thirty years. Wind velocities probably exceeded 160 miles an hour, but there was no way to be certain because the "balloon shed quickly collapsed," along with the roof and house of the U.S. officials trying to monitor the ferocity of San Felipe.

Red Cross officials reported complete and utter devastation: houses destroyed, the main crops ruined, and large industries—such as sugar centrales, tobacco factories and warehouses, and fruit packing plants— demolished, immediately throwing thousands of people out of work. No one had an exact estimate of deaths, but in some ways the dead were lucky, because no one had any idea how to feed the living. The Red Cross estimated 50,000 homes destroyed, and although they had already furnished food and clothing to more than 180,000 islanders, the situation was obviously desperate.[70]

As senators and congressmen worked their way through the graphic photographs displayed by committee staff, Representative Harold Knutson of Minnesota had a question; he understood the need for assistance, but "how about Porto Rican resources. . . . I do not see anything that gives any idea of the capacity of the Porto Ricans to take care of themselves. . . . I say that if Porto Rico can independently handle the difficulty she should be given that degree of autonomy."[71]

After Knutson once again stressed that "this has got to be a real necessity," Representative Lloyd Thurston of Iowa wanted to know about interest on the loans suggested. Was there to be an absolute waiver of payment of interest on deferred payments? Senator Bingham favored a waiver of interest, but he understood Thurston's point that it should be limited to those who had essentially lost everything. For example, "some of the planters would be able to pay interest next year and the citrus growers the year after that."[72]

With these assurances in place, the governor of Puerto Rico, Horace Towner, took the witness stand. To his credit the governor seemed to be ashamed. Indeed, echoing the accusation made by Senator Edmund Pettus against Senator Joseph Foraker in 1900, Towner stressed that "with regard to whether or not you ought or ought not to do this—I hardly think it should be necessary for me to make such an appeal as that. The 1.5 million people of Porto Rico are all American citizens. They are your own fellow citizens . . . [and] they have helped themselves to the full extent of their ability."[73]

Representative Charles Underhill of Massachusetts listened; he then asked Towner about the "moral effect" of the loan. "Do you feel a better feeling will be engendered by this act? . . . We hear rumors and loose talk and propaganda with reference to independence and dissatisfaction with our own Government and our activities down there."

The governor pointed out that the complainers represented a small fraction of the people. Puerto Ricans supported the United States because the island's commercial intercourse was almost entirely limited to the United States. Islanders had no choice but to accept U.S. authority;

and as to the worry of Representative Ralph Gilbert, that unworthy people would receive aid, Towner stressed, "It is vastly important that these coffee growers should be helped in this dire necessity because we want them to remain in Porto Rico. They are white people. They are a good, dependable, meritorious class of people. They need more help than anybody else."[74]

And they eventually got it. With interest.

After thirty years of U.S. rule Puerto Rico seemed to prove the theory of the eternal recurrence of all things. Congress's reaction to the hurricane turned back the clock; it seemed to be reading 1900 when, ironically enough, Theodore Roosevelt, Jr., became governor of Puerto Rico.

The new governor was an admirable, honest man who openly admitted his own and the nation's faults. He had no experience in colonial affairs; he knew nothing about the island, and neither did his colleagues, a group of men and women who failed to blush even when they made the most outrageous and pathetic proposals. For example, one of Roosevelt's aides suggested this plan for creating additional jobs: The colonial government would buy a multitude of canaries, poor Puerto Ricans would teach them to sing the "Star Spangled Banner," and islanders would then sell the gifted birds to rich North American tourists.[75]

Roosevelt tried to be different. He saw no way the natives could do without the United States—independence would condemn more than half a million Puerto Ricans to death[76]—but he also tried to show them that he had no intention of continuing the "hopeless drive" to Americanize the island. He began his inaugural address in Spanish; each night he memorized twenty new Spanish words, and even though he knew he would make mistakes, Roosevelt tried to use the words in the next day's intercourse.[77]

The new governor hated to look at the mail. After thirty years as a U.S. colony, educated Americans still wrote to "Porto Rico, Cuba" and "Porto Rico, Central America," or to "Ambassador Roosevelt, American Embassy, Porto Rico." The postman continually brought requests for Puerto Rican stamps, and a visit from friends who sailed down in a yacht upset both the governor and his devoted wife. At dinner the friends wanted to know who the president of Puerto Rico was. Exasperated, the governor's assistant replied that he was a man called Herbert Hoover.[78]

Roosevelt picked up his pen. In a Sunday piece for the *Washington Star* (dated December 8, 1929), he tried to explain the nature of the people and the still-horrifying impact of the hurricane. Fully a year after the storm hit, he estimated that 60 percent of the children were malnourished, and many were "literally slowly starving." On his more than twenty visits to the island's cities and towns Roosevelt had often seen "pathetic little groups carrying home made coffins"; he had watched mothers carrying little skeletons, all of whom were Americans.

To relieve this distress Roosevelt wanted money, not from the federal government, but from the pockets of mainlanders willing to help the pathetic multitude sandwiched into the tiny island of Puerto Rico.[79] The Golden Rule Foundation had set aside Sunday, December 8, 1929, as a day in which to solicit aid for the helpless islanders. Dig deeply, wrote the governor, because "these hundreds of thousands of children are American citizens."

The children continued to starve. Why? Because Puerto Rico was still a fuzzy dot on America's mental map of the world, and because for all his good intentions and dedicated efforts, Theodore Roosevelt, Jr., was a perfect representative of U.S. colonialism. The hurricane was the island's problem, the United States its only source of "salvation."[80] That the governor's depiction of island life echoed that presented by Joseph Marcus ten years earlier (in Marcus's study for the U.S. Labor Department) never forced Roosevelt to question his or America's basic assumptions about our rights and their future.

On the contrary, although Roosevelt proudly admitted that Americans had all the power, it was, he felt, "ridiculous" to argue that thirty years of power translated into primary responsibility for Puerto Rico's economic and political condition. In one dizzying paragraph he agreed that the U.S. corporations had the best lands, "handsome earnings," and that they did treat the Puerto Ricans "in a rather summary fashion." But the sugar barons had nevertheless brought wealth to the island; they had never enjoyed any competitive advantages, except those abilities given by God; and within the limits set by capitalism they tried to employ the islanders who "found themselves without property."[81]

This intelligent man used his intelligence to deny and distort reality. The United States had all the power but none of the responsibility for Puerto Rico's admittedly overwhelming problems. Overpopulation, the size of the island, the lack of natural resources—along with the hurricane, these explained Puerto Rico's dismal present and its never-to-be-a-state future. To Roosevelt "it was practically impossible to envisage any period in the future"[82] when islanders could assume the financial burdens of statehood. Since it was "base" to hold up such a possibility to such a hopeless people, Roosevelt outlined his alternative vision of the colony's future.[83]

Puerto Rico would be America's "show window looking south."[84] To prove to the rest of Latin America what U.S. ingenuity could achieve the island would assume a dominion status. In this manner there would be enough money to finance a local government, and if Puerto Ricans ruled their own island, the pride of the people would finally be satisfied. Roosevelt understood the feelings of inferiority engendered by colonialism. He therefore wanted to create conditions that provided some opportunities for self-respect and self-esteem.

When would dominion status be achieved? Roosevelt had no date in mind, nor, beyond private philanthropy, did he have any vision of the island's economic future. This was unfortunate because Roosevelt left Puerto Rico in January 1932 to become governor of the Philippines— "For years I had been interested in them. They are the greatest colonial possession that the United States has ever had."[85] He left just when the island's sugar industry entered a period in which its very survival was threatened. The time bomb set by the Americans (and Puerto Ricans and Spaniards and French), who had rooted the island's future in sugar, was about to explode. In federal agricultural planning Puerto Rico took a distant back seat to states like Louisiana. Thus Roosevelt was certainly correct when he noted, "I was really sorry to leave the island . . . and I felt I had left friends there and an interesting problem by no stretch of the imagination solved."[86]

No one was crying for the owners of South Porto Rico Sugar. In 1928 the company netted nearly $5 million in profits, a full 25 percent profit figured on sales and almost 50 percent figured on net worth. Even in 1929, 1930, and 1931 South Porto (and Central Aguirre) did quite well. Not like the banner years of 1927 and 1928 but smack in the middle of the world depression, South Porto Rico in 1932 would never complain about a $2.6 million profit—close to 20 percent on sales, and 20 percent if figured on net worth.[87]

The problem was overproduction in the rest of the world and overproduction in the U.S. colonies as a response to overproduction in the rest of the world. Start with the price paid for sugar. In the United States the price was set by the world market price, plus the tariff added to protect U.S. producers from world competition. Of course, except for Cuba, the United States had used little foreign sugar since 1913,[88] but a country that boasted of free-market competition nevertheless did everything possible to protect mainland and insular (i.e., Puerto Rican, Hawaiian, and Filipino) producers from their exposure to the profit-making opportunities of others.

In the 1920s, as British and Japanese producers put too much sugar on international markets, the world price of sugar declined. What Puerto Rican companies did was compensate for the lower world price by using fertilizers to increase sugar output and machines to more effectively process the increased output.[89] Ultimately this was disastrous; the increased output, added to the world's oversupply, exacerbated an already difficult problem. But as South Porto Rico's profits suggest, the short-term benefits of the increased production strategy worked. Companies like South Porto Rico and Central Aguirre continued to make handsome profits and, in the midst of the depression, both companies always sent substantial dividends to their primarily mainland stockholders.

The problem was the world price of sugar, linked to the willingness of the federal government to protect its producers. As too much sugar lowered prices, the federal government simply increased the tariff. For example, in May 1932 sugar sold in world markets at one-half cent a pound, but in the United States it sold at roughly three cents a pound. Overproduction had helped create a situation in which government subsidies accounted for two-thirds of the price of raw sugar.[90]

Nobody minded the contradiction—survival of the fittest Americans surviving on government relief—but by 1932 it was also clear that even the resources of the federal government could be exhausted. Something had to be done to limit production, and if that was done at the expense of Puerto Rico and the other colonies, the result would be a hundred thousand thrown out of work in a nation that always had 30 percent or more of its people permanently unemployed.

The sugar problem acted like a stone thrown into water. It set off ripples of discontent that moved islanders to challenge not only the absentee owners of sugar but also the very nature of the colonial relationship. After all, to possibly penalize Puerto Rico in order to certainly benefit Louisiana was to underline the political nature of every economic problem.[91] Quite unintentionally the crisis of sugar made islanders more willing than ever to listen to the two men who dominated Puerto Rican politics for the next thirty-five years.

Pedro Albizu Campos returned from his worldwide sojourn in 1930. A year later Luis Muñoz Rivera returned from a self-imposed exile in New York. The revolutionary met the poet, and when one went to jail, the other went to the White House.

It was an extraordinary decade.

NOTES

1. Theodore Roosevelt, Jr., *Colonial Policies of the United States* (New York: Doubleday, 1937), pp. 83–84.

2. Carlos E. Díaz Olivo, "The Fiscal Relationship between Puerto Rico and the United States," *Revista del Colegio de Abogados de Puerto Rico* 51 (April–September 1990): pp. 1–136, esp. p. 47.

3. Ibid., esp. pp. 44–49.

4. See *Congressional Record*, Senate, 6th Congress, 1st session, October 29, 1921, 6998.

5. Ibid., p. 6697.

6. Ibid., p. 6992.

7. Ibid., p. 7003.

8. See Díaz Olivio, "Fiscal Relationship," p. 51.

9. See the papers of E. Montgomery Reilly, Manuscript Division, New York

Public Library (henceforth cited as Reilly papers). I found out about the existence of these papers only by reading Truman Clark's *Puerto Rico and the United States, 1917–1933* (Pittsburgh: University of Pittsburgh Press, 1975).

10. *Congressional Record,* House, 67th Congress, 2nd session, March 3, 1922, p. 5031.

11. Roberto Todd, *Desfile de Gobernadores de Puerto Rico* (San Juan: 1943), pp. 66–69.

12. Delma S. Arrigoitia, "José De Diego: A Legislator in Times of Political Transition" (Ph.D. diss., Fordham University, 1985).

13. Ricardo Alegría, ed. *Temas de la Historia de Puerto Rico* (San Juan: Centro de Estudios Avanzados, 1988), p. 227.

14. Aida Negron de Montilla, *Americanization in Puerto Rico and the Public School System* (Río Piedras: Editorial Edil, 1970), p. 172.

15. See Clark, *Puerto Rico,* p. 53.

16. See Reilly papers, p. 6.

17. Ibid., p. 7.

18. Ibid., p. 7.

19. Reilly letter to Harding dated August 31, 1921. See Reilly papers.

20. Letter is dated September 17, 1921, pp. 3 and 4. See Reilly papers.

21. See H. P. Krippene, "Porto Rico's Playful Politics," *Current History* (January 1922): pp. 610–615.

22. Luis Muñoz Marin, "A Ninety-Eight Percent American in Porto Rico," *New Republic* 29 (January 4, 1922): p. 611.

23. See Charles Goodsell, *Administration of a Revolution* (Cambridge: Harvard University Press, 1965), p. 37.

24. See Clark, *Puerto Rico,* p. 55.

25. See Reilly's letter of November 9, 1921, Reilly papers; for the actions of the chief of police see Alegría. *Temas,* p. 227; for the letters to the editor see, Clark, *Puerto Rico,* p. 56.

26. Letter from Harding dated November 11, 1921, Reilly papers.

27. Letter to Harding dated October 11, 1922, Reilly papers.

28. See *Congressional Record,* House, 67th Congress, 2nd session, for March 3 and April 4, 1922.

29. This analysis relies heavily on the discussion of Luis Ángel Ferrao, *Pedro Albizu Campos y el Nacionalismo Puertorrigueno* (Río Piedras: Editorial Cultural, 1990), esp. p. 74; see, too, Clark, *Puerto Rico,* the chapter entitled "The Kaleidoscope of Puerto Rican Politics," pp. 76–105.

30. See Reilly's letter of September 28, 1922, Reilly papers.

31. See letter to Harding dated May 3, 1922, Reilly papers; also Clark, *Puerto Rico,* p. 62.

32. Letters from Harding dated March 5, 1923, and March 28, 1922, Reilly papers.

33. The Balzac case is reprinted in *Documents on the Constitutional History of Puerto Rico* (Washington, D.C.: Commonwealth of Puerto Rico, 1964), pp. 140–149; the quotes cited appear on p. 146.

34. Ibid., p. 147.

35. Ibid., p. 148.

36. Ibid., p. 149.

37. Clark, *Puerto Rico*, pp. 88–89.

38. See *The Civil Government of Porto Rico, Hearings before the Committee on Territories and Insular Possessions*, Senate, 68th Congress, 1st session, 1924, p. 6.

39. *Civil Government of Porto Rico, Hearings before the Committee on Insular Affairs*, House, 68th Congress, 1st session, 1924, p. 25.

40. Ibid., p. 39.

41. Ibid., pp. 41–42.

42. Ibid., pp. 45 and 47.

43. *Amend the Organic Act of Porto Rico*, House, 68th Congress, 1st session, Report no. 291, March 13, 1924, pp. 2 and 3.

44. *To Amend the Organic Act of Porto Rico*, Senate, 68th Congress, 1st session, Report no. 356, April 7, 1924, pp. 5 and 7.

45. Pedro Albizu Campos, *Obras Escojidas*, Vol. 1, 1923–1936 (San Juan: Editorial Jelofe, 1975), p. 52.

46. This comment appears on page 1 of Gruening's five-page letter. Interior Department Archives, Records of the Office of Territories and Island Possessions, Record Group 126, National Archives, Washington, D.C. The file is 9–8–78.

47. See, for example, Earl Parker Hanson, *Transformation* (New York: Simon & Schuster, 1955), pp. 82–83.

48. For a reasonable discussion of the "illegitimacy" issue see Ferrao, *Pedro Albizu Campos*, pp. 122–124.

49. See *Sugar, Hearings before the Committee on Finance*, Senate, 75th Congress, 1st session 1937, p. 132. Recall that it was Gruening who wrote the letter that President Roosevelt called "extremely good."

50. See Roberto F. Rexach Benitez, *Pedro Albizu Campos: Leyenda y Realidad* (San Juan, 1961); I have also interviewed Ruth Reynolds, Oscar Collazo, and Carlos Velez Rieckehoff.

51. See Clark, *Puerto Rico*, p. 175.

52. Besides the recent study by Ferrao, other Spanish-language studies of Albizu include Manuel Maldonado Denis, *Pedro Albizu Campos: Las Conciencia Nacional Puertorriqueña* (San Juan: Ediciones Compromiso, 1972); Juan Antonio Corretjer, *Pedro Albizu Campos* (Montevideo: El Siglo Ilustrado, 1970).

53. Albizu, *Obras Escojidas*, Vol. 1, p. 42.

54. Ibid., p. 14.

55. Ibid., p. 18.

56. Ibid., pp. 25–26.

57. Ibid., p. 30; see, too, an interview he gave on January 8, 1927. He notes that he made an error when he joined the Unionists: "I confused the shouting created by those who had lost public posts with true rebellion." Vol. 1, p. 35.

58. Ibid., p. 50.

59. See Ferrao, *Pedro Albizu Campos*, p. 47.

60. See, for example, Federico Ribes Tovar, *Albizu Campos: Puerto Rican Revolutionary* (New York: Plus Ultra, 1971), pp. 13–14.

61. See Ferrao, *Pedro Albizu Campos*, esp. pp. 40–41.

62. See Arnold G. Dana, *Porto Rico's Case: Outcome of American Sovereignty* (New Haven, 1928), p. 7.

63. Ibid., the letter appears on pages 58–64 of Dana's pamphlet. The quote used appears on p. 58.

64. Ibid., p. 59.

65. Ibid., p. 62.

66. See *Civil Government of Porto Rico*, Senate, 68th Congress, 1st session, 1924, p. 6.

67. Dana, *Porto Rico's Case*, p. 64.

68. See Clark, *Puerto Rico*, pp. 102–103.

69. See *Relief of Porto Rico*, Joint Committee on Insular Affairs, 70th Congress, 2nd session, 1928, p. 3.

70. Ibid., pp. 9 and 11.

71. Ibid., p. 30.

72. Ibid., pp. 30–31.

73. Ibid., p. 39.

74. Ibid., p. 48; for Underhill see pp. 39–40.

75. Roosevelt, *Colonial Policies*, pp. 98–100.

76. Ibid., p. 117.

77. Mrs. Theodore Roosevelt, Jr., *Day before Yesterday* (New York: Doubleday, 1959), p. 230.

78. Ibid., p. 231.

79. *Congressional Record*, Senate, 71st Congress, 1st session, December 10, 1929, p. 2812.

80. Ibid., p. 2812.

81. Roosevelt, *Colonial Policies*, pp. 102–103.

82. Ibid., p. 116.

83. For a fine overview of U.S. attitudes toward the Puerto Rican economy see Truman R. Clark, "The Imperial Perspective: Mainland Administrators' Views of the Puerto Rican Economy, 1898–1941," *Revista Interamericana* 4, no. 4 (Winter 1975): pp. 505–517.

84. Ibid., p. 119.

85. Ibid., p. 125.

86. Ibid., p. 124.

87. See Moody's *Manual of Industrial Corporations* for 1931 and 1937, pp. 368 and 3007 respectively.

88. See Rafael Alberto Bernabe, *Prehistory of the Partido Popular Democrático: Muñoz Marín, the Partido Liberal and the Crisis of Sugar in Puerto Rico*, Doctoral Dissertation, State University of New York at Binghamton, 1989, p. 154.

89. See John E. Dalton, *Sugar: A Case Study of Government Control* (New York: Macmillan, 1937), pp. 62–65.

90. See Bernabe, *Partido Popular Democrático*, p. 162.

91. Ibid., p. 84.

Chapter 5

Revolution and Reaction

If you are willing to have help of a kind and have no real voice in the government of the nation to which you are appended, why, then, that is one thing. If I were a Puerto Rican that would not satisfy me, just as it did not satisfy Washington, Thomas Jefferson, and Simón Bolívar.
Senator Millard Tydings, Chair, Senate Committee on Territories and Insular Affairs[1]

The message is a syllogism: Puerto Rico is small. Puerto Rico lacks natural resources. Therefore Puerto Rico needs to rely on others for its long- and short-term needs.[2]

Facts often have nothing to do with the centuries-long persistence of this syllogism. Point to an island like Singapore—ten times smaller than Puerto Rico, and also without substantial natural resources—and one consistent reaction is skepticism. Singapore is the exception, Puerto Rico the rule. Just look at our history.

A contemporary manifestation of the syllogism's persistent power is the 1986 congressional testimony of Arturo Guzmán, a Cuban economist. Discussing the island's future, Guzmán said this: "If we could use the analogy of a child that is up for adoption, that child which is sitting in an orphanage, it isn't going to show you much outgoing signs of affection until the child is completely assured that you are willing to accept him as a parent. Look upon us as that child."[3]

Puerto Ricans are not children. But some believe they are. And like the syllogism, it is true if they say so.

Ironically, the most influential discussion of Puerto Rico's alleged inferiority appeared in 1934. Called *Insularismo* (literally insularism), the book tried to analyze, not a dogma, but a controversy.[4] Antonio Pedreira sought to stimulate change by provoking thought, but readers, perhaps justly, focused on the pessimism expressed by Pedreira. Lines like "in proportion to its size, a country develops its riches, and therefore its culture"[5] were quite unlikely to generate the sense of self-confidence required to challenge not only the limits imposed by geography but the limits imposed by almost 450 years of colonialism.

Pedreira, a university professor, looked at Puerto Rico's elite with a decided sense of apprehension. The young seemed to be "a generation of invalids,"[6] a group of men and women lacking the mental courage to understand that the culture was at a historical crossroads. Politically and economically major changes had to be made. The challenging and monumental issue was whether Puerto Rico would move forward by finally fabricating a positive definition of self and society or, instead, languish in a sea of confusion and inferiority. As Luis Muñoz Marín wrote, "Perhaps we are destined to be neither Porto Ricans nor Americans, but merely puppets of a mongrel state of mind . . . perhaps we are destined to discuss Cervantes and eat pork and beans in the Child's [today McDonald's] restaurant that must be opened sooner or later."[7]

Destiny had nothing to do with it. Only people make and *remake* culture. They do it with the weight of the past on their shoulders, yet there is no reason that the past has to shackle the future. Thus, the 1930s are so important in Puerto Rican history because the nation faced a choice, a choice of whether to move into the future on the basis of a corrected past or walk into the future extending a dependent and grateful hand to the New Deal offered by the island's forever helpful Uncle Sam.

Flags can excite a nation. During the war in the Persian Gulf U.S. cars and houses, lapels and department stores, were filled with almost unprecedented displays of small and gigantic depictions of the Stars and Stripes. The flag became the United States, or, more accurately, the flag symbolized the nation's long latent sense of pride in self and society.

In Puerto Rico the nation's flag has always had special significance for any group seeking change. Look at the Cuban flag, for instance, and you notice that it is the reverse of Puerto Rico's banner. Both flags were designed at the same time, tied to poles buried in soil that would soon be free.

Cuba won its independence. Puerto Rico did not. So when Pedro Albizu Campos returned to the island in 1930, he made the one-star banner the symbol of the Nationalist party. Singing the national anthem (written in 1868, the year of the Shout of Lares) as they gazed at the flag, Puerto Ricans might be stirred to action by lines like these: "Most beautiful Borinquen, we have to follow Cuba; you have brave sons who want to fight! Let us no more seem fearful! Let us no more, timid, permit our enslavement!"[8]

No matter how important, enslavement was not the key issue facing the Nationalists on the night of April 16, 1932. The Puerto Rican legislature had suggested converting the nation's flag into the official emblem of the colony. To Albizu this was both a travesty and a humiliation. Indeed, as word spread that the legislature had actually passed this law, Albizu stopped a speech celebrating the birth of José De Diego and immediately called his listeners to action. They should march to the Capitol and stop the legislators from engaging in such a profane action.

Led by Albizu, over 800 protesters soon arrived at the Puerto Rican Capitol. They pushed to get in, police pushed to keep them out, and a young man died. Rafael Suarez Díaz, a follower of Albizu, was crushed to death in the pushing and shoving match. To the Nationalists he became, along with the flag, a symbol of their struggle to defeat U.S. colonialism. However, to contemporary and later critics of the Nationalists, the assault on the Capitol proved that Albizu and his followers showed little respect for the local authorities. The Nationalists were quite willing to use force to achieve their aims.[9]

This perfectly accurate comment needs to be put in social and historical perspective. First, in 1932 Albizu used far less violence than his political opponents. Second, Albizu directed his attacks at the agents of colonial authority; his island opponents assaulted one another. Finally, Albizu never hid his revolutionary stance; even today, a follower of Albizu will proudly indicate that "we wore our guns on the outside" for all to see and none to misunderstand.

The violence started as soon as the 1932 campaign began. In this election the Coalition (the prostatehood Republicans united with the prolabor-prostatehood Socialists) literally battled the proindependence Liberal party. In March the Liberals started a riot when they interrupted what they called fraudulent voter registration drives. The Liberals threw rocks at their opponents and disobeyed the police; in the ensuing melee three people lost their lives. In Vega Baja and Vega Alta the towns were at war. Liberals, Republicans, and Socialists routinely used firearms, sticks, stones, and knives as a means of political persuasion. And in May 1932 near the town of Ciales, three separate riots occurred between Liberals and their opponents. Thankfully no one was killed, but the Liberal leader Luis Muñoz Marín told a reporter that "when the law does not protect, people must protect themselves by using force if necessary."[10]

Albizu would have agreed with Muñoz, but his legitimization of violence revolved, not around protecting oneself against other Puerto Ricans, but around political and economic ideas. As early as 1927 he argued that the United States, a nation with enormous national and international problems, lacked the time or the desire to listen to a "submissive and servile" mass of colonists. To get U.S. attention islanders had to make a definitive break with the colonial regime; only a revolution would alert the United States to Puerto Rico's plight but, this time, islanders would root their actions in a specific set of political, economic, and cultural ideals.[11]

Politically, Albizu agreed with a position soon seconded by Senator Millard Tydings: The United States conquered Puerto Rico.[12] It took the island by military force, and thus from July 25, 1898, the moral and political authority of the United States was utterly invalid. Often (the attorney side of) Albizu Campos harked back to Puerto Rico's 1897 agreement with Spain; the United States had no right to ride roughshod over a valid agreement between two peoples.

His essential point, however, repeated time and again, was the military imposition of alien authority *linked* to an electoral mandate the United States always disregarded. Puerto Rico was a colony, and even when "the Union Party for 25 years won electoral majorities," nothing changed. Puerto Rico remained (to use Governor Horace Towner's phrase) under the "absolute control" of U.S. officials.[13]

Puerto Ricans had a right to counter force with force. Children did as they were told. Adults questioned and, if necessary, forcibly resisted unjust authority. They did so because every human being had a "natural right" to be free; and they did so because foreigners now owned, controlled, and used the economic and human resources of Puerto Rico for their own benefit: "There is no justice because the basic cause of our misery is the displacement of Puerto Rican landowners by the North-Americans as a result of the political system dominating Puerto Rico."[14]

In an extraordinary series of articles written and published over two years (1930 and 1931) Albizu offered a sophisticated and extensive analysis of Puerto Rico's economic predicament. Discussing everything from tariffs to the shipping laws, from agriculture to nationalization, from Britain to Cuba, Albizu always came back to the same point of origin: Economic development was inextricably linked to, and based on, political power.[15]

Albizu understood that economics was a zero-sum game; the resolution of any economic issue produced winners and losers, the haves and the have nots. To Albizu it was impossible to have any chance of economic success without *first* having the political power to control, for example, tariffs, shipping, and the flow of profits from their country of origin. In a telling analysis of international competition Albizu asked this question: "We would like to know how a person that has thought a little about these problems is able to believe for a moment that free trade is able to benefit a nation subject to foreign rule, completely tied, and without political powers of any nature."[16]

For Albizu any nation naturally nourished and protected its own. With political power Puerto Rico could do the same thing because "when it enjoys full sovereignty and it knows how to exercise the powers that this privilege concedes, foreign capital, if it wants to continue inside the national frontiers, has to march in unison with the national interests, even though these are in conflict with the nationality of its own origin."[17]

Economic progress and political freedom were for Albizu two sides of the same coin. The problem was that to have any chance of *self-sustaining* economic progress Puerto Rico first needed meaningful political power, which always brought Albizu back to one of his original ideas: revolution—an overthrow of the colonial regime.

To achieve that overthrow Albizu argued that the nation needed a "normal infusion." After thirty years of U.S. colonialism islanders lacked the sense of self-confidence required for social action. As if a brand, someone had stamped inferior on the insular mind; to Albizu, a man of high intelligence and supreme self-confidence, this was not only personally offensive; it was the biggest barrier to the success of the revolution: "Our country is in a great war with no means of defending itself; only a resurgence of collective morality is able to save Puerto Rico."[18]

To provide that resurgence, Albizu emphasized, idealized, and sometimes overlooked always controversial aspects of Puerto Rico's past. In a speech called "The Concept of Race" he tried (like José De Diego in 1918) to root national self-confidence in a Spanish heritage that overlooked the brutality and exploitation that existed in the island's past *and* its present. To Albizu, underlining Spanish scientific and literary achievements was accurate and helpful; overlooking the equally significant degree of institutionalized Spanish exploitation alienated the very people Albizu wanted to reach.

Islanders old enough to remember the harshness of their Spanish masters had a difficult time with Albizu's concept of the Spanish race; and those who, in 1932, were still being exploited by Spaniards failed to comprehend Albizu's unwillingness to face unpleasant facts. In congressional testimony Frank Dillingham estimated that 10 percent to 20 percent of the sugar plantations were still owned by Spaniards. In a speech, Albizu harshly, accurately, and bitterly criticized the "brothers" who walked arm and arm with the colonial powers; he then walked away from the truth by arguing that they "were pigs from Chicago—Spain had never been a country of pigs. . . . Spain is the nation of the historical vision par excellence."[19]

Besides Spain, Catholicism became a centerpiece of Albizu's efforts to restore a sense of national pride and self-assertiveness. A convert to Catholicism, Albizu genuinely believed what he said; it was also politically significant that Catholicism theoretically provided a unifying force that cut through the class and regional divisions of Puerto Rican society.

However, by making the Catholic religion a central element of Puerto Rico's revived national identity, Albizu raised as many barriers as he eliminated. What about the Masons? The nonbelievers? And, most important of all, the roughly 15 percent of the population that after the U.S. invasion had turned to Protestantism? Were these islanders part of Puerto Rico's heritage? Did they have to reconvert to be 100 percent Puerto Rican?[20]

Through the years Albizu's principles never changed. He was an authentic revolutionary, declaring, "The only transcendental obligation that a man or a woman born in a colony has is to redeem the country from its subjection" in a country still dominated by reformers.[21] Enormous crowds gathered whenever Albizu spoke, and many islanders lived vicariously through the courage and passion Albizu always conveyed. In the 1930s and beyond he was Puerto Rico's colonial conscience; but when it came to actual support, islanders turned to their traditional parties. In the only election in which he participated, 1932, Albizu received only 5,257 votes (out of over 450,000 cast).[22] He could legitimately claim that people voted for their jobs but his showing was nevertheless a great disappointment, a "mistake" he would never again repeat.

Ironically, the island's majority party, the Liberals, made many of the same points stressed by Albizu. Luis Muñoz Marín, for example, published in 1932 a series of economic articles that arrived at conclusions remarkably similar to Albizu's. Independence was not a sentimental but an economic necessity because only with political power would Puerto Rico have the wherewithal to determine its tariff and agricultural policy.[23]

In 1932 Muñoz argued that meaningful political powers were required for self-sustaining economic growth. But by 1934 he proudly accepted full responsibility for federal intervention and control of Puerto Rico's economic and political future. Returning from a trip to Washington on January 22, 1934, he told the more than 30,000 supporters gathered at the dock in San Juan that Puerto Rico was "on the eve of the New Deal."[24]

Muñoz's about-face—if consistency is the hobgoblin of small minds, Luis Muñoz Marín was indeed a giant—occurred in Washington. Contact with men like Undersecretary of Agriculture Rexford Tugwell convinced Muñoz that Puerto Rico's future rested on a close association with the federal government. As early as 1933 and 1934 Muñoz shelved status to focus on economics, and in the process he created what later governor Roberto Sanchez Vilella (1964–1968) called the "panting" of Puerto Rico for more and more federal funding. In Sanchez's words, "It is [in the 1930s] a question of the beginning of Puerto Rico's dependence on Federal assistance."[25]

Many factors made 1934 a year of new beginnings. Muñoz, for example, had first gone to Washington to remove a governor. Robert Gore, who had suggested that Franklin Roosevelt head the Democratic ticket in 1920, asked the new president for a political quid pro quo. What good jobs did the Democrats have now that Roosevelt was president? Gore got Puerto Rico, and throughout 1933 he created so much controversy that his tenure reminded islanders of the reign of "King Monty." Told by his superiors that "Puerto Rico is not believed even approximately ready for statehood," Gore nevertheless pressed Americanization. His opponents were disloyal, those who suggested independence went unhired, and from all appointees Gore demanded an undated letter of resignation. Cross Robert Gore and you were on the street in the time it took to say "unemployed in the middle of the depression."[26]

A neverending barrage of complaints finally forced Roosevelt to replace Gore with a man who soon became even more controversial. General Blanton Winship had fought in the Spanish-American War. He helped defeat the Filipinos in their struggle against the United States, he served in France during the Great War, he returned to the Philippines in the late 1920s, and he was available in 1934 when Franklin Roosevelt felt the need for a strong hand in the Caribbean. Only two weeks after Winship's appointment on February 5, 1934, the president wrote a "confidential" letter to the general concerning the safety of his wife. If "conditions in the island were still so disturbed," perhaps it was better that Mrs. Roosevelt postpone her visit and thus avoid a "demonstration inconvenient to all concerned."

The general told the president not to worry. Although "I shall adopt effective measures for her protection at all times," Puerto Ricans would be glad to welcome her.[27] And why not? She, as much as any other representative of the Roosevelt administration, was responsible for the increase in relief funding Muñoz had trumpeted as the beginning of Puerto Rico's New Deal. The Liberals would stage a welcome for the president's wife every bit as gracious as the welcome accorded to Muñoz Marín when he attended Mrs. Roosevelt's Washington tea parties.[28]

Muñoz was now an insider, a man with the ear of the president's wife. He knew how to make himself heard, and he also knew about the administrative changes proposed for Puerto Rico. After thirty-six years of guidance by the War Department's Bureau of Insular Affairs, Puerto Rico would soon be under the jurisdiction of the Department of the Interior. As Oscar Chapman, the under secretary ultimately responsible for the island, put it in a radio address to the American people: "Economically the island has not fared so well . . . particularly the extension of the sugar industry, while long yielding handsome returns to the stockholders of corporations which increasingly acquired lands on the islands, benefitted the Puerto Rican people little." The Roosevelt administration meant to reverse Puerto Rico's course because "Puerto Rico today [it was 1934] represents the picture of a country gradually depleted of its natural resources, of a country densely populated in which standards of living have gradually sunk lower and lower."[29]

Oscar Chapman sounded like Pedro Albizu Campos!

Washington did in fact understand the legitimacy of the Nationalist leader's charges. In 1934 42 percent of the island's people received relief, but by one government estimate at least 80 percent of the Puerto Rican people qualified for economic assistance if the funds were available.[30]

Equally significant, attempts at a voluntary control of sugar production (the "Marketing Agreement" of 1933) not only had failed to stabilize the industry but also had underlined the importance of political power in the conduct of economic affairs. In setting quotas for production, the sugar beet areas of states like Louisiana had actually seen their production quotas rise; Hawaii, an incorporated territory with only 7 percent of its people receiving relief, was forced to accept production cuts, but these were only half as great as the limits suggested for the unincorporated territory called Puerto Rico. The island was to cut production by a full 20 percent, while as a result of the new Agricultural Adjustment Act, processing taxes intended to help American farmers would affect the island in two different—but always negative—ways. By one estimate the new taxes would add $18 million to the island's imported food bill as they sent back to the mainland $6 million in taxes for products produced in Puerto Rico.[31]

Strikes became the order of the Puerto Rican day. In August 1933 5,000 tobacco workers walked out on their employers. Strikers soon tried to stop the rush of strike breakers, with violence the predictable result. In Lares (also in August 1933) 400 needleworkers not only went out on strike but patrolled the streets looking for anyone who dared to work. And when this strike quickly spread to Mayagüez, the largest city on the island's west coast, an estimated 2,000 workers attacked the shops owned by a native businesswoman. In the ensuing battle workers and police fought each other throughout the day; it was a guerrilla encounter in which, by nightfall, thirty-one people had been hospitalized and one man shot by the police.[32]

In September sugar workers clashed with police as they fought for better wages at the United Porto Rico Sugar Company. Here workers had no chance of success because the company had just filed for bankruptcy. National City Bank threatened to auction off a piece of Puerto Rico's future as, on January 11, 1934, Pedro Albizu Campos spoke to more than 6,000 striking sugar workers. The strikers had pleaded with Albizu to help them resolve a battle that had already lasted for two months. They no longer trusted the island's labor leadership, so they turned to a man who spoke of revolution.[33]

In Washington conditions on the island appeared ominous. Indeed, when the president wrote to General Winship about his wife's safety, he was obviously concerned about much more than Albizu Campos. To Teddy Roosevelt, Jr., Puerto Rico would be America's "show window looking south." To Franklin Roosevelt the island was a window he needed to close.

Privately Roosevelt told Ernest Gruening (the man who would head the island's reconstruction administration) that "the place is hopeless," so hopeless that the president "could only raise his arms above his head to emphasize his feeling."[34]

Publicly Roosevelt suggested a plan to rebuild Puerto Rico. He would creatively use the funds derived from the Sugar Act of (February) 1934 to provide temporary and long-term assistance, knowing that as their part of the bargain islanders like Luis Muñoz Matrín would plea with their people "to help the United States stabilize the world sugar market."[35]

In a confidential memo to the president General Winship said the original number was $150 million![36] The United States of America would give Puerto Rico $150 million for reconstruction if islanders embraced the Sugar Act proposed by Congress. In Washington when the initial outlines of the program was prepared, Muñoz had in his head the $150 million figure—or some other figure for the always gigantic sum changed from day to day—when he returned to the island in early 1934. For example, in debate in the island's legislature he proposed buying the bankrupt United Porto Rico Sugar Company; when opponents asked where the money would come from, Muñoz assured them the sugar act contained funds for the general improvement of Puerto Rican agriculture.[37]

And when opponents pointed out that the harsh production limits set by the act (i.e., the island's production would, as suggested the year before, be reduced by 20 percent) were rooted in Puerto Rico's status as an "insular" rather than a "domestic" producer, Muñoz stressed that the insular status was a key to the benefits Puerto Rico would receive. What Congress proposed to do was take the taxes from the Sugar Act and let Puerto Rico use them for its rehabilitation.[38]

Taxes imposed in Louisiana went to Washington. Taxes imposed in San Juan went to San Juan. Thus, *the key to the island's rehabilitation funding was its colonial status!* This logic repeated the argument made by Senator Joseph Foraker in 1900. As with the customs duties Puerto Rico still received in 1934 (and still received in 1992), the Sugar Act would treat the island differently because it did not, for example, have voting representation in Congress. Make Puerto Rico a domestic producer, and its taxes would follow the dividends paid by absentee owners: Everything would go to the mainland.

In advocating acceptance of the Sugar Act of 1934 Muñoz—and the Liberal party he represented—married Washington. For the next thirty years he would try to renegotiate the terms of that marriage, but once he rooted the source of his reconstruction funding in the island's colonial (or insular or unincorporated) status, he would continually prove the wisdom of his and Albizu's 1932 analysis of the economy: Self-sustaining economic development rested on the imaginative use of meaningful political power.

Take, for example, the 500-acre law. In 1932 Muñoz said the law was a "political myth"; his goal then was to centralize production in large, "semi-public" *centrales*.[39] By 1934 Muñoz wanted to enforce the law as a means of redistributing the island's agricultural lands. The idea was to give thousands of Puerto Ricans a chance to own the small farms that would provide a means for people to provide for themselves.

This laudable idea immediately met with a great deal of support and an equal amount of resistance. U.S. and Spanish and Puerto Rican owners of large tracts of land predictably and fiercely resisted any efforts to expropriate or nationalize or even pay them for their property. As Albizu noted in July 1934, "You will have to proceed to forced expropriation and for that you require legislation that will be a reality only if the President of the United States desires it."[40]

All roads led to Washington. And to the federal courts. Because, even if the President said yes, the 500-acre law was U.S. legislation, to be contested in U.S. courts. Judges raised in Boston and New York would decide Puerto Rico's economic fate, and while they debated, the people would wait for changes in the mother country's legal codes.

Albizu said the Liberals' strategy—best known as the Chardon Plan— put the Puerto Rican people at the "mercy" of the president of the United States. He reminded islanders that the president had stressed that "the economic rehabilitation of the island depended on the economic rehabilitation of the United States."[41] The latter preceded the former, so even with the best of intentions, Albizu said it was "childish" (*pueril*) to expect much from a man who had to deal with "ten million unemployed, forty million indigents living on public charity, a growing Federal deficit, and public debt that no one knew how to pay."[42]

No one listened to Albizu the economist. Instead, Muñoz would take to the airwaves, using the radio for a series of extremely effective "fireside" chats with the Puerto Rican people. Meanwhile, his Republican and Socialist opponents tried to blunt the political impact of the New Deal. They correctly feared that Muñoz and his colleagues would use the promised funds to increase his and the Liberals' political power. At any time jobs equaled votes in Puerto Rico; but in the 1930s jobs equaled survival, the persistence of a people, many of whom were literally starving.

Starvation was also on the mind of a university professor. In March 1934 Clemente Pereda reacted to a suggestion made by the island's Coalition (of Republicans and Socialists) majority: To rehabilitate the island's economy, Puerto Rico should become a state.

Pereda feared for the national, the cultural, survival of the Puerto Rican people. So he went to Plaza Baldorioty in San Juan, positioned himself next to an enormous crucifix, and for seven days fasted as a way of protesting the suggested annexation of his people.

The reaction to Professor Pereda's fast astonished virtually everyone on the island. Each and every day hundreds of people walked, as if in a procession, by the professor and his crucifix. Word spread to the island, and suddenly workers from one end of Puerto Rico to another traveled to San Juan to offer Pereda small religious stamps or other religious objects. Every no-statehood politician made an appearance at the professor's side. Antonio Barcelo (the president of the Liberal party) Muñoz Marín and Albizu Campos: They all paid homage to the professor and his silent struggle to avoid Americanization.[43]

Pereda struck this cord in the island's psyche: "Puerto Ricans don't know how to talk about anything else than Puerto Rico."[44] The same people who accept notions of inferiority will blossom if someone discusses the beauty of a Flamboyan tree, the riches of island cooking, or the remarkable decency of the "average" Puerto Rican. In 1991 islanders on a plane from New York or Hartford or Dayton still clap when their plane touches sacred soil, and they clapped for Clemente Pereda in 1934 because he personified a love of country and culture that is so commonplace it can easily be missed.

Pereda touched this cord by going on a hunger strike. Albizu Campos touched it by suggesting that islanders move beyond the tactics used by Professor Pereda. Albizu naturally applauded Pereda's opposition to statehood. He also applauded the professor's willingness to sacrifice himself for the good of his country. But Albizu nevertheless argued that "it was unfair to hope that others would sacrifice themselves when we lack the will to surpass the sacrifice with guns in our hands." To Albizu "the time had come in which each Puerto Rican had the obligation to be the apostle of his own moral passion."[45]

One very controversial example of Albizu's thrust was the Cadets of the Republic. They were an openly revolutionary army of young men who wore black shirts to symbolize the death of the nation; they had been conscripted into the service of their country by the Nationalist party and were committed to the idea most closely associated with Albizu Campos: "The nation is valor and sacrifice."[46]

Somehow Americans judging Albizu forgot the comment of Nathan Hale: "My only regret is that I have but one life to give for my country." To Winship or Roosevelt, Albizu was a fanatic; to Puerto Ricans, even to many of those who bitterly disagreed with his tactics, Albizu was a patriot. In Washington and in San Juan Americans then considering his prosecution for sedition resisted the insular courts because they knew it would be difficult to ever get a guilty verdict from a Puerto Rican jury.[47] So as prosecutors debated what to do about Albizu, the U.S. Army began to prepare weekly lists of Puerto Rican subversives, J. Edgar Hoover prepared to send G-men, and in the meantime Ernest Gruening arrived with a mandate from the president to do something about America's "hopeless" colony.

As head of the newly created Division of Territories and Insular Possessions, Ernest Gruening said that of his four "wards" (i.e., Puerto Rico, Alaska, Hawaii, and the Virgin Islands), Puerto Rico was his major concern. Gruening believed that Puerto Rico was "unequivocally and permanently United States Territory";[48] moreover, conversations with the president convinced Gruening that Roosevelt saw the Caribbean as "an American lake."[49] The island would forever be a part of the United States, so it was essential to stabilize and, if possible, revitalize our valued island possession.

To provide moral support for the Puerto Rican people he and Muñoz sent them a Christmas present. Through the summer and fall of 1934 islanders had waited for the implementation of the Chardon Plan. Its details promised changes (e.g., besides land redistribution there were detailed and imaginative proposals for industrialization, for tourism, for coffee, *and* for the migration of islanders to less-crowded countries) welcomed at any time of the year, but late December was "dead time" in sugar. And 1934 was an especially bad year for the average sugar worker. Farm owners in search of actual production quotas had a difficult time obtaining credit for their crops. Many workers spent all year idle; so at the end of a terrible period, Gruening and Muñoz lobbied the president for a message to his people.

Roosevelt addressed the message to Luis Muñoz Marín, a man who knew how to cut cane. The Liberal party placed radios on every public plaza in the country; it was later estimated that more than one-half million islanders heard Muñoz translate this message: "I [Franklin Roosevelt] can and do assure you and your people of my complete good will and firm determination that permanent reconstruction shall be initiated at the very earliest possible moment on the basis of the Chardon Plan, the principles of which have received my approval."[50]

Muñoz had the president's word that dressed as Santa Claus, he would provide the assistance Puerto Rico required. Equally important, Muñoz had assurances from Gruening that despite bitter resistance from the U.S. head of the Puerto Rico Emergency Relief Administration, funds for the island's economic transformation would be locally controlled by the Liberal party. Within months Muñoz and his colleagues had established a fine system of kickbacks for every federal job provided. For example, new employees were pressured to join a society called Renovación, a mask used to channel their membership dues to the Liberal party.[51]

Muñoz, remember, had grown up in New York. He would happily use federal funds to feather his own nest, but by mid-1935 the size of that nest had been considerably reduced. The $150 million dollars had now turned into $75 million; however, no one had seen much of that *projected* budget because turf battles (i.e., would direction be from Washington or San Juan?) slowed down the program's actual implementation and, even more ominous, Muñoz was not the only American with an eye on federal funds.

In a letter to General Winship, Ernest Gruening managed to sound like an advocate of independence. He noted that "certain basic grievances which the Puerto Ricans rightly protest against should be rectified." The coastwise shipping laws exempted the Philippines, the Virgin Islands, and Hawaii but nonetheless applied to Puerto Rico. And as if that wasn't bad enough, the same shipping companies that "derived substantial subsidies from Uncle Sam" had the audacity "to raise their freight charges on cement and lumber 65 percent as soon as we announced our reconstruction program."[52]

The race to help Puerto Rico had so many contestants that greed and self-interest unquestionably played a part in the program's death before birth. But the fundamental issue remained political power. By the end of 1935 the $75 million had turned into $37 million, which according to a memo sent by General Winship to the president would actually net the Puerto Rican people only $16.5 million for reconstruction. To Winship, "Puerto Rico had received much less than any state, territory, or other possession, on a per capita basis or on any other yardstick basis that could be applied." The president had to understand that "Puerto Rico must be considered by comparison with other units of the government as having been ignored in the plans for relief and rehabilitation throughout the country."[53]

Albizu Campos was right. His predictions about funding for the Chardon Plan proved tragically accurate. The irony (or, depending on your point of view, the contradiction) is that the very same men who underlined the institutionalized injustices to which Puerto Rico was subjected, Winship and Gruening, had no empathy or understanding for a man who advocated revolution. On the contrary, Winship and Gruening were about to do everything possible to put Albizu Campos in jail for as long as the federal courts would permit.

The University of Puerto Rico at Río Piedras was (and is) an exquisite campus: grand buildings, pillars everywhere, imaginative uses of paint to accentuate architectural detail, and in every nook and cranny of the campus flowers, ferns, and palm trees. Students often took the beauty for granted, but none remained indifferent to an October 24, 1935, battle that saw four young Nationalists killed in a collision with the island's U.S.-led police force.

Two days later the burial of the young Nationalists was a tragedy for their families and a political event for the nation. Close to 8,000 people squeezed into the cemetery of Seboruco, a resting place favored by the workers and other poor inhabitants of this San Juan neighborhood. Albizu Campos spoke of "the massacre of Río Piedras." He told his audience that Colonel E. Francis Riggs, the U.S. head of the police force, had sent the police to the university "with the deliberate intent of assassinating the nationalist representation of Puerto Rico." Thus, the death of the young men repeated Puerto Rico's history: "The liberty of the nation was mixed with our blood and it is also mixed with the blood of the Yankees." To assure justice Albizu asked those who believed in liberty to raise their hand. "We swear," said the audience, "that the assassin will not survive in Puerto Rico."[54]

At La Fortaleza (the governor's residence), Blanton Winship said the Nationalists represented a tiny minority of Puerto Rican society. Nevertheless, the general based his response to Albizu on the strategies his soldiers employed when they helped put down the Philippine insurrection at the turn of the century. Winship immediately and greatly strengthened the police force. Machine guns in their arms, they were called out at the slightest provocation; and whenever Winship traveled in San Juan or on the island, he moved with what another U.S. official called "a preposterously large bodyguard."[55]

The general was scared. In his mind any U.S. official associated with the colonial apparatus was a potential target of revolutionary violence. To help maintain order, therefore, the general fired one soldier and brought in another.

In January 1936 Colonel Otis Cole commanded the forces in San Juan. He had such decided opinions about the Puerto Rican people that when on a January inspection tour Secretary Harold Ickes suggested the transfer of certain installations from the U.S. Army to the Interior Department, Coles stood up at a luncheon and said this to Ickes: "Mishter Shecretary, I don't know a God-damn thing about the Department of the Interior and you don't know a God-damn thing about the army but I want to tell you that if you take away our base, we'll be back here with machine guns to put these people down."[56]

Winship might have approved of that policy, but Cole was not the man to carry it out because he had to be carried out. The moment he finished his tirade, the colonel collapsed in a drunken stupor; his second-in-command, prepared for the event, caught him, and six other soldiers, waiting with a stretcher, then carried their leader off to retirement in colder climates.[57]

The new commander of the U.S. forces was Colonel John Wright, both a military historian and a man of action. Wright soberly readied his troops for any eventuality and also began to prepare what he labeled "weekly summaries of subversive activities, Puerto Rico Area."[58] In conjunction with the G-men provided by J. Edgar Hoover, Wright sent spies into the community. Double agents and paid informants dotted the Puerto Rican countryside, providing Wright with a February (1936) report that meticulously analyzed the extent and intensity of Albizu's support.

The Nationalists were everywhere! For the first ten pages of this report—jointly prepared with agent D. Di Lillo of the Pittsburgh office and Edgar K. Thompson from bureau headquarters—Wright listed one Puerto Rican community after another. On Vieques a baker headed the Nationalist party, in Guayama it was a dentist, and in Barranquitas a school teacher. Many communities had organized squads of Cadets of the Republic, and although their level of armament varied, they left Wright no doubt that the Cadets would use force to obtain their subversive aims. To prove his point he cited seven pages of quotes from *La Palabra* (the word), the Nationalist newspaper.[59]

Wright never caught the contradiction: He was writing "stamped secret" reports about the public pronouncements of Albizu and his supporters. The Nationalists never tried to hide their revolutionary intent. After the speech in the cemetery, for example, Albizu made a public call for young islanders to join his revolutionary army. Wright spent time underground while, for all to see and hear, Albizu and his supporters told anyone willing to listen that their aim was to overthrow the colonial regime, their strategy to force a crisis by attacking, not civilians, but the agents of authority.

The attack came on February 23, 1936. Colonel Elisha Riggs, the police chief Albizu held accountable for the "massacre of Río Piedras," was himself assassinated by two young Nationalists. After their arrest the two young men were taken to jail, where they were promptly assassinated by the officers who arrested them. For their efforts General Winship not only exonerated the policemen guilty of the murders but promoted them to serve on his personal bodyguard squad.[60]

Meanwhile, the U.S. attorney for Puerto Rico, A. Cecil Synder, prepared to indict Albizu for three things: conspiracy to overthrow the U.S. government by force, conspiracy to incite rebellion and insurrection against the United States, and conspiracy to recruit soldiers to engage in armed hostility against the United States. Some people argued that the death of Riggs prompted these charges, but Synder told President Roosevelt, "Contrary to the belief in some circles that this case was

brought because of the murder of Chief of Police Riggs . . . by my request
two Special Agents had come to Puerto Rico on February 3, 1936 and
had already completed their investigation and left Puerto Rico before
Colonel Riggs was murdered."[61]

In Washington Ernest Gruening rightly believed he was out of the
island's information loop. He worried about the nature of the charges
being leveled—why sedition? why not murder?—as General Winship
cabled him to rest easy.

The searches that I have been planning for arms and documentary evidence
were carried out in different municipalities this morning [March 5, 1936] at
daylight—stop—military arms and equipment, a bomb, and very important
documentary evidence were procured from different sources—stop—seven men
including Albizu Campos were arrested and placed under bonds—stop— . . .
the strong evidence which was being gathered up to the time of action and *was
considered conclusive* [my emphasis] is now further strengthened . . . [and] everything is well in hand and all necessary precautions taken and all cases will be
pushed until the present activities of the guilty parties have been suppressed
and they have been brought to justice.[62]

Justice would take place in the federal courts because, as Synder told
the president, "this was not just another criminal case." The United
States faced a crucial moment in Puerto Rican history: "After four centuries as the only Spanish colony that never undertook an armed revolt,
a small coterie was attempting to change by violence the course of the
history of Puerto Rico." Even though the case was "brought under
statues rarely invoked" and even though "we had few precedents to
guide us," Cecil Synder decided to meet a political challenge with a
political indictment: "The defendants were prosecuted because, under
the guise of a political moment, they persistently engaged in armed
violence."[63]

In Washington Senator Millard Tydings knew something about violence. He would, after all, soon tell Puerto Ricans that he could never
accept their political lot. If he were a Puerto Rican he would act like
Washington, Jefferson, and Bolívar.[64]

But Tydings wasn't a Puerto Rican. He was an American; he was a
friend of the assassinated Colonel Riggs; and he was also so angered by
the violence that one side of his mind understood, that his other side,
the one that dominated, suggested a bill to make Puerto Rico an independent nation.

On March 18 Roosevelt and his colleagues discussed Tyding's suggestion at a Cabinet meeting. If only for political reasons—Secretary
Ickes thought it would have a quieting effect on public opinion—they

decided to support such a bill and they even assigned Ernest Gruening to oversee its preparation. However, he was to tell no one he was doing what he was doing; the bill was not to be seen as an administration measure.[65]

Now assigning a man who said that Puerto Rico was "unequivocally and permanently U.S. territory" to write an independence bill was a little like asking Albizu Campos if he supported statehood. But Gruening nevertheless took on the job and by March 27 had submitted a second draft on the bill to Senator Tydings. The emphasis on second is important because despite using the 1936 Philippine independence bill as a guide, the Puerto Rican bill contained economic provisions sure to alienate virtually every islander. Where the Philippine bill mandated a twenty-year introduction of tariffs, the Puerto Ricans, in far worse economic shape, would divorce the United States in four years. Twenty years later Gruening and his assistants had no idea how this provision changed from draft one to draft two. They agreed only that before submitting the bill, "they had carefully gone over it."[66]

About the only people not consulted about independence were the Puerto Ricans. Gruening said in 1956: "What harm was done? The bill was just a proposal and a good way of raising the issue." Tydings went a step further; he said (also in 1956): "The Puerto Ricans weren't consulted when Puerto Rico was annexed to the United States. It was not necessary to consult them about their independence. It was a matter primarily for us to decide, although no discourtesy was intended."[67]

Few if any Puerto Ricans agreed with the Senator's definition of self-determination. In Congress the prostatehood resident commissioner, Santiago Iglesias, called the measure a "cyclone bill"; for short term it represented "a tremendous ingratitude and scorn to the majority" of islanders; long term it was "unjust, arbitrary, ingrate and devastating for Puerto Rico."[68]

Tydings responded by changing his mind. Five days after he assured everyone that the bill would receive prompt attention, he indicated that nothing would be done in 1936. In Washington the bill was supposedly dead on arrival. In San Juan Colonel Wright used his double agents to learn how islanders planned to breathe new life into the supposedly dead independence bill.

At Central High School a new generation of youngsters repeated the actions of 1919. But instead of forming a José De Diego society, these students nailed the one-star banner to the school's flagstaff. When the principal decided to tear it down, students decided first to halt traffic and then to swear an oath of allegiance to help those students suspended for trying to stop their principal. Colonel Wright's translation of the document read: "The hour has arrived to demonstrate our noble sentiments of solidarity. There is no right for not being loyal and for being a traitor. . . . DOWN WITH THE SOLDIERS. DOWN WITH THE AS-SASSINS. . . . DOWN WITH THE NATIONAL GUARD."[69]

Adding a bizarre note to the student strike was the appearance of Representative Marion Zioncheck from Washington. In twenty-four hours the honeymooning representative managed to watch the striking students, call for the marines to restore order, and, as the *Washington Star* reported, "fish, smash up two cars, break down a gate, get challenged to a duel, and, as he passed the time between adventures drinking coconut milk, Zioncheck would toss the empty gourds out the hotel window—to strike any passerby."[70]

The marines landed—but their job was to respond to a radio plea from Zioncheck. SOS! He needed a plane to get him out before somebody killed him! Before he left, the irrepressible Zioncheck could not resist this political commentary: "The United States ought to get in or get out of here. Children are running through the streets yelling Viva Repúblic! and Down With the United States! This is all poppycock. This thing is like a snowball. It grows. You don't see any older folk responsible for all this parading."[71]

Actually, as Colonel Wright told his superiors, there were some old folks involved. At forty-five Albizu Campos failed to qualify, but at sixty-five Antonio Barcelo, the head of the Liberal party, was a legitimate senior citizen. He favored independence and had no trouble sharing a podium with a man indicted for conspiracy to overthrow the government of the United States. In Caguas on May 10 Albizu and Barcelo had effectively agreed to disregard the Tydings Bill. Instead, working off the suggestion made by Albizu in 1924, they called for a "united front," a coalition of all parties who would call a constituent assembly that would immediately proclaim the republic.[72]

Unfortunately for all concerned, unity was not the order of the day. Although the head of the Republican, prostatehood, party had initially declared himself in favor of independence, by mid-May he had exchanged self-rule for silence. The Socialists had their representatives running all over the island, counseling members "to stand quietly but firmly against independence"; meanwhile Muñoz Marín, the other half of the Liberty party, found himself in a jail of his own making.

If Muñoz fought independence, he would be seen as a tool of the colonial power; but if he accepted the Tydings Bill, the "total ruin" of Puerto Rico was guaranteed.[73] This was so because of the bill's harsh provisions *and* because Muñoz's entire and only plan for reconstruction rested on his 1933 marriage to Washington. The redistribution of land, the purchase of *centrales*, the migration of his people, industrialization—all the promises Muñoz had made had in his own eyes no chance of success because with independence Muñoz would have no money to fund the New Deal he and Washington had promised.

Ernest Gruening, angry at Muñoz's reluctance to accept the independence his party trumpeted, asked: "What do you expect? You can't have your cake and eat it too. . . . Of course we can improve the bill by adding some other 'going away presents' and other more generous terms."

Muñoz responded, "You can't impale me on that have your cake and eat it too. That is just what I do want."[74]

And that is just what he would never get. The Tydings Bill was exactly what it appeared to be: a threat. Keep up the agitation for independence and we will set you free, free to enjoy the increasing poverty that was America's colonial behest in 1936.

Muñoz opted for a strategy that, as it split his party apart, produced chaos. He claimed that "it was only through his influence that the Liberal Party was restrained from approving a resolution in favor of joining the Nationalists and immediately calling a constitutional convention."[75] And when his party requested that he accept its nomination for resident commissioner, he not only refused the nomination but refused to participate in the forthcoming elections as well. In his eyes abstention was the best course because the combination of bribes by the sugar industry and fear on the part of islanders guaranteed defeat for his party.[76]

Of course, it might also have guaranteed defeat for Luis Muñoz Marín. The man who declared to Ernest Gruening that "the destiny of Muñoz Marín and the destiny of Puerto Rico are inseparable"[77] did not take defeat lightly. In any event Muñoz opted for abstention; he was going to pursue what he had already been told he could not have: independence with economic justice.

Meanwhile, Tydings never acted on the bill that caused so much controversy; Roosevelt did nothing about legislation that did but did not come from his administration; Barcelo endorsed the constituent assembly; the Socialists bitterly fought independence; and Pedro Albizu Campos, eager to be part of any constitutional convention, could participate only if he somehow managed to avoid jail.

Colonel Wright provided his superiors with a detailed analysis of the trial and of the events leading up to it. On July 8 Albizu and Barcelo met at the Condado Hotel; however, even the colonel's spies were no help because "the details of the conference have been kept secret." Later that same day Albizu visited Barcelo and Rafael Martínez Nadal (the president of the prostatehood Republican party) at their homes. Apparently they did not regard Albizu as a fanatic because the purpose of Albizu's visits was to thank both men for the cablegram they had jointly sent to President Roosevelt: Stop the proceedings against Albizu and the other Nationalists.[78]

No way. As Cecil Synder told the president, "This was the most important criminal case ever tried in Puerto Rico. . . . It has been the major preoccupation of this office for six months." Synder was ready to go, and so too was Colonel Wright. He had forty policemen, "some in uniform, some in plain clothes," outside the federal building. He had one man "mingling with witnesses" on the second floor of the court-house, two men on the first floor, one man at every public plaza in the vicinity, and, in the tiny courtroom, Wright estimated that of the forty spectators, "more than half were policemen and detectives."[79]

The courthouse was secure from everything except the jury. In his first trial, which lasted from July 14 to July 19, Albizu proudly assumed all responsibility for the acts of his party; dressed as always in a black suit, white shirt, and black bow tie, Albizu conducted himself like a Harvard graduate. Whether this impressed the jury is difficult to say because they decided a political case on political grounds: The seven Puerto Rican members of the jury refused to convict a Puerto Rican patriot, the five North American jurors said Albizu and his colleagues were indeed guilty of trying to overthrow the government of the United States.

The hung jury infuriated prosecuting attorney Synder. After all that work and effort he meant to get a conviction, so in the second trial—held only a week after the first one—the jury was somehow composed of ten North Americans and two Puerto Ricans, both of whom were "closely associated with American business interests."

Now in a country of 2 million Puerto Ricans and 5,000 Americans, Synder had achieved a feat of judicial legerdemain. No one ever calculated the odds of such a jury occurring, and no one had to, for as juror Elmer Ellsworth later put it in a letter to President Roosevelt, "My associates on the jury all seemed to be motivated by strong if not violent prejudice against the Nationalists and were prepared to convict them regardless of the evidence."[80] Initially Ellsworth held out for acquittal; in the end, however, he followed his flag instead of his convictions.

The judge wasted no time in handing out sentences. Albizu got ten years in the Atlanta penitentiary and his colleagues received similar sentences. From the courthouse they were first taken to the fortifications at El Morro and then to the jail—La Princesa—that had housed the Puerto Ricans imprisoned by the Spanish in the 1890s.

Few Puerto Ricans missed the irony. But for the Americans, Albizu's conviction was a cause for joy, back patting, and praise for the U.S. judicial system. As Cecil Synder later put it to the president, "It is superfluous for me to add that in this case we did not infringe on civil liberties nor did we attempt to suppress the independence movement."[81]

Headquartered at El Morro, Colonel Wright continued to compile his weekly list of subversive activities. On August 20, he provided evidence that even with Albizu in jail, the rift between Americans and Puerto Ricans continued to widen. First was "a violent conference" between the Women's Federation and Senator William H. King of Utah. On a fact-finding trip to the island King battled with the nonpartisan group seeking to free Albizu. "Visibly enraged" by the women's pleas, King screamed that he would never meet "with assassins." If Puerto Rico wanted independence, the United States would grant it tomorrow, "and all the commercial, political and social relations between the two countries would cease at once." He wished the women "peace and tranquility in Puerto Rico," and they told him that was impossible while Albizu remained in jail.[82]

At a dinner in honor of the senator, Ernest Gruening angrily criticized virtually every political leader in Puerto Rico. Their refusal to condemn the killing of Colonel Riggs "shocked" him. How could they defend a murderer? And how could the heads of Puerto Rico's largest political parties cable the president to scrap the case against Albizu? Gruening was at his wit's end, a crazy-quilt combination of disillusionment and anger at the unwillingness of so many prominent Puerto Ricans to condemn revolution.[83]

The next day Senator King helped the situation by acting like Representative Zioncheck. On a tour of the island intended to demonstrate "how America was alleviating Puerto Rico's lot," King had no apparent interest in, or questions about, the reconstruction program. At stop after stop he grabbed a child and asked, "Do you speak English?" The children, frightened by the strange man in a motorcade, generally said nothing. So at the next stop King, more impatient than ever, grabbed another youngster and said, "Do you speak English? Answer me! Do you speak English?"[84] For Senator King silence was not golden. So as the motorcade stopped at a crossing, he was about to grab another youngster when the children, dancing around the senator, began to shout, "Do you spik Eenglish? Do you spik Eenglish?"

The senator was not pleased. He went back to his car, he went back to Washington, and, as a result of this senator's burlesque, Puerto Rico actually went back to yet another round of teaching in English.

King prodded Interior Department officials who needed little prodding. For roughly four years Spanish had been the medium of elementary school instruction, English a special subject taught in all grades. This never satisfied the U.S. officials, who felt that English should be the prime medium of everyday instruction. So they used King's anger to generate a change in educational policy, a change that clearly underlined the short- and long-term thinking of Franklin Delano Roosevelt.

In a letter written by Ernest Gruening the president told the Puerto

Rican people, "I desire at this time to make clear the attitude of my administration on the extremely important matter of teaching English in Puerto Rico."[85] To the president it was "an indispensable part of American policy that the coming generation of American citizens in Puerto Rico grow up with complete facility in the English tongue." After all, "many of its [Puerto Rico's] sons and daughters will desire to seek economic opportunity on the mainland or perhaps in other countries of this hemisphere." They needed to speak English to succeed "and to profit from their unique geographical situation and the unique historical circumstances which has brought to them the blessings of American citizenship by becoming bi-lingual."[86]

Shades of 1898! The president—he did, after all, sign and broadcast Gruening's letter—wanted islanders to be grateful for the opportunity to learn the three r's in a language they did not understand. Even more important, Roosevelt ended the letter with a crystal clear indication of his thinking about Puerto Rico's future political status. He told islanders that "bi-lingualism will be achieved by the forthcoming generations of Puerto Ricans only if the teaching of English throughout the insular educational system is entered into at once with vigor, purposefulness, and devotion, and with the understanding that English is the official language of our country."[87]

Our country! Future generations! Islanders instantly grasped that despite all the talk about self-determination and independence whenever you want it, Roosevelt was echoing his predecessors: Puerto Rico was a permanent possession of the United States. At any time this was unwelcome news. In April 1937 Roosevelt's letter signaled no change in what all agreed was a chaotic political and economic situation.

The Coalition had won the November 1936 elections in a squeaker that was every bit as violent as the 1932 elections. In October, for example, Liberals and Coalition forces squared off in a gun battle near Vega Alta. Police detachments were rushed in to restore order, but nothing seemed to work. A week later another battle produced two deaths and only God saved a Liberal leader when a Coalition assassin tried to eliminate his political opponent.[88]

The inconclusive results of the elections provided no political direction from the island. Even without Muñoz and his supporters, the "independence now" Liberals had won 46 percent of the vote. But the fractured Coalition majority controlled the island's legislature; and they sent their resident commissioner to Washington, while, on the island, Muñoz was expelled from the Liberal party. His former colleagues understandably argued that his abstention cost them and independence a victory. Muñoz now struggled to create a new political organization based on an old (1933) idea: independence later, money from Washington now.

Muñoz's problem was how to get islanders to be pro-American when one outrage followed another in such rapid succession. On March 21, 1937, a group of Nationalists tried to march in Ponce. Police stopped them and minutes later nineteen people were dead, over one hundred wounded. Reporting for the American Civil Liberties Union, Arthur Garfield Hays said that the "facts show that the affair of March 21st in Ponce was a massacre." Governor Winship had "repeatedly denied" civil liberties for at least the last nine months; the Ponce Massacre was due to the denial by the police of the civil rights of citizens to parade and assemble; and this denial was ordered by the Governor of Puerto Rico."[89]

Roosevelt's letter about Puerto Rico's permanent status arrived only two weeks after the Ponce massacre. His (and Gruening's) timing underlined administration policy: Puerto Rico was, for generations to come, a part of the United States. And for all the talk of a new deal, administration officials told the president that Puerto Rico continued to get a raw deal.

The basis for this charge came from three U.S. sources: Governor Blaton Winship, Secretary of Agriculture Henry Wallace, and, of all people, Ernest Gruening.

As in 1936, General Winship complained that funds allotted for reconstruction never arrived. Talk was cheap because, as Winship told the president, "the Federal government has never extended to Puerto Rico financial aid anywhere near comparable with that extended to the States." Per capita Puerto Rico received $57.41 of federal assistance; Hawaii got $141.50, the Virgin Islands $282.28, and the average state, $222.99. Puerto Rico, the general stressed, was the world's seventh largest buyer of U.S. goods, "exceeding all countries of the Western hemisphere except Canada." Thus, if only because Puerto Rico provided so much assistance to the U.S. economy, the island deserved a better shake from the American people.[90]

Asked to assess the validity of the general's charges, Secretary of Agriculture Wallace told the president that "the total amount of Federal emergency aid to Puerto Rico for the last three years is less per capita than that of any other state or territory, and even this aid includes more than half of the processing tax collected on Puerto Rican sugar."[91]

Again no one listened to Albizu the economist. Washington never found the money for Puerto Rico's reconstruction. Expenditures of roughly a million a month did nothing more than plug a few holes in a swiss cheese dike. The island was going further down hill, and even when it pleaded for help, it always came in last. As Gruening put it to Congress when he pleaded for permission to refine sugar in Puerto Rico:

We specifically object to the restriction on the processing. . . . We think it is a matter of permanent statesmanship, that if Congress can legislate against Territories which are voteless and unprotected . . . we are essentially going back to the factors which caused us to seek out independence from Great Britain, and which caused the rebellion of the colonies from Great Britain, and which caused the rebelling of the colonies against the tyranny and oppression of mother countries in the Old World.[92]

There is no evidence of Albizu smiling in his Atlanta prison cell. (He and his associates were transferred to Atlanta's federal prison in June 1937.) What the evidence does show, however, is that the sugar companies still made substantial profits from their exceedingly large holdings. In a country supposedly at war with the 500-acre law, Central Aguirre, for example, told potential investors in 1937 that it owned 22,000 acres of land and that it controlled another 17,000 acres of land. Profits varied, but 1936 was an especially good year. The company earned $2.5 million, a 37 percent profit figured on sales and a 35 percent profit figured on net worth.[93]

These numbers made stockholders happy. And to the consternation of figures like Albizu Campos, they never dimmed Muñoz Marín's enthusiasm for federal funding of Puerto Rico's reconstruction. Through 1937 Muñoz struggled to create a movement that would rely on the same president who had never provided the funds promised.,

Muñoz would not take no for an answer. He kept coming back to a dry well when, luckily for him, the prospect of war suddenly transformed U.S. thinking. Within three years Puerto Rico was the Gibraltar of the Caribbean, Muñoz a man who told Congress that "the question of political status was not declared an issue for two reasons: In order not to create embarassment to the National Government during a period of great crisis, and in order to allow the people of Puerto Rico to unite under economic aspiration without the confusion of the political issue."[94]

Congress thanked Muñoz for his support. No one wanted to be embarrassed as the United States created in tiny Puerto Rico what soon became the largest naval base in the world, (Franklin Delano) Roosevelt Roads.

NOTES

1. See *Puerto Rico, Hearings before the Committee on Territories and Insular Affairs,* Senate, 78th Congress, 1st session, May 1943, p. 137.

2. See Francisco Quiñones Vizcarrondo, *El Cerebro Puertorriqueno* (Caguas: Imprenta Cartagena, 1989), p. 13.

3. *Puerto Rico's Economy,* Committee on Interior and Insular Affairs, House, 99th Congress, 2nd session, May 1986, p. 337.

4. Antonio S. Pedreira, *Insularismo* (Río Piedras: Edil, 1985), p. 145.

5. Ibid., p. 43.

6. Ibid., p. 147.

7. Luis Muñoz Rivera, "The Sad Case of Porto Rico," *American Mercury* 16, no. 62 (February 1929): p. 141.

8. See María Teresa Babin and Stan Steiner, ed., *Borinquen* (New York: Vintage, 1974), pp. 79–80.

9. See Luis Angel Ferrao, *Pedro Albizu Campos y el Nacionalismo Puertorriqueno* (Río Piedras: Editorial Cultural, 1990), p. 82.

10. See Jaime Ramírez Barbot, "A History of Puerto Rican Radical Nationalism, 1920–1965" (Ph.D. diss., Ohio State University, 1973), p. 75.

11. See Pedro Albizu Campos. *Obras Escogidas*, Vol. 1 (San Juan: Editorial Jelofe, 1975), pp. 44–45.

12. *Puerto Rico, Hearings before the Committee on Territories and Insular Affairs*, Senate, 78th Congress, 1st session, May 1943, p. 50.

13. On the Unionists see Albizu, *Obras Escogidas*, Vol. 3, p. 14; on the nullity of the Treaty of Paris see ibid., Vol. 3, pp. 16–24.

14. Ibid., Vol. 1, p. 69; also Vol. 3, p. 83.

15. See ibid., Vol. 1, pp. 111–164.

16. Ibid., Vol. 1, p. 141.

17. Ibid., Vol. 1, p. 143; An especially good analysis of these issues appears in Luis Nieves Falcon, "El Pensamiento de Albizu Campos," *Pensamiento Critico* 12 (May–July 1989): pp. 2–8.

18. Albizu, *Obras Escogidas*, Vol. 1, p. 87.

19. Ibid., p. 275.

20. For a solid analysis of Albizu and Catholicism see Ferrao, *Pedro Albizu Campos*, pp. 257–291; on the reactions of Protestants see Fernando Pico, *Historia General de Puerto Rico* (Río Piedras: Huracán, 1988), p. 252.

21. Ablizu, *Obras Escogidas*, Vol. 1, p. 92.

22. See Ramírez Barbot, *Puerto Rican Radical Nationalism*, Appendix B.

23. Rafael Bernabe, *Prehistory of the Partido Popular Democrático: Muñoz Marín, the Partido Liberal, and the Crisis of Sugar in Puerto Rico*, Ph.D. thesis, State University of New York at Binghamton, 1989, pp. 118–120.

24. See ibid., p. 211; also see Thomas Matthews, *Puerto Rican Politics and the New Deal* (Gainesville: University of Florida Press, 1960), esp. Chap. 4 and 5.

25. See Roberto Sanchez Vilella, "La Transformación de la Orientación hacia el Desarollo del Partido Popular Democrático, en la Decada del 1940," in Gerardo Navas Davila, ed., *Cambio y Desarollo en Puerto Rico: La Transformación Ideológica del Partido Popular Democrático* (Río Piedras: University of Puerto Rico Press, 1985), pp. 123–129, esp. p. 124.

26. Matthews, *Puerto Rican Politics*, esp. pp. 56–70.

27. Franklin Roosevelt Library, Hyde Park, New York. See President's Personal File, Box 1263, Folder marked Blanton Winship.

28. See Matthews, *Puerto Rican Politics*, p. 105.

29. Oscar Chapman, "Affairs of U.S. Territories," a broadcast over the National Broadcasting System, October 10, 1934; the speech was reprinted in the 1934 edition of *Vital Speeches of the Day*, p. 85.

30. See John Dalton, *Sugar: A Case Study of Government Control* (New York: Macmillan, 1937), p. 218; the 80 percent estimate is from a "memo for the Secretary of the Interior" at the Roosevelt Library, Hyde Park, New York, Official File, 400, Box 24, Folder marked Puerto Rico, April–December 1936.

31. See Bernabe, *Partido Popular Democrático*, p. 177; Dalton, *Sugar*, p. 218.

32. Bernabe, *Partido Popular Democrático*, pp. 191–192.

33. See "Taller de Formación Política," *Huelga en la cana* (Río Piedras: Ediciones Huracán, 1982).

34. See Ernest Gruening, *Many Battles: The Autobiography of Ernest Gruening* (New York: Liverwright, 1974), p. 181.

35. Bernabe, *Partido Popular Democrático*, p. 212.

36. Roosevelt Library, Official File, Box 24, Folder marked Puerto Rico, January–March 1936. The general's letter and long summary are dated January 20, 1936; the $150 million figure is noted on p. 2.

37. Bernabe, *Partido Popular Democrático*, p. 218; also see Dalton, *Sugar*, p. 219; Matthews, *Puerto Rican Politics*, esp. Chap. 5.

38. Bernabe, *Partido Popular Democrático*, pp. 217–220.

39. Bernabe, ibid., analyzes this on pages 120–121; the original analysis of Muñoz's ideas appears in *El Mundo*, September 10, 1932; and *La Democracia*, September 12, 1932.

40. See Albizu, *Obras Escogidas*, Vol. 2, p. 47.

41. Ibid., p. 47.

42. Ibid., pp. 47–48.

43. See Ferrao, *Pedro Albizu Campos*, pp. 185–186.

44. See José Luis González, *Nueva Vista al Cuarto Piso* (Río Piedras: Libros del Flamboyan, 1986), p. 189.

45. Albizu, *Obras Escojidas*, Vol. 2, p. 29.

46. Ibid., p. 108.

47. See, Matthews, *Puerto Rican Politics*, p. 252.

48. See Truman Clark, *Puerto Rico and the United States* (Pittsburgh: University of Pittsburgh Press, 1975), p. 146.

49. See Gruening, *Many Battles*, p. 191.

50. Matthews, *Puerto Rican Politics*, pp. 201–202.

51. The memo about Liberal control is from James Bourne; see Roosevelt Library, Official File, 400, Box 24, p. 2; the comments about graft can be found in Gruening, *Many Battles*, p. 202.

52. National Archives, Interior Department Archives, OTIP, Record Group 126, 9–8–68, Part 7, Box 862.

53. Roosevelt Library, Official File, 400, Box 24, pp. 1 and 2 of the long and detailed memo.

54. See Albizu *Obras Escojidas*, Vol. 2, pp. 122–123.

55. National Archives, Interior Department, DTIP, Record Group 48, Folder marked PR, 1934–1936, p. 3 of this nine-page document.

56. See Gruening, *Many Battles*, pp. 194–195.

57. Ibid., p. 195.

58. Estado Libre Asociado de Puerto Rico, Comisión de Derechos Civiles, *Informe*, San Juan, February 1989; the lists appear in the appendices to this very extensive study.

59. Ibid., I am quoting from the report dated February 10–February 20, 1936.

60. Roosevelt Library, Official File, 400, Box 24, Folder marked Puerto Rico, 1938.

61. Ibid., the comment is on p. 2 of this report.

62. National Archives, Interior Department, DTIP. See Nacionalists, Albizu.

63. Cecil Synder, Roosevelt Library, Official File, 400, Box 24, Folder marked Puerto Rico, p. 3.

64. See *Puerto Rico, Hearings before the Committee on Territories and Insular Affairs,* Senate, 78th Congress, 1st session, May 1943.

65. See Matthews, *Puerto Rican Politics,* pp. 253–254; see Ickes to Gruening, National Archives, Interior Department, File 9–8–68, March 19, 1936.

66. Frank Otto Gatell, "Independence Rejected: Puerto Rico and the Tydings Bill of 1936," *Hispanic American Historical Review* 38 (February 1958): pp. 26–44, esp. pp. 31–33.

67. Ibid., p. 33.

68. *Congressional Record,* House, 74th Congress, 2nd session, April 27, 1936, p. 6244.

69. See *Informe,* Weekly Summary of Subversive Activities, dated May 21, 1936, pp. 2 and 3.

70. See the *Washington Star* for May 13, 1936.

71. See the *Washington Star* for May 14, 1936.

72. See *Informe,* summary of May 21, 1936, p. 4.

73. National Archives, Interior Department, DTIP, 9–8–68, Part One.

74. See Gruening, *Many Battles,* p. 199.

75. Matthews, *Puerto Rican Politics,* p. 258.

76. See, for example, Gatell, "Independence Rejected," pp. 33–44.

77. See Gruening, *Many Battles,* p. 197.

78. See *Informe,* Weekly Summary, July 16, 1936, p. 1.

79. Ibid., pp. 4 and 10.

80. The letter, dated October 17, 1938, is at Princeton University. See American Civil Liberties Union, Vol. 2053.

81. Synder, Roosevelt Library, Box 24, p. 3.

82. See *Informe,* Weekly Summary for August 20, 1936.

83. Ibid., p. 7.

84. Earl Parker Hanson, *Transformation* (New York: Simon and Schuster, 1955), pp. 54–55.

85. See Gruening, *Many Battles,* p. 206.

86. National Archives, Interior Department, DTIP, 9–8–65.

87. Ibid., this is a one-page letter.

88. See Ramírez Bardot, *Puerto Rican Radical Nationalism,* pp. 79–80.

89. American Civil Liberties Union, *Report of the Commission of Inquiry on Civil Rights in Puerto Rico,* New York; it is dated May 22, 1937.

90. See Roosevelt Library, Official File, 400, Box 24, January–May 1937; also Box 24, Folder marked Puerto Rico, 1938. The general sent detailed complaints for 1936, 1937 and 1939.

91. See a memo from Wallace to Winship forwarded by the president. Dated February 8, 1937, it is at the Roosevelt Library, Official File, 400, Box 24, Folder marked Puerto Rico, January–May 1937.

92. See *Sugar, Hearings before the Committee on Finance,* Senate, 75th Congress, 1st session, August 1937, p. 133.

93. See Moody's *Manual of Industrial Corporations* for 1937, p. 2974.

94. See *Nomination of Rexford G. Tugwell as Governor of Puerto Rico*, Senate, Committee on Territories and Insular Affairs, 77th Congress, 1st session 1941, p. 49.

Chapter 6

Prisoners of War

And of this island shield Puerto Rico is the center. Its possession or control by any foreign power—or even the remote threat of such possession—would be repugnant to the most elementary principles of national defense.
President Franklin Roosevelt, 1943[1]

Soldiers sought a short cut. After four years of horror and 10 million dead, strategists wanted a quick end to the next war. Destroy the enemy at once and the world would never repeat the lingering slaughter called World War I.

Aviators had this idea: Forget soldiers. Bomb the home front (a phrase that did appear in dictionaries prior to 1919) and you ended the war by annihilating the industrial base that made modern war possible. In the United States General Billy Mitchell mock bombed New York. Like the "armored knights in the Middle Ages," aviators were the special breed who would make wars briefer, more humane, and even less expensive. To prove his point Mitchell "wiped out" New York on July 30, 1921. His planes used 1,000- and 2,000-pound fragmentation bombs, as well as "those of the gas and flame variety." According to Mitchell, New Yorkers who survived the onslaught fled to Yonkers, eager to forever avoid another attack of terror from the sky.[2]

Through the 1920s and into the late 1930s theories of air warfare were just that, theories. In London and Vienna, Tokyo and Naples, city planners did hold air raid drills, but it took the horror of Guernica (in the Spanish Civil War, on April 26, 1937) to fully awaken the world to the

Pandora's box called air power. In Great Britain the attack was labeled
an odious manifestation of German barbarity; in the United States soldiers continued to teach the efficacy of the tactics employed at Guernica,
while in the Caribbean, President Roosevelt watched as squadrons of
airplanes mock bombed San Juan.[3]

The results of the February 25, 1939, air raid only showed on the
"umpires' master charts." But the roughly 175 planes over San Juan had
engaged in a battle theoretically central to the survival of the United
States. As strategists saw it, the enemy could do what we could do.
Suppose the Germans had friends in Brazil? They could slowly build up
their forces in South America; they could then take Puerto Rico, and,
suddenly, America's southern flank would be exposed. Instead of the
enemy, unarmed civilians in Miami or Atlanta would now be the targets
of strategic or, more accurately, obliteration bombing.

People in San Juan slept through the mock attacks. But once the
president came home, there was no way to sleep through two major
changes in U.S. military thought. Geography and technology had in-
voluntarily placed the island on the world stage, and through 1991 it
would stay on that stage, a key to U.S. defense, and in Admiral Arthur
Knoizen's phrase,[4] a "university of the sea" for the mock bombing that
continues as I write and you read these lines.

The first report that affected Puerto Rico appeared in December 1938.
Admiral A. J. Hepburn chaired a committee that told the president the
island was on the navy's "A-List."[5] Air bases in the Caribbean were an
"obvious necessity," and given the dearth of U.S. possessions in this
area," Puerto Rico was an obvious choice. In fact, "in its study of the
Caribbean the Board found only one site capable of being made into an
air base suitable for the normal operation of patrol planes." The winner
was Isla Grande, a soon-to-be 400-acre air station smack in the center
of San Juan. The board noted that a base this far eastward in the Caribbean would be of "major strategic importance" because it would provide
facilities for one or two carrier groups and facilities for two squadrons
of planes, with provision for "immediate emergency expansion for at
least four patrol plane squadrons."[6]

"Emergency" was the operative word. Less than two months after
the president's trip, the Puerto Rican legislature approved the sale of
the Isla Grande land to the navy, while in Washington the president
made an even more surprising announcement: General Blanton Winship
was stepping down as governor of Puerto Rico. His replacement was
Admiral William Leahy, the retiring chief of naval operations. Leahy
was a confidante of the president, and despite articles that cited his
administrative skills, the accurate consensus was that Leahy would oversee the military transformation of Puerto Rico.

In the war, island politicians saw an opportunity and a responsibility. In May 1939 the island's legislature, still controlled by the coalition of Republicans and labor, passed a resolution that noted, "Whereas the Government of the United States has decided to establish in the island a military department of the first order for purposes of defense," what about rethinking statehood? After all, "without that friendship and without that loyalty which the people of Puerto Rico feel toward the metropolis, the Island could not be considered as a stronghold in spite of the armed forces which might be established therein."[7]

Since Roosevelt had already stressed the need for generations of English instruction before Puerto Rico could become a state, no one answered the legislature's message. But when the Rotary Club of Ponce offered its young men to the army and navy, some answer was required. So after careful consideration, the secretary of war, Harry Woodring, told the Ponce volunteers that the army would not establish recruiting centers in Puerto Rico. Apparently, Puerto Ricans made excellent soldiers when they served with other Puerto Ricans. But, said Woodring, "it is very doubtful whether these same Puerto Ricans would be satisfied in the U.S. The change of climate, environment and diet, the absence of their relatives and friends and deprivation of the privilege of marrying and raising families might well cause nostalgia and discontent." Therefore, for the Puerto Ricans' own good, Woodring told them to stay home.[8]

Why climate and distance had no disqualifying effect on soldiers from California or Minnesota or Alaska was a question the secretary of war never answered. Islanders naturally and correctly assumed that racism was once again at work, but given the realities of war, they let the army and navy take their lands but reject their children.

Even on the high-priority items, the work took time. On May 23, 1940, Admiral Leahy told an enquiring colleagues that the "island now has the accurate appearance of a mud hole produced by pumping the bottom of the bay onto a tide water island." Leahy figured another year "to make the island give the appearance of anything more than a mud flat"; despite the primitive conditions, fliers were already using Isla Grande as a base for aviation operations.[9] A local wag did complain to a *Fortune* reporter that "they aren't building any air-raid shelters for the Puerto Ricans"; there were also no shelters for the Americans, however. Soldiers and workers lived in tents as they feverishly struggled to complete the field before the war began.[10]

Trouble was, before anyone laid asphalt over the mud, military strategy had once again changed. The island, already vital to U.S. air defense, suddenly became the center of the navy's Atlantic strategy. Hyperbole became reality as the navy sought to turn the eastern shore of Puerto

Rico into a Gilbraltar that would serve as the axis of U.S. *and* Allied naval operations.

In a classified report, Admiral John W. Greenslade told the president that "complete control of the Caribbean area is fundamental to our national defense." The Caribbean was a "highway," a body of water "literally filled with seaborne traffic essential to our economic life and welfare." The Admiral thus suggested that the United States build a major operating base in the Puerto Rico–Virgin Islands Neighborhood. "This base is considered to be of paramount importance and fundamental to our Naval Strategy in the Atlantic." The base, a giant from the moment Greenslade conceived it, should include facilities for thoroughly protected anchorages; it should have "a capacity for emergency and interim repairs under war conditions of all classes of ships and aircraft"; and, finally, the base also should be able to support "air, submarine, and light forces permanently stationed there for the purpose of securing us against strategical surprise and covering our lines of communication to the Southeast."[11]

Now "permanent" is a big word. Did the admiral mean forever? Or just until the war was over? Puerto Rico already had too many people on too few acres. Islanders were willing to do their part, but only until the war ended. Then the navy had to leave.[12]

No problem. The navy agreed to depart when the war was over, so islanders let them confiscate or buy an incredible quantity of Puerto Rico's scarce acreage. By mid-1941 soldiers and especially sailors owned huge tracts of land stretching from one side of the island to the other: near Catano, 353 acres for an "Intermediate" navy landing field; in San Juan, another 700 acres near the city's port facilities; at El Morro, the entire 50-acre tract with 3 acres especially reserved for officers' quarters; in Carolina, 672 acres for a navy receiving station; and, for the operating base, the navy confiscated two-thirds of Vieques and another 8,000 acres near Fajardo. Total holdings on the "baby" and the main island: nearly 30,000 acres for what admirals adroitly named Roosevelt Roads.[13]

Work began at once. The navy decided, for example, to put one of the world's largest dry docks on its new operating base. It started work on a facility 1,100 by 150 feet,[14] and before the dry dock was even built Congress made it clear that the only temporary thing about the bases was the promise made by the navy. In an August 1941 exchange between Senator Millard Tydings and governor-to-be Rexford Tugwell, the senator asked questions about independence. They batted the issue about and then Tydings made this point: "Of course I have assumed in this question [i.e., Puerto Rico's independence] that we would have naval and air bases." Tugwell's one-word response was "Absolutely."[15]

Also testifying in these hearings was the president of the Puerto Rican Senate, Luis Muñoz Marín. If he was bothered by the gap between what the navy said on the island and what Tydings said in Washington, he never said so. Muñoz focused on economics and on the promises he had made to the Puerto Rican people.

In 1938 Muñoz had founded the Partido Popular Democrático (the Popular Democratic party, or PPD). Still wedded to the "ideal method" he had first conceived in 1933—"reconstruction; economic justice; independence to be taken up later in Congress"—Muñoz now emphatically put the status issue on hold. His public rationale for avoiding status was to focus on economics, but the senator also knew how to take advantage of political opportunities. The aged Santiago Iglesias (he died the next year, in 1939) had an impossible time trying to hold together the fractures in the labor movement. So, Muñoz used his considerable charm and intelligence to calm the Socialists nerves as he got their votes. Forget the "misleading" issue of status; a vote for Muñoz and the "Populares" was a vote for economic change funded by the federal government Socialists loved.[16]

To win, however, Muñoz needed more than the Socialists. He needed the poor, who had so often sold their votes to the sugar corporations. So in 1940 Muñoz ran one of the most creative campaigns in Puerto Rican political history. He set up grassroots organizations in seventy-five municipalities and 786 rural "barrios." He spoke to the people in everyday Spanish, and he emphasized his ties to Puerto Rico and its culture. The party's newspaper was *El Batey* (the *batey* was the ballfield used by the Taino Indians in precolonial times), its slogan was Bread, Land, and Liberty, and its emblem the profile of a *jíbaro*, a poor, rural Puerto Rican dressed in a straw hat.[17]

Muñoz deliberately identified with a portion of the population that other politicians had often neglected. He mobilized thousands of new voters, but he still used his old ideas. In May of 1940, for example, *El Batey* told its estimated 100,000 readers that "Muñoz could secure federal aid, just as money Muñoz promised had been forthcoming for reconstruction." And a worried Admiral Leahy wrote to Secretary of the Interior Harold Ickes:

The insular territory does not have and will not have sufficient funds to finance such a project [i.e., buying corporate sugar lands and redistributing them to *jíbaros*]. Mr. Muñoz Marín in his political campaign openly advocates the acquisition of corporate land by the Federal government. . . . This or any similar plan would involve many millions of dollars.[18]

Where did Muñoz expect to get the money? If Roosevelt had let him down on reconstruction in the 1930s, why would the president deliver now? Echoing the reservations expressed by Pedro Albizu Campos in 1934, why would the federal government, busily preparing for the most expensive war in human history, have the extra money required to substantially fund social change in Puerto Rico? And even if he got the money, how would Muñoz channel it into self-sustaining growth without political power? In 1940 Puerto Rico remained a colony under the "absolute control" of the United States. What had changed between 1934 and 1940? What meaningful political power did the island suddenly have?

Muñoz never answered these questions. In the words of one of his boosters, "The party realized it would have to buy the land but gave relatively little thought to the means of payment." Even "the Populares' plans for Federal aid were quite vague but they were the only plans they [the Populares] mentioned."[19]

Like many a politician—Puerto Rican, U.S., or French—Muñoz Marín was short on specifics, long on rhetoric. All he wanted from voters was a chance to make good on his promises, and to the surprise of many, he got it. In the 1940 elections the Populares won almost 40 percent of the vote, but most importantly, they won control of the insular Senate. Although Muñoz was arguably the most powerful politician on the island, to retain and increase that power he somehow had to do what he had no idea how to do!

Where was he going to get the money to finance serious change? And what were the small farms going to produce once Muñoz took them away from their parasitic absentee owners?

Before Congress in August 1941 Muñoz was a model American. The first reason he listed to explain the PPD's focus on economics was his desire not to embarrass the federal government at a time of national emergency. Also, as the senators presumably knew, he had also promised Admiral Leahy that, (1) he would go along with the federal government whenever he could and (2) he would raise neither the issue of independence nor the issue of statehood during the next two years.[20]

Muñoz agreed to "play ball." The issue was the attitude of the senators and representatives. What did the 77th Congress plan to do about Puerto Rico? Oddly, the first thing they did was criticize themselves. Discussing the economy Senator Tydings said, "We are not attempting to solve the problem even in a remote way."[21] Representative Fred Crawford of Michigan began his volunteered testimony by echoing Ernest Gruening and Albizu Campos: The shipping law were unjust and should be changed "unless we are willing to contribute anywhere from twenty to thirty or forty billion dollars per annum toward the subsistence of these people." Crawford had no idea how so many human beings, sandwiched into such a small space, could ever support themselves, but "getting down to some things that we have done, I think our legislative approach from an industrial standpoint in Puerto Rico has been nothing short of diabolic."[22]

Diabolic! With Congress admitting its devilish attitudes, Muñoz should have been in good shape. Only four months before, in April 1941, the insular legislature had passed a land law. Based on decisions by the U.S. Supreme Court Puerto Rico planned to enforce its 500-acre legislation and redistribute corporate holdings among the people. Critics noted that substantial portions of the retrieved land would still be used to grow a dead-end crop—sugar—but at the very least these profits would theoretically stay on the island, to be used for projects that would produce self-sustaining growth.[23]

Muñoz began his testimony by explaining how "we train the electorate." In the past people had sold their votes; now, because of the Populares' educational efforts, islanders acted on self-interest rather than corporate interest. This sounded good to Senator Homer Bone of Washington, but what about the children? "Are babies in Puerto Rico being raised to go to work at 6 or 7 years of age? Is that the only way in which we are able to develop our insular possessions?"

Muñoz answered, "We are trying to stop that." Senator Bone said, "That is shocking to me." Muñoz responded, "It is shocking."[24]

Muñoz always demonstrated a remarkable ability to listen patiently to utter nonsense. By betting on Washington he had painted himself into a corner; so when he and Bone got to talking about financing the land law, this was Muñoz's response. He knew that Tugwell thought it would cost much more than $50 million; nevertheless he believed that sum would do the trick. And "if Congress wants to contribute we would be very glad; and we could do it faster." But the island was going to pay its own way. The legislature had allocated $7 million to buy the acreage, and from this revolving fund Puerto Rico would retrieve the land and give it back to the people.[25]

Senator Bone and the rest of his colleagues apparently liked this response because no one asked Muñoz one question about the specifics of his plan. For example, of the $7 million allocated, $5 million was in bonds that *could* be authorized. At $7 million a year it would take a minimum of seven years to purchase the land? And where was the insular government going to get the extra money required to fund subsistence farmers and the industrialization program, which was also a part of Muñoz's dream for Puerto Rico?

Muñoz wisely offered no specifics. He had none. Senator Bone, shocked by what he had heard, nevertheless reminded Muñoz, "It is a problem for your country to settle as much as you can and not dump it into the lap of Congress any more than you have to."

Muñoz said, "And that is my view."[26]

Presumably Muñoz wanted Congress to believe that the Populares were different; they would stand on their own two feet. Whatever the case, as the United States and Puerto Rico moved toward Pearl Harbor, Muñoz traveled with the Chardon Plan and, as in 1934, with no money to fund it.

Meanwhile, Congress had a diabolically clean conscience.

Two things saved Luis Muñoz Marín: the war and America's thirst for liquor. By January 1943, for example Muñoz wrote an article for the *New Republic*, underlining the "plight of Puerto Rico." The island's life-line was ships, but between submarine sinkings and the withdrawal of every possible boat for the African campaign, the island had only one-third of the boats it normally used. The island was starving. Indeed, "in Puerto Rico we do not have a "submerged third," we have a floating and sometimes drowning 90 percent and a buoyant 10 percent."[27]

Before Muñoz's article was even published both Congress and the Interior Department recognized the accuracy of Muñoz's statements. In November 1942 Secretary Ickes sent his "special representative," William A. Brophy, to assess the degree of Puerto Rico's distress and to help pave the way for congressional hearings that would focus on the island's political, economic, and social conditions.

In his diary Brophy explained the source of Washington's concern. In September 1942 the island had received only 5,000 tons of food for a country that relied on imports. "Something urgent had to be done if the island was to be saved—and 2,000,000 on an island which is an eastern defense bastion for the Panama Canal cannot be permitted to starve, riot and revolt."[28]

Brophy had hoped for help from the Interior Department's Division of Territories; he soon decided, however, that it was

nothing but a glorified [not much glorified] bookkeeping and clerical office which had no organization at all. . . . The real crux of the situation is that they have no plans for the doing of anything. . . . It's just like the Indian Service used to be except that they do not even have a job in the field. Indeed the man who has "charge" of the Puerto Rican section has never been in Puerto Rico, speaks no Spanish, and is a bookkeeper.[29]

Brophy knew diabolical when he saw it. So he tried to devise plans that bypassed the department he worked for, and he also tried to stop Representative Carl Domengeaux of Louisiana from starting the riot Brophy sought to prevent. At a dinner held for the congressional del-egation that had come to San Juan to listen to the Puerto Rican people, Domengeaux managed to fondle women, get drunk, curse out Governor Tugwell, and racially abuse the speaker of the insular House, Ramos Antonini. When he saw Ramos's dark skin, Representative Domengeaux said, "It's pretty dark in there, come out so that I can see you."[30]

Like Marion Zioncheck and William H. King in the 1930s (See Chapter 4), it was relatively easy to dispose of congressional racists and loud-mouths. Harder to resolve was the economic condition of the Puerto Rican people. Brophy, for example, after spending six months studying the island, finally came to this conclusion: "Puerto Rico is a sinkhole—just radical measures alone can save it, and whether they like it or not, they have to have fewer kids or have them die earlier."[31]

Rum saved the day.[32] It was not a radical measure, but it was the bonanza that Congress offered and Muñoz gladly accepted.

This is what happened. The war cut the United States off from its normal supplies of hard liquor. As Muñoz stressed, it also significantly reduced a principal source of the island's everyday tax revenues: The excise taxes Puerto Rico got from imports and exports. So with congressional approval, Puerto Rico was allowed to keep 70 percent of the rum tax, and since Americans were big drinkers, the island watched its revenues skyrocket to totally unprecedented proportions. In 1939 the island saw Congress put $1.7 million into the U.S. Treasury; by 1942 the figure was $13.9 million, and by 1944 the figure was $65.8 million. Of this last figure, $65.7 million was derived from rum.[33]

Congress helped save its Caribbean bastion by eventually quadrupling the rum tax, and Muñoz, a very audacious man, took credit for Puerto Rico's paying its own way! Indeed, even before the biggest part of the windfall arrived, he wrote that islanders were for the first time in their history taking care of their own unemployed. "Puerto Rico has shown that she does not ask for aid from the federal government until she has taxed herself to the limit."[34]

Nonsense. At best Muñoz had a temporary bonanza that depended not only on the will of Congress but on a continuation of World War II. What rum gave Muñoz was a windfall, breathing room, and a responsibility.

Up to and through the war Puerto Rico was still a colony and still under the absolute authority of the Congress. But rum gave Muñoz the money to put some substance on his very vague plans for Puerto Rico's economy. Equally important, the island's military significance gave Muñoz a degree, albeit small, of political leverage his predecessors never enjoyed. After broadcasting its fight for the four freedoms, the United States did not want to be put in a position where it had to suppress a colony. Muñoz and his party majority finally had some cards to play, and that meant they would have to assume—along with Congress and the presidents—responsibility for opportunities won *and* for opportunities lost.

At La Fortaleza Governor Tugwell tried to explain the difference between a controlled and a planned economy: "The one is necessarily
dictatorial; the other, I have contended, can be democratic and indeed
is necessary to modern democracy."[35] Tugwell argued for government
ownership of new enterprises; along with islanders like Teodoro Moscoso, head of a new government agency called the Puerto Rico Development Company, Tugwell and Muñoz used the rum revenues to fund
a variety of new, state-owned corporations: a glass factory, a paper and
pulp factory, a shoe and leather operation, and facilities for the manufacture of cement and structural clay products.

The glass and paper operations were a "natural" offshoot of the rum
bonanza. The government would use its resources to build facilities that
complemented its profitable core, and with the revenues from these
operations, the government would slowly redistribute the land as it
simultaneously started other enterprises that provided new opportunities, all based on resources and skills possessed by Puerto Rico and
its people.

So far so good. The problem—apparent from day one—was whether
these state operations were part of a planned economy or simply a
stopgap measure on the way to industrialization by private, read absentee, capital.

Tugwell expected no miracles from a planned economy, but the island's new facilities were nevertheless part of a strategy that revolved
around overall state control of the society's economic resources. At all
times Tugwell "emphatically" and even dogmatically opposed incentives to outside capital because once you let that capital in, you more
easily lose the political and economic power essential to the realization
of your economic plans. Control was difficult in any society; in a colony
it was absolutely essential because by definition a colony lacked many
of the political powers required for economic planning.[36]

Tugwell harbored a contradiction: He favored a planned economy in
a society controlled, not by San Juan, but by Washington. This contradiction bothered Tugwell; it did not bother the islanders who worked
with the governor, though, because from the outset their primary goal
was to foster investment. If they controlled that investment, fine; if not,
they still wanted the investment.

Teodoro Moscoso, for example, later asked himself a rhetorical question: "Why did the government have to assume responsibilities which
normally fall within the province of private enterprise?" Because in 1943
there was no other game in town. To Moscoso and to Muñoz government
control "was conceived as an instrument for pump priming private enterprise into action."[37]

Moscoso clearly stated his plans—and his policy differences with Tugwell—in a June 14, 1943, appearance before the House committee inves-

tigating the island's political, economic, and social conditions. In an exchange with Chairman Jaspar Bell of Missouri, Bell asked about stock owned by the Puerto Rican government in one of its new corporations: "Would you sell it?" Moscoso answered: "Absolutely. What we want to do is establish industry. Who does it, if it is the devil himself, I do not care."[38]

Now the devil was not an appealing partner to many industrial planners. But Moscoso not only seemed perfectly willing to consider any outside investor but offered Bell a plan that he "personally" developed to attract industry to Puerto Rico. The "amendment" that Moscoso read to the congressmen said that "income, provided that it is invested in new interests, shall be exempt from taxation."[39]

Moscoso openly admitted his plans were still inchoate. When Bell asked, "If the concept is for increasing employment and increasing production you would go so far as to extend that idea to all those that invested their income in the expansion of these industries?" Moscoso responded: "I have not given any thought to that particular phase of it. I do not see why not if the industry was good."

Congressman Crawford: "You are going to increase employment?"

Moscoso: "That is right."[40]

Moscoso (and Muñoz) and Tugwell all wanted the same thing: more jobs for the Puerto Rican people. They differed fundamentally in the time period they allotted to produce those jobs and in the role of political power in economic affairs. Tugwell argued that to have a self-sustaining economy you first needed political power.[41] Moscoso (and Muñoz) seemed to believe that you could have the economic change and then control it in a politically satisfactory way. And even if you lacked control, you still got the jobs.

It took four years to finally resolve this economic battle. Meanwhile, rum revenues gave Muñoz and the Populares the money they needed to easily defeat their opposition. Muñoz simply argued that just as he had pledged, the Populares delivered on their promises of economic change. Land was being turned over to the poorest people, factories were being built, and absentee owners were put in their parasitic place.

In reality the Populares were "winging it"; they considered deals with the devil while at Roosevelt Roads sailors reneged on deals that placed mammoth obstacles in the path of whatever economic *or* political plans Muñoz and his colleagues devised.

The navy wasn't leaving, even though Roosevelt Roads was closed before it even opened!

Through 1941 and 1942 the workforce at Roosevelt Roads climbed from 200 to 3,000 men and women. Operating out of a tent camp construction crews soon dredged the harbor, completed an air field, built the gigantic dry dock, put in roads, fabricated a bombproof power plant, devised a net and mine depot, and forcibly transported more than 10,000 citizens of Vieques to St. Croix.

For those remaining on the island sailors offered work in the quarry that provided the rock needed for a breakwater designed to connect the baby to the main island. The British as well as the U.S. fleets considered "Rosey Roads" a possible operating port; therefore, through 1942 native and mainland workers struggled to complete the Caribbean cornerstone of America's defensive network.

At times morale was low. A newspaper started by the U.S. forces— the *Vieques Breeze*—tried to convince laborers that no matter how useless their efforts seemed, they were nonetheless making a significant contribution to the war effort. And if that wasn't motivation enough, they should also consider the effect they were having on islanders. As Dr. L. Davis put it in January 1943, "The advent of this project here has taught men and women to read the clock. Juan has learned that he must get to work on time, while Juanita has learned that his meals must appear on time."[42]

A Father Tackney observed that the natives had waited in idleness until, "in May of 1941, the base came." In less than two years, the men of Vieques "learned more than they would have in twenty years here on the island alone." They could now operate "strange" machines. According to Father Tackney, thanks to the Americans, "a common phrase among the people is 'Estilo Americano'—which means the American way. Socially we continentals have given them a new outlook on life."[43]

Unfortunately the natives' streak of good luck was about to end. By mid-1943 "it was clear to Allied leaders that due to the location of most Allied operations, a base of the intended size would not be necessary." So "almost impulsively," the navy mothballed Roosevelt Roads before it even finished the breakwater that still juts out from a corner of Vieques. The base was thus put on caretaker status at the very same time as war department officials made it clear to Senator Tydings that they did not want to give back what they no longer needed.[44]

In May 1943 Tydings wanted to definitely settle Puerto Rico's political status. In his eyes "the arrangement between the United States and Puerto Rico was one of the most unsatisfactory relationships between two governments that I have ever encountered, on the face of the earth."[45] It was a terrible situation that Congress would never resolve by a grant of statehood. In fact, for all the talk of respecting the will of the people, Tydings made this statement to Rafael Carrión, an advocate of statehood: "But the American Congress isn't going to give you statehood. There is no use butting about it; they are not going to give it to you."[46]

And later in the same discussion, Tydings said: "I appreciate how you feel and let me say this to you: If it were possible to make the poll of the House and the Senate and ask every man, "Do you see any immediate prospect for granting statehood to Puerto Rico?"

Mr. Carrión: "The answer would be no."

Senator Tydings: "The answer would be no."

Mr. Carrión: "No, definitely."[47]

Because Tydings himself "wants to go under that kind of hand-out government year after year after year," he proposed to make Puerto Rico an independent nation. He saw no other way to change a "disgraceful" situation. Puerto Rico "was a blot on the American system."[48]

The senator was serious. He was also quite contradictory because before he spoke to Carrión, he had already told the War Department that he would postpone doing anything about the blot on the U.S. system. When Senator Tydings asked if the military wanted to "keep the status quo there during the period of hostilities," John J. McCloy, then an assistant secretary of war, responded: "That is right. I would like to make this suggestion also, that you do not limit it to precisely the date of the armistice, the cessation of hostilities. We ought to have a 'look-see' in regard to what the Caribbean area is at the end of the war, who occupies the adjacent islands, who is controlling the Atlantic, and so forth."[49]

Senator Robert Taft thought this was a good idea, but he noted that

what I cannot see is how you can effectively permit an independent nation to be operated in a base so important in which you are using so many parts of the island. . . . I can understand a certain amount of autonomy, but I cannot understand how you can reconcile complete independence of the Island with the effective and necessary use of Puerto Rico for a military control of the Caribbean."[50]

It was a terrible problem that was finally brought to a head in a dialogue between McCloy and Tydings. The senator said, "Of course what you are saying is even if the people of Puerto Rico want independence and even though they give you all the bases that you want, there still might arise a question where you would want a watershed or a valley."[51]

McCloy reluctantly agreed. Indeed, when Tydings noted that "in the end you would rather have no independence at all. That is a logical conclusion is it not?" McCloy said, "yes; from a purely military point of view. The soldier wants to have a chance, without consulting anybody, to issue his orders."[52]

And the Puerto Ricans? Well, they have to take those orders. When Senator Taft asked if the Virgin Islands could provide a Puerto Rican substitute, McCloy answered, "I would be bold enough to say no to that question."[53]

In his own proposals for Puerto Rico the president never mentioned independence. He merely suggested the "greatest possible degree of home rule";[54] Roosevelt was, for example, heartily in favor of a law first brought to Congress in 1924: The Puerto Ricans would elect their own governor. To push this change and also to redefine the role of federal authorities in Puerto Rico, Roosevelt had appointed a committee that made these positive suggestions. In the future the president's powers would be limited to "vetoing only such measures passed by the local legislature as were beyond the proper field of local self government." And to assure that the Puerto Rican governor did a good job, Roosevelt proposed a new executive office for the island: that of the U.S. commissioner general. This official would apparently work side by side with the elected governor, since he had responsibility for the execution of the laws of the United States, for the coordination and supervision of federal civilian agencies, "and [for] their correlation with the activities of insular agencies."[55]

This confusing proposal died even before it reached its committee resting place. Few people understood it, and even fewer were pleased by the economic suggestions of Interior Secretary Ickes. Testifying in mid-1944 Ickes stressed the need for industrialization. Since the island's meager agricultural resources would never support so many people, Congress should support the native efforts to create a new and improved Reconstruction Finance Corporation. However, even if the industrialization plans worked, "there would still be a surplus without work. The population increased 30,000 to 40,000 each year." Nobody knew what to do with all these people, although "Puerto Ricans would be desireable additions to any nation and many outlets for them exist on this hemisphere."[56]

Was one of those outlets in the United States? Were American citizens welcome in their own country? If they were, Ickes never said so. He suggested that "the Federal government should investigate the feasibility of making agreements with other American republics which might be interested in the migration, under suitable conditions, of those Puerto Ricans who voluntarily decide that they want to make their future in South and Central America."[57]

For Ickes Puerto Rico would still be owned by North America as its citizens moved to South America! This incredible proposal underlined the poverty of the administration's thinking while, on Vieques, Abe Fortas, later Supreme Court Justice, explained the poverty of the Viequesans. He noted that the navy owned 21,000 of the baby island's 32,000 acres. And yes, "the Navy has recently determined that a large portion of this acreage is no longer needed by it but by acquiring so large a portion of the island and taking it out of civilian use and occupancy, the Navy effectively destroyed the economy of the community."

As Fortas explained, the island depended on sugar, yet "not only did the Navy acquire most of the sugar lands but it acquired the best of the sugar lands. Since the acquisition of these lands by the Navy there has been no cultivation of sugar cane and no means, therefore, whereby the civilian population of the island could sustain itself."[58]

Fortas was involved because he had to "strongly recommend against" the islanders' request to get back the island's best land. Fortas said no because the municipality had no way to use the lands even if the navy returned them. After all, the navy paid no taxes. That meant the municipality had no money to do anything, and even if it did, the navy might want lands again. Fortas proposed a government-sponsored project that rehabilitated the island even as it "did not disturb the [navy's] underlying title." In essence, the government would help the islanders to get back on their feet, but if the navy again needed the land, the islanders again had to leave.[59]

As a final footnote to this sordid situation another federal official, Major General Philip Fleming, suggested that "while the Government, doubtlessly, cannot hope to recover its investment in the property, this office is of the opinion that the property should not be disposed of without the payment of a money consideration."[60] The municipal government, rendered penniless by the navy, was to pay the army for the lands the navy had promised to return.

Just before he made his Vieques decision Abe Fortas (then an undersecretary in the Interior Department) also made a decision about the fate of Pedro Albizu Campos. For years the department and the president had received letters asking or demanding that Albizu be pardoned. Since the requests often came from prominent South American officials, Roosevelt wanted to consider the pleas for clemency. The problem was the defendant. With the president's approval the attorney general stipulated that Albizu had to ask for a pardon. "This he persistently declined to do for the reason that the United States had no jurisdiction in Puerto Rico, and if he acknowledged any kind of supervision by the United States Government it would be an acknowledgement of the jurisdiction of the United States over him."[61]

As people on the island would say, Albizu remained "vertical." He also remained in jail. Forfeiting his customary good conduct allowances Albizu served the maximum sentence, which expired on June 3, 1943. When he went to New York—he was not allowed to return home— Albizu still had four years of probationary sentence left. The problem was that Albizu never reported to his or any probation officer. To do that would be to admit the legitimacy of U.S. authority; so in New York Albizu disregarded federal officials as, according to what the attorney general told the president, he openly "engaged in activities in the City of New York in furtherance of his objective of overthrowing the Government of the United States in Puerto Rico."[62]

By September 1944 Albizu had already been free for a year. Fortas got involved because of a worried letter from Governor Rex Tugwell. Did the attorney general really mean to arrest and resentence Albizu? Tugwell thought this was a terrible idea because "it would have a deleterious effect on our relations with Latin America and would strengthen the independence group within the Popular Party."[63]

Fortas told Tugwell not to worry. What had happened was that two marshalls' left forms with Albizu "requesting that they be executed by the probationer." Albizu disregarded the request and that prompted rumors that Albizu would be returned to Puerto Rico for resentencing. This was not going to happen. The administration understood "the consequences that would occur in Puerto Rico if [the judge] ordered Albizu returned to Puerto Rico for revocation of his parole." The Justice Department therefore agreed that "the best thing would be to let the matter remain inactive until after . . . insular elections and at that time the whole matter might be the subject of a review."[64]

The insular elections were Tugwell's real worry. As he told Fortas in another letter, dated September 14, 1944, "One of the current surprises" was the resurrection of the independence movement in the island. A year before, for example, in a message to a proindependence Congress, Muñoz had told the assembly, "I wish the Congress great success in expressing to the American people the ideals that are indisputably those of the majority of Puerto Ricans."[65]

With letters but no active participation, Muñoz had apparently tried to cap the independence enthusiasm within his own party. It didn't work. In the Popular party's 1944 convention Muñoz's candidate for resident commissioner had been soundly defeated. He reluctantly accepted Jesús Piñero as a substitute, but according to Tugwell, "The independentistas were very wild and wooly and ran away with the whole show, putting Muñoz on the defensive, and, although they appear not to have known it, putting him into a state of near panic for some time."[66]

Tugwell said that he tried to stiffen Muñoz's spine. In a series of meetings the governor explained to the senator that the island's voters should be told that status was not an issue in the 1944 elections, just as it had not been in 1940. What the independence advocates wanted to do was "say enough during the campaign so they could claim after election that they had a mandate from the people." Muñoz might actually be risking a legislative approval of independence; that terrible prospect had to be avoided at all costs so Tugwell "put it on the grounds that during the next few years he would need to have a free hand for negotiation concerning new status arrangements, that this was likely to be a rather complex negotiation, and he could not afford to be pushed from behind all the time by a crowd of intransigents."[67]

Muñoz did and did not do what Tugwell suggested. Voters were continually told that status was not an issue in the election; a vote for the Populares would not be interpreted "in any form, or under any circumstance," as a vote in favor of any political status. But acceding to the demands of the independence majority, Muñoz also promised that no later than the structuring of the peace Puerto Ricans would hold a plebiscite to decide finally "what the people want via the full exercise of their rights and for the better realization of their future."[68]

Because status was not an issue because Muñoz was an able politician, because rum helped him deliver on his economic promises, and because the opposition was in utter disarray—what chance did statehooders have when men like Tydings said that statehood was out of the question?—the Populares achieved a colossal victory in the 1944 elections. They won over 65 percent of the vote and overwhelming control of the insular Senate (seventeen of nineteen seats) and House (thirty-seven of thirty-nine seats).[69] Luis Muñoz Marín reigned as undisputed master of the island's politics. But his opponents expected that he would fulfill his pledge. The plebiscite had to be held. And soon.

Senator Tydings beat everybody to the punch. Before Muñoz could himself avoid or his opponents press for a plebiscite, Tydings introduced another Puerto Rican independence bill. The measure did call for full retention of U.S. military bases, but in sharp contrast to his 1936 measure, this time the senator proposed a twenty-year transition period on trade; as in the Philippines the tariff rates would increase 5 percent a year until, in 1965, Puerto Rico and the United States treated each other like independent nations.

Muñoz was less than elated. To the extent they existed, his economic plans relied on federal assistance tied to the acquisition of private (read U.S.) capital.[70] For example, in late 1944 Muñoz and his colleagues had rejected a comprehensive Tugwell plan that argued that "the continued dependence on outside assistance only aggravates the economic problem, since it does not promote reforms, the expansion of resources, or the necessary adjustment of the population to the development of the sense of responsibility and self-sufficiency that is a *prerequisite for the achievement of the other objectives* [emphasis in original]."[71]

Whether under state or private ownership Tugwell and his colleagues argued that further dependence on outside sources would only perpetuate Puerto Rico's economic agony. Muñoz and Moscoso disagreed. Indeed, in the same month Tydings introduced his independence bill (January of 1945), Puerto Rico's Development company decided to provide free factory buildings for private enterprise. Since there was no rum money to construct these facilities, the company planned to apply to the War Emergency Program (WEP) for the seed money required to attract private investors to the island.[72]

As in 1933, in 1945 Muñoz still accepted the syllogism that argued that islanders could never survive on their own. He lacked the will to try because 500 years of colonialism had already convinced him that he and his island could never succeed on their own. Thus, the Tydings Bill threatened Muñoz's only hopes for economic progress as it simultaneously threatened his hold on political power.[73]

Muñoz's problem was how to fight the bill but still maintain the support of the Populares independence majority. After all, whereas in 1945 other colonies pleaded for their independence, and would be happy to get ten years for transition, here was Tydings offering a twenty-year stretch to adjust to self-sufficiency. Muñoz's proindependence colleagues had almost immediately cabled their sense of enthusiasm to Senator Tydings, so to fend off the rush to independence, Muñoz adroitly made this argument: In the elections he had made a solemn pledge to support a plebiscite; thus, unless Congress let islanders vote for all three options, Muñoz saw no way to keep faith with the Puerto Rican people.[74]

Not bad. Muñoz was, after all, a superb politician. But his colleagues also knew a political trick or two. Indeed, on March 8, 1945, they unleashed a historic bombshell that made life difficult not only for Luis Muñoz Marín but for the U.S. Congress as well.

Independence advocates first presented Congress with two lists, one of Puerto Rican senators, the other of Puerto Rican representatives. Of nineteen senators, eleven came out in favor of independence; of thirty-nine representatives, twenty-two favored divorce from the United States. And in a third list, this one from seventy-three of the island's Popular mayors, fully forty-two supported independence.[75]

All told, 57 percent of Puerto Rico's democratically elected representatives had decided in favor of independence. This was a first in island history, a clear and unequivocal manifestation of the will of the islanders' representatives. Given the pressure exerted by Muñoz for Populares to vote no, supporters of independence could legitimately now argue that even the 57 percent figure masked the real feelings of the Puerto Rican legislature.

Muñoz would still come to Washington seeking a plebiscite. But a Congress that never tired of talking about self-determination now had the colonial ball neatly thrown in its lap.

Hearings began in May 1945. If nothing else Senator Millard Tydings was a blunt, outspoken man. At one point in the hearings he explained to islanders that most Americans had little if any interest in Puerto Rico; fifty years into the U.S. occupation and the senator's constituents still thought the island was in the Pacific.[76] Of course, ignorance could be bliss; perhaps North American ignorance would allow islanders to get what they wanted just because nobody cared for, or knew anything about, Puerto Rico.

Tydings quickly eliminated even the ignorance option when he told his listeners about a poll he had personally conducted. He wanted to be fair; he wanted every fact to be on the table, readily open for inspection. Thus he declared, "I found no Senator and no Representative, up to now, who favors eventual statehood for Puerto Rico, so we ought to eliminate that status from our consideration, because it doesn't seem fair to the Puerto Rican people, as I see it, to hold out such a possibility, which in my judgement, will never be realized."[77]

Tydings made a good point. But what about self-determination? Or if not democratic decency, at least political expediency? With the Populares in control and the legislature already on record in favor of independence, why not preserve democratic appearances? Tydings had told islanders that "statehood, in my opinion is absolutely the deadest issue next to Hector's ghost I know of in the United States of America at this time. . . . The fact is that at the moment there is no sentiment here for statehood and there is not any prospect."[78]

Given the absence of any sentiment for statehood, what did Tydings, and the Senate, and the House, have to risk? The answer is the will of the Puerto Rican people.

It was quite doubtful that islanders desired statehood. On the off-chance that they might express such a desire, Tydings wanted to cut political embarrassment off at the pass. Eliminate the statehood option and you eliminated any chance that after a fair election on the island, the United States would have to publicly disregard the will of the Puerto Rican people. A nation that loudly broadcast the four freedoms did not want to admit openly that they did not apply in the Caribbean. In the words of Interior's William Brophy, "My rough ideas are that the Caribbean Sea is ours . . . and that we must bear burdens not only in Puerto Rico but throughout the rest of the Caribbean, as we have done either directly or indirectly for a long time past."[79]

The colony had become a burden, a burden the United States had to stoically accept. For example, when Muñoz Marín testified before the Tydings committee, he made an intelligent and forceful plea for a plebiscite. This sounded "absolutely sound" to Senator Tydings, except that Muñoz forgot who made the rules in their relationship. Congress had to take the initiative in any plebiscite because there was no point in voting for a status Congress refused to concede. "In that situation you would be in the position of having assumed that whatever you asked for we would give you and we would be in the position of breaking faith if we did not give it to you."

Tydings refused to offer options Congress would defeat. His colleagues refused to offer any options at all. Senator Allen Ellender explained his position in this way: "It strikes me if we should say to Puerto Rico, let us know what you want, and then we refuse to give them what they ask, we will put ourselves in a bad light." Ellender reported on a poll of his own: "My guess is at this moment that Congress would not give the Puerto Ricans full independence nor statehood. It would be in between as far as I can see. The Congress may give you the right to determine whether or not you desire independence by giving you the right to vote on the question."[80]

What was the point of voting if Congress eliminated choices before any one made a choice? Senator Dennis Chavez answered this one in an exchange with Muñoz Marín: "I can see plenty of reasons why there should be a large opinion in Puerto Rico for independence, but even if there is we still have the responsibility of almost half a century, and we should not evade that responsibility by saying: Now you are going to be independent; go free and do what you please."[81]

The United States had its responsibilities to fulfill, so as a good will gesture to Muñoz—to allow the committee to "study" the plebiscite proposal—Tydings introduced the plebiscite measure, though steadfastly refusing to give it or the independence bill any serious consideration. His excuse, cited in a letter to the island's Committee for Independence, was that he had devoted his energies to the Philippine independence bill and to the resurrection of their war-ravaged society.[82]

The independence majority was angry, first at Tydings and second at Muñoz Marín. In their eyes Muñoz's submission of the plebiscite proposal, linked to his seeming advocacy of a dominion status, bordered on treason. The nation finally had a golden opportunity to achieve its long-sought goal, and Muñoz turned his back on the ideal he supposedly favored. To Gilberto Concepción Muñoz favored a "colonial measure" at the very moment independence was Puerto Rico's for the asking.

Muñoz answered these charges in a September 11, 1945, statement to *El Mundo*. He accused the independence advocates of "obstructing and sabotaging" his efforts in Washington. If they really believed in democracy, they should let the people decide among all three alternatives. And if they were not willing to do that, he was not willing to let them remain in the Popular party. Choose the plebiscite or choose independence, but make a decision because "it is utterly impossible for one man to be in favor of both things. . . . It is utterly impossible for a man to be in favor of both my being supported and attacked on my efforts to have this pledge fulfilled."[83]

In the name of democracy Muñoz split with the *independentistas*. He said he wanted all alternatives to be represented when he had already been told by one senator after another that at a minimum statehood was out of the question. So Muñoz proposed an unrealizeable alternative because he had no intention of severing his ties to Washington. If Congress did as it promised, he would tell voters that true to his pledge he had labored hard for the promised but refused plebiscite. And if Congress somehow granted a three-way plebiscite, Muñoz felt confident that voters would support the dominion status he did in fact favor. Either way, Muñoz looked good, and all the while, he never cut his umbilical cord to Washington.

Meanwhile, in the White House President Harry S. Truman was getting an earful from his advisers. Special Counsel Samuel I. Rosenman told the president that "Senator Tydings spent 20 excited minutes telling me how terrible it would be, that the Congress would never consent to statehood for example, and that it would be improper to submit statehood as a possible alternative to Puerto Rico knowing full well we would not give it to them."[84]

Tydings was at least consistent. Tugwell, as early as July 4, 1942, had told islanders that "the Declaration [of Independence] did not end colonialism; but it removed that system to a moral category which made it indefensible."[85] Tugwell, however, defended the indefensible when he signed a statement accepted by himself, by Tydings, by the Interior Department, and, on October 16, 1945, by Harry S. Truman.

The president was both cautious and contradictory. "It was the settled policy of this Government to promote the political, social and economic development of people who have not yet attained full self government, and *eventually* [my emphasis] to make it possible for them to determine their own form of government." The president then took pride in what the United States had done for the Philippines: "The people of the Philippines determined that they desired political independence, and accordingly, the Government of the United States made provision to this effect."[86]

But what was the United States going to do about the will of the Puerto Rican legislature? A clear majority in favor of independence was an undeniable fact. Were we going to be able to take as much pride in Puerto Rico as in the Philippines?

Absolutely. As long as Congress said yes before the Puerto Ricans did. In the president's words, "In the interest of good faith and comity between the people of Puerto Rico and those of us who live on the mainland, Congress should not submit proposals to the Puerto Ricans for adoption by them which the Congress is not prepared to enact finally into law."[87]

But Congress had already eliminated statehood as an option. And nobody was too keen on independence. Where did that leave our respect for self-determination?

It left it in the hands of the Puerto Ricans, who, according to J. Edgar Hoover, had forced the issue on February 25, 1946. Involved because the plebiscite was apparently a subversive activity, Hoover informed the attorney general that the island's legislature had passed a bill providing for a three-way plebiscite: statehood, independence, or dominion. Another bill, acting on Tugwell's planned resignation, called for a governor elected by the Puerto Rican people. Rumor had it that $200,000 was already appropriated to carry out the law, and Hoover said that "in the event additional details are received concerning this matter, they will be furnished to you."[88]

A note scrawled on the memo asked, "Does the boss know about this?"

In Washington and San Juan both bosses knew about it, but the one in San Juan responded by once again supporting contradiction. In an interview with ABC television on January 3, 1946, Governor Tugwell had said, "I do not see how we Americans can get out of the dilemma we are in. We believe in liberty, in home rule, in self determination. But we are holding on to Puerto Rico without the expressed consent of its two million people. That is no position for an American to find himself in."[89]

Tugwell's way out of the dilemma was to exercise the rights guaranteed to the governor in the 1917 Jones legislation: Tugwell vetoed both bills. For example, the plebiscite bill had to be rejected because it "provided for a unilateral expression of opinion in Puerto Rico without the consent of the Congress."[90]

The Puerto Ricans responded by overriding the governor's veto. That meant the buck stopped at Harry Truman's desk, and true to his decisive nature, the president not only made a decision but disregarded the serious reservations of his secretary of the interior. Julius Krug understood Tugwell's arguments, but what about appearances? What would the rest of the world think? To Krug sustaining the governor's veto would be considered by Puerto Ricans, other South Americans, and Europeans "as a denial of an often expressed principle." He grasped the dangers of free choice but thought they could be eliminated "if the plebiscite was preceded by an educational campaign" that explained the consequences of statehood, independence, and dominion status.[91]

Truman explained his veto of the plebiscite bill in this manner. He had "consistently favored and recommended to the Congress" that it let the Puerto Rican people decide their own future. However, Truman had also consistently said that before islanders made a choice, Congress had first to tell them what their choices were. So far Congress had refused to act, and that meant vetoing the proposed plebiscite because any approval of the bill "might be erroneously construed by the people of Puerto Rico as a commitment that the United States would accept any plan that might be selected at the proposed plebiscite."

The Puerto Ricans had once again forgotten that first came the will of Congress and then, and only then, came the will of the Puerto Rican people. To hold a plebiscite without Congress first stipulating its terms would be to create a situation in which, "if the plan thus selected should not be acceptable to Congress, it could then be argued that the United States was not keeping faith with the expressed will of the people of Puerto Rico."[92]

The president's strained logic—we will keep faith with the people's will by not allowing them to express it—killed the plebiscite proposal. Muñoz Marín struggled to keep the measure alive, but it was an uphill battle at best, made even more difficult by the publication of a devastating economic analysis prepared at Senator Tyding's request by the U.S. Tariff Commission.

The report repeated, yet again, that the island's economy was a nightmare produced by overpopulation. Colonialism, absentee ownership, the promised but never delivered assistance from Washington—these were at best downplayed because, in the words of one of Muñoz Marín's colleagues, the study deliberately tried to "justify the status quo." Since only a perpetuation of the island's colonial status could assure even a modicum of well-being, Congress should face up to the "immensity of the task," which, even if Congress did nothing, "should not deter the islander's leaders from shouldering it [the immense task] and continuing to make whatever progress is possible."[93]

Congress told the Puerto Ricans to be patient. Wait a while longer and we will see what we can do. That was fine in Washington, but in San Juan Luis Muñoz Marín was under tremendous pressure. The *independentistas* were on the verge of forming their own political party (they actually did so in October 1946), and the lack of political action translated into a lack of political direction. Islanders of all persuasions demanded to know Muñoz's plans. What were his aspirations now that Congress had refused to allow him and his party to keep their word to the Puerto Rican voters?

Muñoz explained his position in a two-part *El Mundo* series called "New Paths toward Old Objectives." Statehood and independence were meaningless terms unless accompanied by the economic assistance Puerto Rico so urgently needed. But with statehood ruled out, Muñoz felt certain that Congress would never provide an independent Puerto Rico with the short- and long-term support required for its industrial development. Thus, Muñoz bet his and Puerto Rico's future on the establishment of the Associated People of Puerto Rico. In 1946 this was still a transitory and not a permanent status. The island's ultimate destiny would be decided only when the economic conditions essential to political stability were attained.[94]

Muñoz's articles finally confirmed the decision he had first made in 1933. After all, whether relying on private or public resources, on a plan for the resurrection of sugar or the industrial transformation of Puerto Rican society, the one constant in Muñoz's thinking was short- or long-term dependence on the public and private resources of the United States of America. As opposed to Albizu Campos or so many members of his party, Muñoz never demonstrated a faith in his own or his people's ability to take charge of their own destiny. Indeed, despite Washington's refusal to keep its word (e.g., the funds promised in 1934); despite blatant racism; despite military expropriation of the island's best lands; despite an educational system in which students learned geometry in two languages, English in the morning, Spanish in the afternoon; and despite a humiliating refusal to let islanders express their own will in a plebiscite, Muñoz kept coming back for more. As if in a revolving door, he went round and round, hoping that Congress would finally say, "Come in. Here are the funds you deem indispensable to Puerto Rico's well-being."

One island scholar wrote that Muñoz identified with a poem written by his father in 1898. He was Sisyphus, pushing the rock up the hill in a sterile struggle wherein he was always doomed to defeat. Nonetheless, he kept struggling because that was Puerto Rico's bitter destiny.[95]

This suggestive hypothesis is just that, a hypothesis. The certainty is that Muñoz—and the people who voted for him—chose dependence. Given the island's colonial status, it would be difficult to argue that that was a free decision. But it was voluntary because no one could argue that Congress and the presidents had not, for the first fifty years of the colonial relationship, behaved in a consistent and predictable manner. In sharp contrast to the situation in 1905, or even 1917, Luis Muñoz Marín and his supporters knew exactly what they were getting into. Thus, they must share with the United States responsibility for Puerto Rico's postwar development.

Harry Truman wrote the final footnote to this part of U.S.–Puerto Rican history. With Tugwell on the way to the University of Chicago, the president was under great pressure to appoint a Puerto Rican to the governorship. Truman listened to a wide variety of suggestions—one letter in the president's files pushed for Eleanor Roosevelt as Puerto Rico's governor—but he finally decided to play politics with the nomination. Higher-ups in the Democratic National Committee reminded Truman that the position was a political plum; agreed, "most American candidates sought the governorship as a reward for political favors and not because they were qualified for the position." Nevertheless the president should follow precedent and appoint an incompetent person to the governorship.[96]

Truman first offered the post to Dillon S. Meyer, a public officer who had assumed a number of federal positions. When Meyer hesitated, Interior Secretary Krug reminded him that "I can't think of any finer stepping stone than this." Meyer still refused the president's offer, so next on the list was a member of the Treasury Department, O. Max Gardner. When this fellow also refused the governorship, Truman at last settled on a Puerto Rican, Resident Commissioner Jesús Piñero.

Opposition to Piñero was both immediate and intense. Some said he would be a "stooge" for Muñoz. The Democratic National Committee, ever anxious to keep control of a political plum, was more subtle: Members said Piñero was a Communist. The man would turn the island red.[97]

Truman, however, stuck to guns. He never even blushed when, on the anniversary of the U.S. occupation of the island, July 25, 1946, the Puerto Rican people were told that the appointment of Jesús Piñero was "concrete evidence of President Truman's belief that islanders were fully capable of administering their own governmental responsibilities."[98]

NOTES

1. Message from the President, see House, 78th Congress, 1st session, 1943, Document no. 304, p. 2.

2. See the *New York Times*, July 30, 1921, p. 18.

3. See, Lee Kennett, *A History of Strategic Bombing* (New York: Scribner's, 1982); on Guernica see Philip Knightley, *The First Casualty* (New York: Harcourt Brace, 1975), pp. 191–216.

4. See *Hearings to Review the Status of Navy Training Activities on the Island of Vieques*, House, Committee on Armed Services, 96th Congress, 2nd session, 1980, p. 100.

5. See *Report on Need of Additional Naval Bases to Defend the Coasts of the United States, Its Territories, and Possessions*, House, 75th Congress, 1st session, Document no. 65, December 27, 1938, p. 4.

6. See A. J. Hepburn, *Letter from the Secretary of the Navy*, House, 76th Congress, 1st session, Document no. 65, p. 16.

7. See the National Archives, Record Group 126, DTIP, 9–8–119.

8. See the National Archives, Record Group 126, DTIP, 9–8–118.

9. National Archives, Record Group 126, DTIP, 9–8–119.

10. See "Puerto Rico," *Fortune*, May, 1941, p. 91.

11. The Naval Historical Center, Operational Archives Division, Box labeled Roosevelt Roads, Washington, D.C.; dated January 6, 1941.

12. On the U.S. Navy's promises see Admiral Leahy's memo to President Truman in April 1948. Naval Historical Center, Operational Archives Division, Washington, Files marked Roosevelt Roads—Admiral Leahy's Report, p. 2.

13. See "Need for a Study of Land Holdings of Armed Forces in Puerto Rico," National Archives, DTIP, Record Group. 126, 9–8–48.

14. See Paolo E. Coletta, ed., *United States Navy and Marine Corps Bases, Overseas* (Westport, Conn.: Greenwood Press, 1983), p. 272.

15. *Nomination of Rexford Tugwell as Governor*, Senate, Committee on Territories and Insular Affairs, 77th Congress, 1st session, 1941, p. 67.

16. See Thomas Matthews, *Luis Muñoz Marín* (New York: American R.D.M. Publishers, 1967), p. 37.

17. See, for example, Carlos Zapata Oliveras, United States—Puerto Rico Relations, 1898–1945," *Horizontes* 29, no. 59–60 (October 1986): pp. 105–135, esp. pp. 120–121.

18. See Matthew Edel, "Land Reform in Puerto Rico, 1940–1959," *Caribbean Studies* 2, no. 3 (1963): p. 41.

19. Ibid., p. 32; Leonardo Santana Rabell, *Planificación y Política* (Río Piedras: Editorial Cultural, 1989), esp. p. 142.

20. Harold L. Ickes, *The Secret Diary of Harold L. Ickes*, Vol. 3 (New York: S&S, 1947), p. 389; Nomination of Rexford Tugwell, p. 49.

21. Tugwell, *Nomination of Rexford* p. 35.

22. Ibid., pp. 34 and 37.

23. See Rexford Tugwell, "Report on the Five Hundred Acre Law," *Puerto Rican Public Papers* (San Juan, 1946).

24. Ibid., pp. 42–43.

25. Ibid., p. 47.

26. Ibid., p. 47.

27. Luis Muñoz Marín, "Plight of Puerto Rico," *New Republic*, Vol. 108 (January 1943): pp. 51–52.

28. President Harry S. Truman Library in Independence, Missouri. See Papers of William Brophy, Box 14, Folder marked Brophy Papers. The quote cited appears on p. 6 of the diary.

29. Ibid., pp. 13–14.

30. Ibid., p. 19.

31. Ibid., p. 20.

32. H. C. Barton, *Puerto Rico's Industrial Development Program, 1942–1960* (Cambridge: Harvard University Press, 1959), p. 2.

33. See the National Archives, DTIP, 9–8–6, Box 349.

34. See Muñoz Marín, "Plight of Puerto Rico," p. 52; Matthew Edel, "Land Reform in Puerto Rico," esp. p. 43; Also, David F. Ross, *The Long Uphill Path* (San Juan: Editorial Edil, 1969), esp. p. 74.

35. Harry S. Truman Library, President's Personal File, Box 768.

36. See Ross, *The Long Uphill Path*, p. 79; Santana Rabell, *Planificación y Política*, esp. pp. 130–142; Emilio Pantojas García, *Development Strategies as Ideology* (Boulder, Colo.: Lynne Rienner, 1990), pp. 45–55.

37. *Hearings before the Select Committee on Small Business*, Senate, 88th Congress, 2nd session, April 1964; esp. pp. 295–296.

38. *Hearing before the Subcommittee of the Committee on Territories and Insular Affairs*, House, 78th Congress, 1st session, June 14, 1943, p. 845.

39. Ibid., p. 850.

40. Ibid., p. 852.

41. See Santana Rabell, *Planificación y Política*, pp. 129–130.

42. See the *Vieques Breeze*, January 24, 1943, p. 1.

43. Ibid., February 7, 1943, p. 1.

44. See "Roosevelt Roads U.S. Naval Station," Command History File, 1943–1973, OPNAV Report 5750–5, Naval Historical Center, Operational Archives Division, Washington, D.C., pp. 1–2; the almost impulsive comment is in Coletta, *Navy and Marine Corps Bases*, p. 273.

45. *Puerto Rico, Hearings before the Committee on Territories and Insular Affairs,* Senate, 78th Congress, 1st session, May 1943, p. 53.

46. Ibid., p. 52.

47. Ibid., p. 55.

48. Ibid., p. 55.

49. Ibid., p. 11.

50. Ibid., P. 15.

51. Ibid., p. 17.

52. Ibid., p. 17.

53. Ibid., p. 18.

54. See *Message from the President,* 1943, p. 2.

55. Ibid., p. 3.

56. *Hearings before the Committee on Insular Affairs,* House, 78th Congress, 2nd session, May 1944, p. 1642.

57. Ibid., p. 1642.

58. See No. 264, H.R. 4863, *To Provide for the Donation of Certain Property of the United States in Vieques,* House, 78th Congress, 2nd session, 1944, p. 1.

59. Ibid., p. 2.

60. See No. 267, House Resolution 4863, *To Provide for the Donation of Certain Property of the U.S. Government in Vieques,* House, 78th Congress, 2nd session, 1944, p. 2480.

61. Roosevelt Library, Official Files, Box 3645, Folder marked Campos, Pedro.

62. Ibid., p. 5.

63. Ibid., but this is from a letter from Fortas to Tugwell dated September 12, 1944.

64. Ibid., the one-page Fortas letter to Tugwell.

65. Luis Nieves Falcon, "El Futuro Ideológico del Partido Popular Democrático," *Diagnóstico de Puerto Rico* (Río Piedras: Edil, 1970), pp. 242–243.

66. Roosevelt Library, Tugwell Papers, Box 47, Folder marked PR, Abe Fortas; the one-page letter is dated September 14, 1944.

67. Ibid., Tugwell to Fortas, September 14, 1944.

68. See Nieves Falcon, "El Futuro Ideológico," p. 243; also see, for example, Robert W. Anderson, *Party Politics in Puerto Rico* (Stanford, Calif.: Stanford University Press, 1965).

69. See, for example, Roberta Ann Johnson, *Puerto Rico: Commonwealth or Colony?* (New York: Praeger, 1980), p. 29.

70. Santana Rabell, *Planificación y Política,* p. 142; Teodoro Moscoso, "Puerto Rico Chooses Free Enterprise," a speech delivered by Moscoso in 1957, p. 3; also William H. Stead, *Fomento: The Economic Development of Puerto Rico* (Washington, D.C.: NPA, 1958).

71. Santana Rabell, *Planificación y Política,* p. 133; my translation and my emphasis.

72. See Ross, *The Long Uphill Path,* p. 84.

73. See, for example, Johnson, *Puerto Rico*, p. 105.

74. Carlos Zapata Oliveras, *United States–Puerto Rico Relations in the Early Cold War Years* Ph.D. diss., University of Pennsylvania, 1986, pp. 122–126.

75. Ibid., pp. 131–132.

76. *Independence for Puerto Rico, Hearings before the Committee on Territories and Insular Affairs*, Senate, 79th Congress, 1st session, May 1945, p. 311.

77. Ibid., p. 291.

78. Ibid., p. 249.

79. Zapata Oliveras, *United States–Puerto Rico Relations*, p. 126.

80. Ibid., p. 377.

81. Ibid., p. 384.

82. Zapata Oliveras *United States–Puerto Rico Relations*, pp. 155–156.

83. *El Mundo*, September 11, 1945.

84. See Harry S. Truman Library, Independence, Missouri, Papers of Samuel S. Rosenman, Box 3; the memo is dated October 3, 1945.

85. See Tugwell "Five Hundred Acre Law," p. 93.

86. Truman Library, Rosenman Papers, Box 3; a copy of the president's statement is included in the Rosenman files.

87. Ibid., p. 2 of the president's statement.

88. Truman Library, President's Secretary's Files, Box 169, Folder marked FBI–Puerto Rico; the memo is dated February 26, 1946.

89. Roosevelt Library, Tugwell Papers, Box 62; see p. 5 of the interview.

90. Zapata Oliveras, *United States–Puerto Rico Relations*, p. 174.

91. Ibid., p. 175.

92. Truman Library, Papers of Samuel S. Rosenman, Box 3.

93. See U.S. Tariff Commission, *The Economy of Puerto Rico* Washington, D.C.: GPO 1946.

94. See *El Mundo*, June 28 and June 29, 1946.

95. Gerardo Navas Davila, *La Dialetica del Desarrollo Nacional* (Río Piedras: Editorial Universitaria, 1978), pp. 106–107.

96. Zapata Oliveras, *United States–Puerto Rico Relations*, pp. 209–210.

97. Ibid., pp. 213–218.

98. Ibid., p. 218.

Chapter 7

Absolutely Clear

This bill does restrict, and let us have that very clear, the people of Puerto Rico to a constitution which is within the limitations of the Organic Act of Puerto Rico. Their fundamental status is unchanged.
Congressman Jacob Javits, June 30, 1950

It is important that the nature and general scope of S.3336 be made absolutely clear. The bill under consideration would not change Puerto Rico's fundamental political, social and economic relationship to the United States.
House Report 1832, March, 1952[1]

Nobody had a name for what Royal Little did. "Conglomerate" would eventually gain widespread use, but in the late 1940s "free form corporation" was the label attached to Little's innovative business methods. What he did, using the Textron Corporation as an umbrella, was seek out companies with three characteristics: large tax losses on their books, stock selling for a low price, and managers eager to make a quick buck. Little then bought the targeted enterprise with a bank loan, paid off the loan by selling the just-purchased company's most marketable assets, and, with the leftovers, tried to make money with the factories that had cost him nothing.[2]

On paper Textron looked like a mammoth enterprise, and to some extent it was a viable corporation because Little's bargains were sometimes profitable operations. The problem was that Little had no exact idea what he wanted to do. He just kept buying companies.

In 1945 and 1946 Little purchased the Nashua (New Hampshire) Manufacturing Company. *Fortune* failed to understand this purchase because none of Nashua's products bore any relation to Textron's needs. What *Fortune* missed was Little's pace-setting motivation: This time Royal Little sold off assets, not to retire a loan, but to pay for another purchase.

Little's financial wizardry soon put thousands of workers on the street. When the union complained to Senator Charles Tobey of New Hampshire, the senator promptly held hearings, and those hearings focused not only on Little's banking practices but also on another question of even more significance to the workers of New Hampshire: Did Little close the New Hampshire mills because of his planned move to Puerto Rico? Was that possession's new tax incentive policy going to take jobs away from mainland Americans?[3]

In Puerto Rico Teodoro Moscoso and his associates were thrilled. After two years of feverish efforts the island's Aid to Industrial Development (AID) Program finally found a big fish in its nets. As a company historian later wrote, "It would be difficult to over-estimate the joy that was in San Juan when Textron signed—or the ease with which the Development Company officials agreed to terms more generous than they had granted or would grant to any other firm."[4]

Since economics is a zero-sum enterprise, Puerto Rico's presumed gain was New Hampshire's loss. Angry Americans wanted action, and even though the hearings soon established that Little's move to Puerto Rico was never a central motive for his sale of Nashua—paraphrasing *Fortune*, Little was simply strip mining Nashua and its resources[5]— worried union representatives raised issues that immediately underlined the inherent weaknesses of Puerto Rico's development plans. From Textron on, the problems were obvious; the tragedy is that no one acted on the information that men like Emil Rieve tried to bring to everyone's attention.

Rieve was the general president of the Textile Workers of America. He had a mainland labor force to keep on the job and a passionate opinion about the long-term impact of Puerto Rico's industrialization plans. As Rieve told Senator Tobey:

After they build up the Puerto Rican mills then they are going to bring in the material up here and compete with our own people in this country. After the government [Puerto Rican] stupidly, in my opinion, buys the mills for them, builds them for them, exempts them from taxes, it will permit these products to come into this country and compete with our people. Frankly, as far as that is concerned, I don't think the country has heard the last from me on this Puerto Rican situation. I intend to fight it.[6]

Rieve's words brought applause from the audience, an audience that had already heard Senator Tobey say that the United States was Puerto Rico's "wet nurse." Of course, Toby had no problems assisting such a "notedly poor place," but

the point remains that what they are doing is killing things off up here and building up things down there. Doesn't it seem rather an anomaly that the taxpayers of the United States should help Puerto Rico but then let Puerto Rico come in and siphon off our industries by giving subsidies and tax advantages and bait to do it. What do you say? Am I right or wrong?[7]

Representing the Interior Department, Irwin Silverman, the chief counsel, was on the defensive. When Tobey pushed him about cheap labor, Silverman had to admit that the lure of below-minimum-wage labor could take jobs away from mainland Americans. And when Toby pointed out that it was the "windfall from rum" that underwrote the development company's efforts, Silverman very reluctantly agreed that the senator was right: "By that very largess we are implementing the Puerto Rican government so that it can eliminate income taxes on corporations that come in there."[8]

But Tobey had to remember the nation's goal and Silverman's efforts. First, there was "a period of tutelage as we [in the Interior Department] call it . . . which as a ward and guardian relationship we have to assist and help, and part of the tutelage or the fee for their learning how to handle their own affairs is this 12 years' [tax exemption] bait."[9]

In addition, Silverman was doing his best to get the cheap labor out of Puerto Rico. He explained that he was trying to find markets for Puerto Rican women. "Every woman from Puerto Rico sent to the United States means that five people—because the average is one woman will bear five children—are being taken care of; five mouths ultimately, over a period of years. Thousands of them are coming to our shores." And if Silverman had his way, thousands of Puerto Rican men would soon move to Alaska! Keeping the men and women apart meant no children, and it also provided work for a number of people on the Alaska Railroad.[10]

Silverman did his best, but the debate's nature and location (i.e., in Washington and not San Juan) underlined *the* fundamental flaw in Puerto Rico's development strategy: It lacked the political power needed to control its economic development. Consider what Puerto Rico's planners called their "fishing net approach" to industrial development: "It involves disseminating information about Puerto Rico and the industrialization program as widely as possible and then following up wherever interest is shown."[11] Now, with this approach Puerto Rican planners admitted they had no overall strategy, no "strategic industry" scheme to create, within, say, twenty years, a self-propelled economy. That was a major flaw in what was soon called Operation Bootstrap, and both Luis Muñoz Marín and Moscoso must assume primary responsibility for rejecting the economic analysis of men like Rexford Tugwell and Pedro Albizu Campos.

As late as 1964, however, Puerto Rican planners were still assuring Congress that despite the model of seven Southern states—states that had created 200,000 new industrial jobs between 1947 and 1954—and despite massive unemployment, "Puerto Rico specifically withheld the benefits of its tax exemption and incentives from runaway firms which would, by their transfer, create unemployment in their original location."[12]

If Puerto Rico was a real state, or even an incorporated territory, it could have imitated the behavior of North and South Carolina. But as a colony whose tax-incentive program revolved around congressional consent, as a possession whose political future (e.g., an elected governor) rested on securing change from an always reluctant Congress, island planners knew their place. They came to Congress hat in hand, anxious to assure men like Senator Tobey that they put the mainland's interests ahead of their own "by discouraging scores of U.S. manufacturers who intended to move their facilities to Puerto Rico and close their plants in the United States."[13]

By definition Puerto Rico took the crumbs, the leftovers from America's industrial plate. Indeed, even if the island had possessed a grand strategy for development, it would have been quite difficult to implement it because as a result of its colonial status, Puerto Rico took what it could get, not what it wanted nor what it might have needed. As one commonwealth economic development agency (Fomento) planner told Congress, "The firms that respond may be famous or unknown, employ 5 workers or 500, produce ladies undergarments or automobile parts."[14] Who knew? And who cared? The idea was to create jobs, and the lack of political power, linked to a rejection of the planned economy sought by Tugwell, meant that Puerto Rico based its development program on businesses that mainland Americans rejected.

Who came to Puerto Rico? The answer to that question is the Royal Littles of capitalism, the greedy entrepreneurs out to make as much money in as short a time as possible. By the mid–1950s it was the "unanimous opinion" of Fomento planners that tax exemption was the "main motivation" moving U.S. leftovers to the island. Indeed, even though the island's *before-tax* rate of return on investment was twice that of the mainland, investors came because they wanted to make four and five times the mainland profit. As an internal Fomento study noted, "Gold rush psychology is apparently still a part of the American scene and the possibility of making a killing seems to be much more of an attraction to many businessmen than does the rather high probability of a more moderate return."[15]

People out to make a killing had little interest in Puerto Rico's long-term development. Muñoz clearly understood this when he told colleagues that "for Puerto Rico's development to take place, we must allow three hundred sons of bitches to become millionaires."[16] Fine! Do it! But also establish a quid pro quo. Make certain that Puerto Rico got its hands on some of that profit because, by definition, a son of a bitch would not turn it over unless he or she was forced—by law—to do so.

The problem, noted as soon as Puerto Rico passed its tax legislation, was that the island's laws included no quid pro quos. In a 1948 article entitled "Taxpayer's Paradise in the Caribbean," two attorneys explained to men like Royal Little the beauty and uniqueness of Puerto Rico's program: "Tax exemption as used in the economic warfare between communities in the past, may be compared to the new Puerto Rican law only as older weapons of international warfare may be compared to the atomic bomb."[17]

Profits exploded in Puerto Rico. The terrible irony was that a 1921 law passed to give Americans a better chance against native and foreign competition would now be used to give Americans decided advantages over the locals, who, theoretically, were creating a self-sustaining economy.

Take the exemption from federal taxation. This made any accountant's heart beat faster because besides being "technically legal," a new business had the "affirmative statutory invitation" of the United States and of Puerto Rico.[18] Both countries wanted you to avoid taxes, but to achieve complete tax exemption, to make certain that Puerto Rico never got a dime of your profit, "*the corporate activities of the subsidiary should be carefully conducted with a view to liquidation rather than continuation of operations* [emphasis added]."[19]

This line was written in 1950. New businesses started out with an eye on liquidation because of a clause in the original 1921 legislation. If a corporation tried to return dividends in any one year, those dividends were subject to full federal taxation. But according to Section 112(b)(6), "No gain or loss shall be recognized upon the receipt by a corporation of property distributed in complete liquidation of another corporation." The 1921 idea was to give a break to corporations closing up shop in the Philippines. Presumably, if they were liquidating, they were in bad shape, so why not let them keep the little they had.

Arguably acceptable in the Philippines, this provision was a disaster in Puerto Rico. Accountants told their clients that "as a general rule the receipts of shareholders who are not bona fide residents of Puerto Rico will be maximized by foregoing dividends and liquidating the company or selling their stock after the termination of the exemption period or at such earlier date as they wish to realize on their investment."[20]

Lie—but be careful about it! This was also part of the advice offered to U.S. corporations about to establish a Puerto Rican subsidiary. The IRS frowned on liquidations that had no other purpose than avoiding taxes. It tended to ask pointed questions about enterprises that did exactly what the accountants and lawyers suggested—made plans to liquidate before they even opened for business.

To avoid such embarrassing questions attorney Robert Baker reminded clients that "merely because the liquidation of a Puerto Rican subsidiary results in tax savings is not a valid reason to conclude that the transfer was adopted in order to avoid federal taxes." You, the client, of course knew that was the case. But if the IRS proceeded on such a theory, they would invalidate all attempts to come within the tax laws they themselves had created. Liquidations were, after all, legal. So plan for a tax-free departure as soon as you open the subsidiary's books and never treat the liquidation differently from any other attempt to avoid taxes. Remember, above all, "that the courts have long ruled, in such cases, that the meaning of a line in the law is that you may intentionally go as close to it as you can if you do not pass it."[21]

And if you did pass it, remember that you could always get help in Puerto Rico. For the man telling clients how to liquidate worked for the Puerto Rican government. Indeed, Robert Baker was the director of the island's Office of Industrial Tax Exemption.[22]

Muñoz and Moscoso were asleep at the wheel. Why, after all, would absentee factory owners behave any differently than the absentee owners of Central Guanica or Aguirre? Even a cursory glance at the evidence presented at Senator Tobey's 1948 hearings showed that the Royal Littles of capitalism would happily dance, all the way to the bank, on any tax line established in Washington or San Juan. To get profits into the hands of locals, to have any chance of creating a self-sustaining economy, Muñoz and Moscoso had to get their hands on some of those profits before, following the advice of the island's director of taxation, corporations used liquidation as the legal route to a tax-free bonanza.

This absurd situation, which was at the heart of Operation Bootstrap, existed because Muñoz and Moscoso lacked meaningful political power because they were in a desperate hurry to make good on their promises to the Puerto Rican people and because they believed that corporations would come to the island only if they got what they wanted. Thus, instead of judging the efficacy of the tax exemption program in terms of its contribution to self-sustaining growth, Muñoz and Moscoso asked: What do the investors want? What can we do to make them happy?[23] Focusing on numbers—ten factories in 1947, thirty-one in 1948—Muñoz and Moscoso refused to listen to the criticisms made as soon as they began Operation Bootstrap.

One internal study noted that "tax exemption in Puerto Rico had an anemic justification as a rational subsidy." Why? Because "there was an inverse [and perverse] relationship between need and assistance."[24] Companies most in need of help, the ones who failed to turn a profit in the first years of operation, would never get a nickel in tax exemption subsidy. But the companies who made the largest profits not only got the greatest subsidy (i.e., no taxes) but also received an additional motivation to liquidate their profitable operations as soon as their tax exemption expired. After all, the only way to get the money out tax free was to close up shop (or ask the federal and Puerto Rican governments to offer more incentives to keep companies that just by asking the question had indicated the depth of their commitment to Puerto Rico's economic development).

This was perverse indeed. It was also by any standard irrational. To make things worse, the Puerto Rican government played politics with the tax laws. The island's Industrial Tax Exemption Act contained a list of forty-two designated industries, each singled out for tax exemption because of its unique potential for development. So far so good. But what about already-established businesses? Did an *existing* operation in a designated industry also receive tax exemption, or was it only the new industries?

The law was fuzzy here, and locals understandably complained about the advantages being offered to outsiders. Americans were getting tax exemptions while islanders were getting tax bills. To solve this political problem Muñoz and Moscoso allowed their underlings *to exempt existing firms.* Indeed, a Fomento employee noted that "without the benefit of any inquiry, the policy followed was to exempt existing firms as soon as tax exemption was granted to a new manufacturer in the same designated industry and the new firm established industrial facilities."[25]

Say you were an American planning to manufacture shoes in Puerto Rico. Once you—just one of you—had your plants established and a factory set for production, existing shoe manufacturers would also receive tax-exempt status. One fellow had been in business since 1932 "and realized sizable and consistent profits all during the decade of the forties." He nonetheless got tax exempt status; he stopped paying $50,000 a year in island taxes, and he never promised to expand his operation, or hire new workers, because he already had a mature company in an economy that was inviting competition from abroad.[26]

As the Fomento employee noted, "Tax exemption for such a firm had a weak justification." In economic terms yes. In political terms, no. Muñoz made a lot of friends by extending tax exemption to existing operations. If he simultaneously reduced his tax revenues and undercut

Operation Bootstrap, well, that was a small price to pay for more of the political stability so essential to luring U.S. investors. Remember, too, that by 1959 and 1960, most of the exemptions of existing as well as new operations expired. Puerto Rico would then tax the thriving corporations generated by its tax exemption programs, and the government would thus be in the enviable position of having substantial resources to develop a self-sustaining economy. Muñoz would have used the sons of bitches instead of being used by them.

He would have used them, that is,

. . . If the most profitable corporations didn't liquidate, which is exactly what they planned to do.

. . . If the people in Nashua, New Hampshire, and in other mainland communities threatened by Puerto Rican labor didn't press for higher wages on the island, which is exactly what they suggested they would do.

. . . If the profitless new industries somehow survived, even though they failed to receive the subsidy they desperately needed.

. . . If it were possible to develop an economy with a "fishing net" approach to industrial development. As one Fomento employee noted, the firms established in the early years "at best represented entrepreneurial mediocrity, at worst, they were a motley troupe of entrepreneurial migrants."[27]

. . . If Puerto Rico established precise quid pro quos for its tax exemption gift, which was difficult when Teodoro Moscoso made speeches noting that "tax exemption requires only a minimum of administration," for example into the mid-1970s Fomento did not even have a list of the island's tax-exempt corporations.[28]

. . . And, finally, if Puerto Rico avoided the political turmoil that would turn away even the most greedy capitalist.

Muñoz can and should be faulted for failing to heed the warnings of his many *contemporary* critics. But recall the period. The critics voiced their concerns from inside the island's government, and virtually no one, except Royal Little's accountants, read tax exemption articles printed in law journals. On the contrary, in Washington and San Juan Luis Muñoz Marín generally received rave notices for his efforts to create a U.S. Caribbean showcase; few senators or congressmen knew anything about the island, and it would be ten years before the fault lines in Operation Bootstrap played havoc with the rosy statistics of substantial economic growth.

In the meantime, Muñoz focused his efforts on political and military affairs. He became the island's first elected governor, he made the advocacy of independence an illegal activity, he supervised the writing of a constitution, he achieved his long-desired Commonwealth status, he got the United Nations to take Puerto Rico off its list of non-self-governing territories, and he reluctantly gave in to virtually every demand made by U.S. sailors and soldiers.

It was a long list of "achievements." It began with a trip Admiral William Leahy made to the island in April of 1948.

Admiral Leahy was Harry S. Truman's troubleshooter and, as a former governor of Puerto Rico, the perfect man to settle disputes that threatened to forever damage relations between islanders and the U.S. military. For example, right after the war ended later governor Roberto Sanchez Vilella asked sailors to make good on their promises and leave El Morro. The land had no military value and the state of national emergency was long over: Would the sailors kindly give back what they had borrowed? Not if they could help it. Officers enjoyed the golf course they had constructed, their living quarters were superb, and using "crude and arrogant" manners they informed Sanchez "that for the officers to play golf and enjoy the club was indeed a national necessity."[29]

Leahy's job was to settle what the president called "real estate problems."[30] He was to survey the twenty-five separate installations borrowed, confiscated, or purchased from the Puerto Ricans as a result of the 1941 state of emergency and report back on what was needed and what was not.

Some of the admiral's decisions were easy. El Morro should be returned to the Puerto Rican people at once. Six acres used as a barracks—the facility was right next to San Juan's main park—should be returned to the island's government. Punta Escambrón, the "best beach" in San Juan, and the only one available for the general public, should be, if possible, returned by the U.S. Army. The beach was used only for enlisted personnel, and locals understandably resented soldiers swimming while they themselves watched.[31]

Again, the admiral only made recommendations. The army, for example, read the admiral's report and told President Truman that besides the beach, they had a "battery of permanently emplaced 6 inch seacoast guns" at Punta Escambrón. They didn't want to return the guns and they didn't want to lose "the $70,000" they had spent to improve the beach. Thus, "since the battery is required for harbor defense purposes and the site contains the only beach available to enlisted personnel, it is recommended that the Army retain this facility."[32]

The army won. And so too did the navy in a dispute that concerned acreage far more significant than even the best beach in San Juan. In May 1947 Secretary of the Navy James Forrestal had told Interior Secretary Julius Krug that sailors meant to make "*permanent* [my emphasis] use of land on Culebra and Vieques for naval maneuvers."[33] The navy had once again changed its mind about the Roosevelt Roads facility: The base would be permanently required. The navy revoked the permission it had given Viequesans to use grazing lands on their island, and, most important of all, the navy wanted anyone living on the land evacuated at once. Maneuvers began at the turn of the year, and "it would be entirely impractical to open these areas for pasture because of the very short periods between bombings, landings, and bombardments throughout the year."[34]

On Culebra the navy wanted another 700 acres on the tiny island they already dominated. Sailors said they needed the land for amphibious training and bombing. Leahy told the president that he was "unable to see any military necessity for the acquisition of additional property on the island of Culebra," but his colleagues disagreed. A handwritten note on the copy of the report at the Naval Historical Center states that "this [the 700 additional acres] is needed for impact bombing, protection of the observers, and further to be able to keep out natives."[35]

The navy never had a reputation for subtlety. Success, however, was another matter. In fact, despite repeated requests from Governor Jesús Piñero to rescind their decision, the navy persisted and Piñero generally confined his complaints to internal channels because of a warning received from James Davis of the Interior Department. In a letter dated January 20, 1948, Davis "fully shared the Governor's disappointment that the Navy has not demonstrated a more cooperative attitude"; and even though "I think it may be entirely possible to exert some pressure through your friends on the Hill, I would advise against any congressional blast which might have an adverse effect on other matters in which you want congressional help."[36] Translation: If you want to get rid of the Jones Act auditor who came along with the permission to elect a governor, if you want to have any chance to write a constitution for yourselves, and if you want help on the economy, shut up about even the most flagrant violations of the navy's word.

For a while Piñero did keep quiet. But the military's requests were so extensive—for example, there was also a major battle about the return of lands required for the island's proposed international airport—that Piñero refused to give in. He took his case to the president, telling Truman, "I have a serious social and economic problem on my hands, caused by the occupation of four-fifths of the island of Vieques by the Navy."[37]

The president's final word on Puerto Rico's "real estate problems" was a July 7 letter to the secretary of the navy. The secretary immediately gave it to his admirals, and they used it to club Piñero into submission. In a conversation tape recorded the same day the admirals showed the president's letter to Piñero, Admirals D. E. Barbey and Maher discussed tactics and strategy. They had a press release the governor had to approve, and they saw no way he could refuse to do so, but what were Oscar Chapman and Irwin Silverman (of the Interior Department) doing in Puerto Rico? And why was Chapman "staying with the Governor?" If he was on the island in an official capacity, Admiral Maher said, bring him in on the press release. Otherwise, "you may be able to terminate his visit by showing him what the President has authorized."

Admiral Barbey: "I should think so!" Admiral Maher: "I think his business is all finished."[38]

Not quite. Later that day Admiral Barbey had a meeting with Piñero, Chapman, and Silverman. Admiral Barbey announced,

I informed the Governor that I had a copy of the letter from the President to the Secretary of the Navy in which he outlined the action he desired [e.g., the navy got the 700 acres on Culebra] to be taken in connection with matters of mutual interest to the Insular Government and the Navy. I further told him that I had received a telephone call from the Navy Department in which they proposed that a joint press release be made on this matter because of local interest, and that I had with me a proposed press release which in effect was a summary of the President's directive.[39]

This opening salvo caught Piñero by surprise. He had never seen the letter before, nor, apparently, had Chapman or Silverman. However, once the governor read both the letter and the press release, he refused to accept the navy's victory. That was ok with Admiral Barbey. He understood the governor's "disappointment." But there was also reality to be taken into consideration. Or as Admiral Barbey told Admiral Maher later in the day, in another tape-recorded conversation: "I suggested that it would be quite unwise for him to take a position in opposition to that of the President."

A man who knew a raw deal when he saw one, Piñero hesitated. He looked for support from the Interior Department, but the president's letter had silenced the governor's now former allies. "Mr. Silverman agreed that such action [opposition] would not be advisable whereupon the Governor suggested that the press release could come out of Washington."[40]

Give the governor credit because despite this presidential club, Piñero still tried to find a way to beat Truman, the navy, and the Interior Department. It was, however, a losing battle, made clear in the final lines of the president's letter: "It is my desire that the Navy Department continue, as heretofore, to give consideration to the plans and requirements of the Insular Government . . . with the view that assistance may be rendered to these plans and requirements when *consistent with the requirements of national defense* [my emphasis]."[41]

Put promises, poverty, and human rights up against the requirements of national defense and the Puerto Ricans lost—each and every time, and not only in the court of presidential politics. In the naval maneuvers conducted in and around Vieques and Culebra, the "good guys" had names like Jones, the "bad guys" names like Fernández. And in another set of 1948 maneuvers, the Americans defended themselves against the Puerto Ricans, who, in this case, were the invading Communist forces![42]

There were alternatives. Piñero, for example, instead of finally saluting his commander-in-chief, could have sided with Albizu Campos. The leader of the Nationalist party had returned to the island in December 1947, and as dedicated to revolution as ever, he preached overthrow of the colonial government. He understood that like the Unionist party earlier in the century, the Puerto Rican legislature had asked for independence in 1946, only to be told that Congress decided the meaning of self-determination. Thus, when gubernatorial candidate Muñoz Marín lectured Albizu about Puerto Rican democracy, the revolutionary answered him in this manner: "It is a supreme insolence for Muñoz Marín to speak of democracy. Muñoz Marín must stop saying such insolences and if he does not do it, we will stop him."[43]

To Albizu the Americans had spent ten years (1937–1947) acting in character. Revolution was the only response to a half century of U.S. colonialism. If Muñoz supported the Americans, then Muñoz had to go—peacefully if possible, by force if necessary.

Muñoz responded by arguing that the Nationalist leader threatened the political and economic changes the Populares had labored so long and hard to achieve. No one was going to invest money in an unstable political situation, and Congress would never concede the island's right to develop a constitution unless Puerto Ricans, among other things, gave into the navy's demands and stopped telling the truth. Muñoz, for example, would soon tell Congress that "by all modern definitions of what constitutes colonialism, it [the Federal Government's] has not been a colonial policy in Puerto Rico." In fact, although "the Federal Government has at times been more helpful than at other times, at all times its attitude has been one of helpfulness toward Puerto Rico."[44]

Whatever his motives, a man willing to rewrite history in such a thorough fashion (e.g., in 1929 Muñoz had written that "Puerto Rico is a sweat shop that has a company store, the United States"[45]) was capable of anything, even a law that *El Mundo* said was designed "to inspire terror in the minds of Puerto Rico's citizens."[46]

Using the United States as their frame of reference, Muñoz (still head of the insular Senate) and his colleagues modeled La Mordaza (the gag law) after the Smith Act legislation of 1940. But instead of fearing Fascists and Communists, the Populares feared the violence promised by Albizu and, even more importantly, the renewed spread of independence sentiment. For example, when Albizu was invited to speak at the University of Puerto Rico in April 1948, students replaced the U.S. flag with Puerto

Rico's banner. When university authorities not only refused to let Albizu speak but ordered Puerto Rico's flag removed, the turmoil reached such proportions that the university's rector indefinitely shut down the university.[47]

Signed into law by Governor Piñero on June 10, 1948, La Mordaza presented Puerto Ricans with a contradiction in terms. In the middle of the colony's first chance in history to elect their own governor, they could do whatever they pleased so long as they remembered that "it was a grave felony, punishable by a maximum of ten years in jail or a maximum fine of $10,000, to encourage, plead, advise, or preach the necessity, desirability, or suitability of overthrowing, paralyzing, or destroying the insular government, or any political subdivision of this, by means of force of violence."

In addition, it was also a grave felony to "print, publish, edit, circulate, sell, distribute, or publicly exhibit any writing or publication which encourages, pleads, advises, or preaches the necessity, desirability, or suitability of overthrowing the insular government."[48]

Accompanying the law was an enforcement apparatus that had—and continues to have—a chilling effect on Puerto Rican society. In 1991 many islanders, whether on a street in Ponce or a bar in Hartford, still refused to openly discuss their independence sentiments. It has become a widespread assumption of the culture that espousing these beliefs means definite trouble for the speaker and potential problems for his or her family.

Muñoz and his colleagues helped create this assumption in 1948 by (1) passing the gag law and (2) attaching to it an enforcement apparatus that substantially silenced a very talkative society. What Muñoz did was instruct his minions to monitor the conversations and discussions of potential or presumed "subversives." In one of the first cases brought under La Mordaza, Dr. Arturo González, attending an independence meeting, said that Muñoz was "a cheat and without shame." What this had to do with violence was difficult to see; indeed, after the 1948 elections the official who wanted to arrest Dr. González admitted that nothing had been discovered to charge the doctor with a violation of La Mordaza.[49]

But the suspicion? And the fear thrown into the minds of others? The law scared people so much that two years before Senator Joseph McCarthy created a similar atmosphere in the United States, and four years before Arthur Miller staged *The Crucible*, Muñoz and his supporters started their own witch hunt in Puerto Rico.

The terrible irony of the law was that it could never stop Albizu or his followers. A man who wore his guns on the outside, a man who preached revolution in New York City as he simultaneously disregarded the existence of federal parole officials, was not going to change his politics nor zipper his lips. As an April 1948 Naval Intelligence Report from the San Juan office indicated, although the Nationalists were not on the attorney general's list of subversives, their "advocation of violent overthrow of the U.S. Government certainly classify them as such. . . . Albizu has not been apprehended by the FBI for fear of creating a "martyr" situation." However, "he and his followers are being watched closely and in the event of *probable* violence, a special law enforcement squad is organized to arrest him immediately [my emphasis]."[50]

Muñoz knew that Albizu would never remain silent. How could he not after listening to Albizu for more than twenty-five years? The real and intended impact of the gag law was on anyone who sought independence; as Muñoz himself said in 1943, the independence ideals were "indeniably those of the majority of Puerto Ricans."[51] But, in 1948, the majority could threaten the political and economic changes Muñoz deemed essential to Puerto Rico's future. Thus, long before anyone fired a shot, Muñoz sought to maintain stability by silencing the majority. Since, over forty-three years later, people are still hesitant about voicing their independence ideals, one could certainly argue that Muñoz achieved his goal.

In the political campaign itself Muñoz promised action on the ideal he was simultaneously trying to suppress. On July 4, 1948, he told his listeners that "all of us, absolutely all of us, wish that this obsolete system which we call a colonial system is ended. The form of political relationship in which the United States holds Puerto Rico is not just. Neither is it intelligent. It is unjust and unintelligent."[52]

To rectify the situation Muñoz called for another plebiscite. But speaking to voters who would tolerate no halfway measures, this plebiscite would include only two choices: independence or statehood. Agreed, the plebiscite would occur only when Puerto Ricans thought their economic conditions had improved to the point where they could sustain independence or statehood. But once that stage was reached, the end of colonialism was in sight. As Muñoz put it in a commitment he and the Populares repeatedly made to the Puerto Rican electorate, "I am going to ask the people of the United States, if the Puerto Ricans allow us to do it with their votes, to establish this high precedent to finish in the world the liquidation of the colonial system which began to be liquidated the 4th of July of 1776."[53]

Muñoz also promised a constitution, jobs, and political stability. He deftly wielded the handful of appealing promises that enabled him to become the island's first elected governor and the Populares to win another overwhelming if tarnished victory. Over 70 percent of the electorate voted Popular (statehooders got 16 percent of the vote, and the first time on the ballot the Independence party got 12 percent of the vote), but there were so many abstentions that Muñoz resorted to blaming the immigrants: It was all those Puerto Ricans in New York that explained the low voter turnout. Equally important, La Mordaza, Albizu, and the turmoil at the university created such a fear of "blood in the streets" that many islanders voted for the Populares only to prevent the triumph of the Independence party.[54]

In Puerto Rico Muñoz's victory was an overwhelming mandate for a constitution, jobs, social stability, and a choice—in the near future—between independence and statehood.

In Washington Muñoz sang a very different tune. One scholar argues that Muñoz and Resident Commissioner Antonio Fernos-Isern lied because they saw no way to obtain from a conservative Congress the changes they had promised to the Puerto Rican people.[55] Thus, they said one thing in Washington and another in San Juan or Mayagüez because there was no other way to obtain the assistance they deemed essential to Puerto Rico's future.

Whatever their motives, the historical record proves that Muñoz and Fernos-Isern made a fundamental about-face during 1949. They disregarded the promised plebiscite and only got the promised constitution by forgetting what they had told the Puerto Rican people during the 1948 elections. For example, in July 1949 Muñoz told the president that Puerto Rico's real goal was "a new state" (it had no name yet), and in March 1950 Fernos-Isern told his congressional colleagues that in asking for the "organization of a constitutional government in Puerto Rico," he wanted everyone to understand that "the Federal provisions of the present organic act would be reaffirmed under my bill. They are *needful regulations* [my emphasis] for the establishment and maintenance of proper relations between the island and the mainland and the Federal government." Why? Because all Puerto Ricans wanted was "to adopt a local constitution and *reaffirm their station within this Union* [my emphasis]."[56]

In his testimony before the committee that would authorize Puerto Rico to draw up a constitution, Muñoz tried to wiggle out of the handcuffs he had put on himself and Puerto Rico. Asked by Representative William Lemke, "May I sum it up this way: You prefer self government under the Federal Government of the United States?" Muñoz answered, "That is right," but not a state because "we have no mandate from the people in that direction."

Lemke: "But rather as a possession or territory of the United States."

Muñoz: "Certainly not as a possession, sir. I do not believe that some Americans can be a possession of other Americans."[57]

Of course they could! The Organic Act to which Muñoz and Fernos-Isern had wedded themselves specifically said (and continues to say) that "the provisions of this Act shall apply to the Island of Puerto Rico and to the adjacent islands *belonging* to the United States." The Interior Department Office which controlled Puerto Rico was called the Division of Territories and Island Possessions; and the corporations that Muñoz and Moscoso were bringing to the island were called (and still are called) "possessions corporations."

Muñoz was caught in a web of his own weaving and, try as he might, the only way to avoid the obvious was to lie about it. For as an Interior Department official put it to a citizen curious about Puerto Rico's political status, "Since Puerto Rico is not the seat of the government of the United States, and has not been admitted to statehood by the Congress, nor given its independence thus becoming a foreign country, it must remain a territory."[58] And an unincorporated one at that.

Muñoz tried to find another word for his "new state," but Congress again and again emphasized the limited significance of Puerto Rico's proposed constitution:

Congressmen Fred Crawford: "At no time have I ever thought Puerto Rico could ever support statehood. Certainly Puerto Rico cannot support any type of independence. She would have to be a puppet of some other country. But Puerto Rico can be a *colonial possession* [my emphasis] and have a great deal to say about her own government under which the Puerto Ricans live."[59]

Congressman Javits: "How does the Congress inhibit them in this particular statue? It says that the only thing we agree to now is that you shall have a constitution within the organic act. . . . Congress controls the organic act whether it passes this bill or not, and it will control it when that Constitution is returned to it."[60]

Senate Committee on Interior and Insular Affairs: "The measure [for a constitution] would not change Puerto Rico's fundamental political, social and economic relationship to the United States."[61]

Congressman Walter Judd: "Is it not true that this bill merely recognizes the fact which everybody knows in his daily experience, namely, that you cannot expect to take a child in the third or sixth grade and move him up to the twelfth grade or into college or into a postgraduate school without going through the various grades between?"[62]

Oscar Chapman, secretary of the interior: "The bill *merely* [my emphasis] authorizes the people of Puerto Rico to adopt their own constitution and to organize a local government. . . . The bill under consideration would not change Puerto Rico's political, social, and economic relationship to the United States."[63]

To Congress Puerto Ricans never got out of grammar school. As Silverman told Senator Tobey in the hearings about Textron, they needed a period of further "tutelage" from their U.S. teachers and they would get it. Nonetheless, as they learned how to behave like adults, they remained a colony of the United States. This conclusion rests on a logical assessment of the evidence: *If Puerto Rico was a colony before the bill was passed, and the bill made no fundamental changes in Puerto Rico's political, social, and economic relationship to the United States, then Puerto Rico had to be a colony after the bill was passed.*[64]

More than anyone else, Luis Muñoz refused to concede that Congress meant what it said. How could he return home and tell the island that all he got was more of the same. So he told his own people that "the agreement ought to be interpreted in the form that is most liberal and most favorable to Puerto Rico and to the fraternal understanding between Puerto Rico and the United States. . . . No one ought to interest themselves in interpreting the agreement in another way."[65]

No one. Except the Congress of the United States, the Interior Department, and the president, all of whom had explicitly told Muñoz that there was only one interpretation of the agreement: Nothing fundamental had changed.

Called Public Law 600, the bill to permit islanders to write their own constitution passed on July 3, 1950. Attached to the bill was the new Federal Relations Act, which still said the same old thing: Puerto Rico "belonged" to the United States. However, islanders would have the right to a local government if they first registered to vote, in November 1950, and then approved, in a planned referendum, the government's desire to write and establish its own constitution.

Before voters had a chance to do anything, Albizu and his followers tried to stop the process that would, in their eyes, perpetuate Puerto Rico's colonial status. As J. Edgar Hoover put it in a November 8, 1950, report to President Truman, "At 12:00 noon on October 30, 1950, an attack was made on the Governor's Palace at San Juan." Four Nationalists were killed, and "at this point the National Guard was called out by Governor Luis Muñoz Marín." The guard immediately tried to stop the attacks directed against island police and against federal facilities. "At Jayuya the Post Office was set afire and the Post Office, Selective Service Office and the Farm Security Office all burned. In San Juan there was an exchange of gun fire between the National Guard, Police and Vidal Santiago, one of the Nationalists who was wounded [trying to assassinate Muñoz]." By November 1, the insular police were busy "rounding up all known Nationalists," Albizu Campos was himself under arrest, and "no further acts of violence were reported in Puerto Rico."[66]

But in Washington, D.C., two Nationalists assaulted Blair House, the temporary residence of President Harry S. Truman. Oscar Collazo fired at one guard while his companion, Griselio Torresola, fired at two other officers guarding the president's residence. Torresola was killed at once, so was one of the guards; two other officers were injured and Collazo lay on the ground, also gravely wounded.

Almost forty years later Oscar Collazo tried to explain his motivation: "It was not important if we did or did not reach President Truman. That was secondary. It was sufficient to create a scandal that focused world attention on the colonial case of Puerto Rico. And the assault was a success."[67]

In the sense that it focused attention on Puerto Rico, Collazo was correct. But instead of moving people to address the issue of colonialism, the attack on Blair House and the Nationalist assaults all over Puerto Rico moved U.S. newspapers and congressmen to label Albizu and his associates a bunch of "ruthless terrorists." Commentators focused on the means used, rather than the reasons for, the assaults;[68] meanwhile, in the United States and on the island, officials rounded up literally thousands of real or suspected Nationalists.

Muñoz understandably took great precautions; Albizu did, after all, stage a revolution. But in his efforts to stop the violence Muñoz used the gag law to silence not only those who had participated in the revolution but those who, for example, had merely applauded at Nationalist meetings. When the referendum on the constitution took place, on June 4, 1951,

the island was being subjected to a rule close to that of martial law. . . . In this atmosphere the Independence Party, second largest on the island, decided to boycott the proceedings for drafting a constitution because . . . in such an atmosphere it can hardly be said that the Puerto Ricans were being given an opportunity to make a free choice of government.[69]

Congress and Muñoz were nevertheless gratified by the results of the referendum. Fully 76 percent of those who did vote supported efforts to create a constitution; in August 1951 the Populares won seventy of the ninety-two delegates elected to the constitutional assembly, and when the statehood delegates asked for amnesty for persons imprisoned under the gag law, Muñoz responded by coining this phrase: "They are not political prisoners but imprisoned politicians."[70]

Serving an eighty-year prison sentence, Albizu remained in jail; the constitution was ready for the people's approval by the turn of the year, and in March 1952 Puerto Ricans overwhelmingly endorsed the work of their representatives.

The trouble started when Congress got the constitution. Delegates had included a provision, in Section 20 of the Bill of Rights, that every islander had the right to obtain work. This infuriated many congressmen who in their desire to erase this right underlined what the new constitution did and did not mean for Puerto Rico. Congressman Halleck of Indiana said that "Puerto Rico is not independent. Puerto Rico is not a sovereign state. They are yet a protectorate of ours."[71]

There was the word again: protectorate! Muñoz kept arguing that Congress could never act in a unilateral fashion.[72] Meanwhile Congress kept telling him who was superior and who inferior in the relationship between the United States and Puerto Rico. Congressman Crawford, for example, discussed repeal of the law that gave Puerto Rico the right to keep all excise taxes. He noted, "Suppose you did repeal that law; suppose Puerto Rico misbehaved, let us say, and you decided to call them to task, to spank them a little bit."[73]

Well, you could spank them! And not only because Congressman Crawford said so. In the Senate hearings regarding Puerto Rico's constitution and its significance, James Davis, head of the Interior Department's Office of Territories, assured the senators—who pressed for this assurance—that

nothing you are doing here in any way weakens or breaches the full power of Congress under the Constitution of the United States. . . . It [the island's government] will be changed in only *very minor respects* [my emphasis]. . . . The alteration in the situation is not in the powers of Congress. . . . It is in the right of the people of Puerto Rico to write the laws under which they are to be locally governed.[74]

Write them yes. Finally approve them no. Congress erased the right to work clause, Muñoz called the constitutional assembly back into session; they did as they were told, and on July 25, 1952, the fifty-fourth anniversary of the U.S. invasion, Puerto Rico proclaimed itself a commonwealth. In a symbolic gesture at the end of the celebration, Muñoz raised the Puerto Rican flag beside the American and, on the island, the two banners flew as equals.

To maintain this image Muñoz had one primary problem: reality. For example, as soon as President Truman signed the law approving Puerto Rico's constitution, Muñoz pushed the administration to take the island's case to the United Nations. Get Puerto Rico off the list of colonial states so that the Populares could tell anyone who asked that the island's new status had the world's endorsement.

Truman and his administration happily and eagerly obliged Muñoz. However, problems appeared as soon as administration and island officials compared their proposed presentations to the United Nations. On September 25, 1952, responding to a proposal from Muñoz Marín, James Davis, director of the Interior Department's Office of Territories (the phrase "and Island Possessions" had been dropped from the division's name), told the governor how and why he had edited Muñoz's work.

First, "the statement that Puerto Rico has ceased to be a territory of the United States has been deleted. . . . If Puerto Rico has not become an independent nation or a State of the Union, and we are all agreed that it has not, then as a matter of domestic constitutional law it must still be a territory of the United States." Davis stressed that the key point was Puerto Rico's "unique" territorial status. The governor had to remember that "the letter you will send to the President will become a public document and we want to be sure that it contains no statements that are controversial or not susceptible of clear documentation, unless it is absolutely essential that the statement be made in order to make our case."[75]

Second on Davis's list—and what a nice touch—was an added reference "to the action of the Constitutional Convention coming after the action of Congress, showing that it was an agency of Puerto Rico that took final action to bring the Constitution into effect."

Thus, even though Congress repeatedly indicated that it had the ultimate authority—for example, the statements of Congressmen Charles Halleck and Javits—we will tell the United Nations that Puerto Ricans ultimately govern themselves.

Third, and this was the biggest disagreement of all,

the flat statement that Puerto Rican laws cannot be repealed or modified by external authority, and that Puerto Rico's status and the terms of its association cannot be changed without Puerto Rico's full agreement has been modified to indicate that this is Puerto Rico's view.

In any case, like the reference to Puerto Rico's status as a territory of the United States, this statement need not necessarily be in the letter. You have a right to express your opinion, of course. . . . The alternative would be to take out the sentence entirely. The decision is yours.[76]

Muñoz waited to answer this letter. In the middle of a heated election campaign he certainly wanted to put his best foot forward at the United Nations. And he did. His party won fully 67 percent of the vote, but the Independence party, with the gag law in effect and under a state of almost martial law, nevertheless won 19 percent of the votes cast. That was not only a significant achievement for the Independence party; it was also an achievement that made U.N. certification all the more urgent and important.

Muñoz's letter to Davis (dated January 17, 1953) resolved none of the differences between the governor's and the administration's interpretation of Commonwealth status.[77] In fact, the battles continued into the Eisenhower administration, and even then they were never resolved. Jack Tate, legal advisor to the State Department, told Muñoz and Fernos-Isern in February 1953 that "neither the Federal legislation or the legislative history of these laws [i.e., the laws about the island's constitution] support the flat statement that there is a compact between the United States and Puerto Rico, with the consequences that Congress has waived its constitutional authority."[78]

Muñoz disagreed. Tate held fast. And the State Department's view prevailed, except that when Ambassador Henry Cabot Lodge took Puerto Rico's case to the United Nations, he began to use Muñoz's interpretation of Commonwealth status. The incredible irony—Lodge contradicted what Congress had repeatedly told Muñoz and Fernos-Isern, while the two Puerto Ricans focused on Commonwealth powers they never mentioned to Congress—existed because the United States could not say in public what it told Muñoz in private. To admit that Puerto Rico was an unincorporated territory, and to further indicate that Congress had ultimate authority over Puerto Rico's destiny, was to admit what Lodge had to deny: that Puerto Rico was still a colony because its constitution never changed its fundamental status.

Lodge handled America's about-face with aplomb. He and his colleagues assured the delegates that Fernos-Isern's presentation was perfectly correct: There was a compact between Puerto Rico and the United States, the new status would grow and be modified, and, most important of all, it could only be changed by mutual consent.[79]

Delegates listened but, oddly enough, the debate soon revolved around a procedural issue crucial to every member of the United Nations: Who was competent to judge whether a people did or did not govern their own destiny? The nations that still owned colonies wanted to keep the power to judge status in a committee they controlled. Meanwhile, the nations represented by the articulate Indian delegate wanted the entire U.N. General Assembly to judge such a crucial issue.

Suddenly, instead of a question of self-rule, U.N. approval of Puerto Rico's new status was linked to the question of competency. What the United States hoped to do was get members to approve of Puerto Rico but reject the competency clause that was now part of the same resolution. So to get support for Puerto Rico's noncolonial status, the United States threatened nations that still owned, and wanted to continue owning, colonies:

The U.S. affirmed that it was in the administering members' best interest to support the resolution—even if the damaging competence clause remained—because a rejection might encourage independence movements in non-self governing territories and reinforce the view prevailing among many United Nations' members that full self government could be achieved through independence.[80]

Puerto Rico would be "free" as long as other nations remained in chains! That was the United States' deal, with one additional contradiction. To get the votes of developing nations Ambassador Lodge said that President Dwight Eisenhower would grant independence any time the Puerto Ricans wanted it.[81]

On November 27, 1953, the United Nations took Puerto Rico off its list of non-self-governing territories. The island's was the first case to be completely settled by the world body, and as long as no one inspected what went on in private, it was an admirable achievement for the United States and for the Commonwealth of Puerto Rico. Eisenhower had reaffirmed U.S. commitment to self-determination, and Muñoz had the United States on record in support of his interpretation of Commonwealth status.

With the U.N. endorsement settled, the next step was to advertise Puerto Rico. Entire issues of popular journals celebrated the wonders of the Commonwealth, while Muñoz stressed that this (now permanent) solution to the status problem had enabled Puerto Ricans to leap over the historical barriers that impeded others: "Upon leaving the barren shores of colonialism, Puerto Rico decided to bypass the turbulent waters of nationalism altogether."[82]

"Unique" was the operative word in almost any discourse celebrating Puerto Rico's political achievement. As intelligent as ever, Muñoz used the cold war to his advantage—look at what we and the Americans have done without communism!—and Washington happily went along. Indeed, Muñoz became Latin America's spokesman for the American Dream, a governor who without a blush in sight lectured the Senate Foreign Relations Committee on proper approaches to economic development. Private enterprise, for example, was an efficient tool for change; "we are all for it." But don't force others to accept it. Let them use Puerto Rico as a model. "You see, we were never faced with the idea that it [free enterprise] was a doctrine that had to be followed. We were allowed to try it in our own way and then change our mind because of our own experience."[83]

That experience did produce problems. Due to intense public pressure, Muñoz pardoned Albizu Campos in September 1953, and no shaper of U.S. public opinion asked why a so-called terrorist received support from all segments of Puerto Rican and Latin American society. And when, on March 1, 1954, four Nationalists wounded five congressmen in an attack on the House of Representatives, the attackers were described as fanatics. Their aim was to call the world's attention to Puerto Rico's colonial status, but instead of noting the similarities between the note found in the purse of Lolita Lebron, "My life I give for the freedom of my country," and the American admonition "Give me liberty or give me death," newspapers headlined that "Eisenhower Target for Fanatics Also."[84]

The 1950s became a time to celebrate Puerto Rico; in a series of 1955 hearings about minimum wages, Muñoz actually heard himself called a "Godsend to the Puerto Rican people."[85] But he also heard Congress tell him who was inferior, and who superior, in the "compact" between the island and the United States. As one economist stressed, in the "sweatshop" phase of Operation Bootstrap the companies that came to Puerto Rico used a great deal of cheap labor to increase their profit margins; they relied on below-minimum wages, and as in the 1948 Textron hearings, that upset Congress: "To continue this situation in Puerto Rico is just inviting American firms to go down there and put up subsidiary plants and exploit the cheap wage rates in Puerto Rico. . . . Can you justify the continuation of that kind of system."[86]

Muñoz fielded this question by avoiding it; he favored wage rates that rose as soon as possible, and he stressed that his government never accepted runaway industries, but the low wages were another matter: "Any rigid figure is profoundly dangerous to the further economic development of the people of Puerto Rico." With this sentence Muñoz again underlined the point made by Albizu in the 1930s. An economic program that revolved around the political will of mainland decision makers was profoundly vulnerable and never self-sustaining. Muñoz, for example, despite all the claims of Commonwealth powers, told the House of Representatives, "I am not questioning the legality" of Congress setting wage rates, but he also noted that the morality of such a policy was dubious at best, especially in an area that "vitally" affected the Puerto Rican people.[87]

Before and after Commonwealth Muñoz came to Washington because Congress had the powers and he did not. He was as dependent as ever, and as vulnerable as ever, because Operation Bootstrap was not putting nearly enough of his people to work. Chairman Graham Barden told Muñoz:

I believe on one occasion after I had gone around the island and seen hundreds with machete knives cutting grass on these sides of the roads I came back and told you what I had seen and asked you why you did not get a mowing machine that would cut so much more grass so much faster. You looked me very calmly in the eye and said, Well, if I do, what I am going to put them to doing?[88]

One answer was keep them on the farm. The Populares came to power on the issue of land reform so, on the acreage owned by the government, they employed far more people than was necessary. However, instead of developing a means for farm workers to indefinitely earn a decent living, the government simply subsidized inefficient enterprises because the Populares lacked any strategy to use agriculture as one source of the nation's revitalization. Workers flocked to the cities because rural opportunities never materialized, because the emphasis on industrialization undermined any prestige attached to agricultural occupations, because the land under cultivation decreased, and because the Populare administrators acted like Frank Dillingham and his mainland associates.[89]

An anthropologist who investigated one of the Land Authority operations noted that the "foremen identified themselves with the foremen
of the old hacienda." They lived in the big houses, on the streets formerly
closed to the Puerto Rican people, and they always wore the *capacetes*
(the helmets) previously used by administrators of the *haciendas*. Indeed,
"the demand for the capacetes was such that the supply was exhausted
in all the local stores and in those in adjacent towns. The capacete as a
symbol of authority and prestige among the bosses was claimed at all
levels of the administration."[90]

Imitating Frank Dillingham was no way to produce self-sustaining
social change. So New York City became another alternative offered to
islanders in search of work. During the 1950s Puerto Ricans began what
soon became a revolving-door system of migration to the mainland.
Hundreds of thousands of islanders came to New York, New Jersey,
and later Connecticut; but even in the banner years of migration, almost
as many islanders returned home. In 1957, for example, 440,000 people
came, while 391,000 went home. The figures for 1958 were 468,000 coming and 442,000 returning.[91]

However, by 1958, almost 400,000 islanders had settled on the East
Coast of the United States. That was an extraordinary 20 percent of the
Puerto Rican people, but even that massive outflow of population—a
"safety valve" available to almost no other developing nation—failed to
hide the island's continuing labor problems. Muñoz understandably
bragged about a doubling of the nation's gross national product (GNP)
and a more than doubling of the average wage rate, yet he just as
understandably never bragged about the almost imperceptible drop in
official unemployment (12.9 percent in 1950, 12.8 percent in 1958) and
the steady decline in labor-force participation, from 53 percent in 1950
to only 47.2 percent in 1958.[92]

Muñoz had problems. He knew it. And, as in 1932 or 1952, he came
to Washington for the assistance he required.

Congress called it the Fernos-Murray Bill, the first of many efforts to
achieve what the Populares soon called the permanently "enhanced
Commonwealth." The idea was to obtain the political power required
for economic change. Puerto Rico asked Congress for greater control of
its labor force and for the extension of unemployment benefits to the
island; it asked for greater control of its tariffs; it asked to be exempted,
"upon request by the Commonwealth," from any trade agreement it
deemed necessary; and, time after time, the bill asked for powers in
language that no one understood.[93]

Of course, the bill was just a proposal. Portions could be changed.
No problem. So it was, as long as Congress remembered that, as Governor Muñoz told—of all people!—Senator Ernest Gruening of Alaska,
"the commonwealth status which we have chosen is not a colonial status

because of the compact principle on which it is based. We have chosen another form of liberty not called independence."

Did Congress agree? Was it going to affirm Muñoz's interpretation of Commonwealth status?

Not on your life. Indeed, these 1959 hearings assumed great importance for the island because they were the first public indication that Congress would not, and given its interpretation of the Constitution could not, *ever* permanently enhance Commonwealth status. The compact was a fiction in the mind of Luis Muñoz Marín. For in no uncertain terms Senator Henry Jackson exploded the governor's interpretation of the island's "new" status.

Consider this comment by Senator Jackson to Muñoz:

Let me put it this way. I know what you have in mind. I mean the commerce clause is not to be taken literally. Commerce has been defined, and naturally it must be defined, in the light of the conditions as exist at the time. But the only section that I put my finger on is Article IV, Section 3 of the Constitution that provides that Congress shall have power to dispose of and make *all needful rules and regulations* [my emphasis] respecting the territory or other property belonging to the United States.[94]

Puerto Rico belonged to the United States. If Muñoz wanted to call it a Commonwealth, fine. But whatever the term used, the island remained an unincorporated territory for whom Congress made all needful rules and regulations. That was the law. And Senator Jackson could and would not change it. He told Muñoz:

I want to thank you for your statement and I just want to say here that my questions go to the fundamental constitutional problem that is very disturbing to me. I do not want you to get the idea that I do not necessarily feel that some of these changes should not be made. *That is not the point* [my emphasis]. The point is that if we make them, should we make provision for a situation where Congress cannot again deal with that situation unless consent is given by the Commonwealth of Puerto Rico?[95]

This was a rhetorical question. With the approval of his colleagues and the government departments that commented on the Fernos-Murray Bill, Senator Jackson killed Commonwealth on June 9, 1959. He refused to permanently relinquish any of Congress's powers, and in the process he made extraordinarily important political and economic decisions for the Puerto Rican people.

Politically, Jackson contradicted Muñoz's interpretation of Commonwealth. How could there be a compact if Congress alone had the authority to make all needful rules and regulations? In addition, using Muñoz's criteria, the island remained a colony if there was no compact.

Economically Senator Jackson's decisions also stymied Puerto Rico's chances for change. Many of Mūnoz's ideas made economic sense; at the very least they offered some way to avoid perpetual tax exemption for corporations that moved to the island. But because the economic ideas were politically unacceptable, the island had to keep begging for no imposition of minimum wages; when they expired in 1960 and beyond, island planners simply extended the periods of tax exemption without gaining—once again—significant quid pro quos in the process.

Island planners believed they had no choice. Tax exemption was, after all, the primary tool that Congress offered. However, tax exemption not only perpetuated the problems first perceived in 1948 but also created a new one: Instead of investing, or at least keeping their money in Puerto Rico, the corporations were sending it to Guam, another U.S. possession acquired during the Spanish-American War. From Guam the money was invested in Europe, and it then went back to Guam and, finally, to Puerto Rico, when the corporations did what the accountants of 1948 had suggested: liquidate their operations.[96]

By 1960 the Populares were already at a dead-end, denied economic change and unwilling to consider the political options—statehood or independence—that offered some hope of self-sustaining growth.

Muñoz, however, had a wild card up his sleeve. If John Kennedy won the election, the young president might prod Congress into giving the island the powers it so urgently needed. The New Frontier was, after all, a child of the New Deal; and, despite thirty years of broken promises, Luis Muñoz Marín never lost faith in the Democratic party's willingness to shape and transform Puerto Rican life.

NOTES

1. House, 82nd Congress, 2nd session, Report no. 1832, Washington, 1952, p. 2; The Javits quote can be found in the *Congressional Record*, House, 81st Congress, 2nd session, June 30, 1950, p. 9585.

2. Robert Sobel, *The Entrepreneurs* (New York: W&T, 1974), p. 356.

3. *Hearings before a Subcommittee of the Committee on Interstate and Foreign Commerce*, Senate, 80th Congress, 2nd session, 1948, Part 1, pp. 68–69.

4. David Ross, *The Long Uphill Path* (San Juan: Edil, 1969), p. 121.

5. See *Hearings*, 1948, p. 70.

6. Ibid., p. 64.

7. Ibid., p. 63.

8. Ibid., p. 762.

9. Ibid., p. 784.

10. Ibid., p. 781.

11. *Tax Treatment of U.S. Concerns with Puerto Rican Affiliates, Hearings before the Select Committee on Small Business*, Senate, 88th Congress, 2nd session, April 1964, p. 269.

12. Ibid., p. 68.

13. Ibid., pp. 68–69.

14. Ibid., p. 269.

15. See H. C. Barton, *Puerto Rico's Industrial Development Program, 1942–1960,* Harvard University, October 29, 1959, p. 17.

16. Raymond Carr, *Puerto Rico* (New York: Vintage, 1983), p. 203.

17. See Robert M. Baker and James E. Curry, "Taxpayer's Paradise in the Caribbean," *Vanderbilt Law Review* 1 (1947–48):p. 195.

18. See Harry J. Rudick and George S. Allan, "Tax Aspects of Operations under the Puerto Rican Exemption Program," *Tax Law Review* (New York University School of Law) 7 (1951–52):p. 404.

19. See Robert M. Baker, "Puerto Rico's Program of Industrial Tax Exemption," *George Washington Law Review* 18, no. 4 (June 1950):p. 470; see also, Rudick and Allan, "Tax Aspects," pp. 419 and 426.

20. Rudick and Allen, "Tax Aspects," p. 426.

21. Baker, "Industrial Tax Exemption," pp. 471–472; see, too, the first part of this article in the *George Washington Law Review* 18 (1949–50):pp. 327–370; see, too, Rudick and Allen, "Tax Aspects," pp. 434–435.

22. See Baker, "Industrial Tax Exemption," Part 1, p. 327.

23. Luis P. Costas Elena, "IRS Section 936 . . . (Part IV), *Revista del Colegio de Abogados de Puerto Rico* 42, no. 4 (1981):p. 625.

24. See Milton Taylor, *Industrial Tax Exemption in Puerto Rico* (Madison: University of Wisconsin Press, 1957), p. 143.

25. Ibid., p. 62.

26. Ibid., p. 45.

27. Ibid., p. 13.

28. Moscoso's remark appears in a 1957 speech entitled "Puerto Rico Chooses Free Enterprise," p. 10; on the lack of a list see Costas Elena, "IRS Section 936 . . . (Part II)," p. 130; for a sustained, contemporary critique of Fomento's lack of emphasis on quid pro quo see Taylor, *Industrial Tax Exemption.*

29. *Hearings before the Panel to Review the Status of Navy Training on the Island of Vieques,* House, 96th Congress, 2nd session, 1980, p. 176.

30. Harry S. Truman Library, Confidential File, Box 3, dated July 7, 1948.

31. Navy Historical Center, Operational Archives Division, Washington, D.C., Box marked Roosevelt Roads, File marked "Admiral Leahy's Report," see esp. pp. 1 and 2.

32. Truman Library, Confidential Files, Box 3, memo 5/20/48.

33. National Archives, Record Group 126, 9/8/48, dated May 27, 1947.

34. Ibid., 9/8/48.

35. See "Admiral Leahy's Report," p. 15.

36. National Archives, Record Group 126, 9/8/93.

37. Truman Library, President's Secretary's Files, Box 169, April 22, 1948.

38. Naval Historical Center, Operational Archives Branch, Washington, D.C., Box marked Roosevelt Roads, Tape-recorded conversations labeled "Transcript of Telephone Conversation Between Radm Darbey (Comten) and Radm Maher," dated July 26, 1948.

39. This is from Admiral Barbey's summary of the meeting; the document is

labeled "Conference with Governor Pinero," dated July 27, 1948. It was found at the Naval Historical Center.

40. Ibid., the memo of the conversation, p. 2; there is also a second phone conversation dated July 27, 1948; see p. 3.

41. Truman Library, Confidential Files, Box 3, p. 2.

42. See Arturo Melendex López, *La Batalla de Vieques* (Río Piedras: Edil, 1989, 2nd ed.), pp. 95 and 91.

43. Ivonne Acosta, *La Mordaza* (Río Piedras: Edil, 1987), p. 40.

44. See *Puerto Rico Constitution, Hearing before the Committee On Interior and Insular Affairs*, Senate, 81st Congress, 2nd session, 1950, p. 7.

45. See Luis Muñoz Marín, "The Sad Case of Porto Rico," *American Mercury* 16, No. 62 (February 1929):p. 139.

46. Acosta, *La Mordaza*, p. 78.

47. See, for example, Ruth Reynold's, *Campus in Bondage* (New York: Hunter College, 1989); also see Acosta, *La Mordaza*, pp. 50–52.

48. Acosta, *La Mordaza*, p. 62.

49. Ibid., p. 104.

50. Truman Library, President's Secretary's Files, Box 169, April 18, 1948.

51. Luis Nieves Falcon, "El Futuro Ideológico del Partido Popular Democrático," in *Diagnóstico de Puerto Rico* (Río Piedras: Edil, 1970), pp. 239–268, the quote appears on pp. 242–243.

52. See *Puerto Rico Constitution, Hearings before the Committee on Public Lands*, House, 81st Congress, 2nd session, 1950, p. 94.

53. Ibid., p. 95; also Roberta Ann Johnson, *Commonwealth or Colony?* (New York: Praeger, 1979), p. 35.

54. Acosta, *La Mordaza*, p. 106.

55. Carlos Ramón Zapata Oliveras, *United States–Puerto Rico Relations in the Early Cold War Years*, University of Pennsylvania, 1986, p. 269.

56. *Congressional Record*, House, 81st Congress, 2nd session, March 14, 1950; I found this statement at the Truman Library, Files of Stephen Springarn, Box 19; for the remark about the "new state" see Zapata Oliveras, *United States–Puerto Rico Relations*, p. 270.

57. *Hearings, Committee on Public Lands*, 1950, pp. 19–20.

58. National Archives, DTIP, Record Group 126, 9–8–68.

59. *Congressional Record*, House, 81st Congress, 2nd session, June 30, 1950, p. 9593.

60. Ibid., p. 9586.

61. *Providing for the Organization of a Constitutional Government by the People of Puerto Rico*, Senate Committee on Interior and Insular Affairs, Report 1779, 81st Congress, 1st session, June 6, 1950.

62. *Congressional Record*, June 30, 1950, p. 9599.

63. Truman Library, Papers of Stephen Springarn, Box 19.

64. Zapata Oliveras, United States–Puerto Rico Relations, pp. 289–290.

65. Eugenio Fernández Mendez, ed., *Crónicas de Puerto Rico* (Río Piedras: University of Puerto Rico, 1969), pp. 627–649; see p. 639.

66. Truman Library, President's Secretary's Files, Box 169, p. 9.

67. See Antonio Gil de Lamadrid Navarro, *Los Indomitos* (Río Piedras: Edil, 1981); and Oscar Collazo, *El Retorno del Patriota* (New York, 1984).

68. See, for example, William Hackett, *The Nationalist Party*, a report prepared for Representative Fred L. Crawford of the House Committee on Interior and Insular Affairs, 1951, p. 1.

69. Acosta, *La Mordaza*, pp. 166–167.

70. Ibid., p. 236.

71. *Congressional Record*, 82nd Congress, 2nd session, May 13, 1952, p. 5121.

72. Perhaps the clearest statement of his views are in a letter to the Interior Department dated January 17, 1953. See the National Archives, DTIP, Record Group 126, 9–8–68, Box 351.

73. *Congressional Record*, 82nd Congress, 2nd session, May 28, 1952, p. 6179.

74. *Approving Puerto Rican Constitution, Hearings before Committee on Interior and Insular Affairs*, Senate, 82nd Congress, 2nd session, 1952, p. 47; for the agreement of Fernos-Isern see *Congressional Record*, May 28, 1952, p. 6180.

75. National Archives, O of T, Record Group 126, 9–8–68, Box 351.

76. James Davis, National Archives, O of T, Record Group 126, 9–8–68. Box 351, p. 2; for many of the UN documents see Carmen Gautier Mayoral and María del Pilar Arguelles, *Puerto Rico y La ONU* (Río Piedras: Edil, 1978).

77. National Archives, O of T, Record Group 126, 9–8–68, Box 351.

78. See Zapata Oliveras, *United States–Puerto Rico Relations*, p. 368.

79. Ibid., pp. 380–381.

80. Ibid., p. 397.

81. Ibid., p. 398.

82. See *Review of Foreign Policy, Hearings before the Committee on Foreign Relations*, Senate, 85th Congress, 1st session, 1958, pp. 374 and 381–382.

83. Ibid., pp. 382–383.

84. See the *New York Times*, March 2, 1954.

85. *Amendment to Increase the Minimum Wage, Hearings before the Committee on Education and Labor*, House, 84th Congress, 1st session, 1955, p. 705.

86. Ibid., p. 713; also James Dietz, *Economic History of Puerto Rico* (Princeton, N.J.: Princeton University Press, 1986), p. 248.

87. Hearings, 1955, p. 707.

88. Ibid., p. 708.

89. See Matthew Edel, "Land Reform in Puerto Rico, 1941–1959, Part Two," *Caribbean Studies* 2, no. 4 (1964):pp. 28–50; also Richard Weisskoff, *Factories and Foodstamps* (Baltimore: Johns Hopkins University Press, 1985).

90. See Eduardo Seda, *Social Change and Personality in a Puerto Rican Agrarian Reform Community* (Evanston, Ill.: Northeastern University Press, 1973), p. 155.

91. See Johnson, *Commonwealth or Colony?*, p. 118.

92. Dietz, *Economic History of Puerto Rico*, p. 275.

93. *Puerto Rico Federal Relations Act, Hearing before the Committee on Interior and Insular Affairs*, 86 Congress, 1st session, 1959, esp. pp. 2–16.

94. Ibid., p. 49.

95. Ibid., p. 51.

96. Department of the Treasury, *The Operation and Effect of the Possessions Corporation System of Taxation*, First Annual Report, June 1978, esp. p. 11.

Chapter 8

Stink Bombs and Heart Attacks

> The U.S. has repeatedly and pridefully declared its policy on
> political status to be that of self determination. Yet here is
> a record of a decade of hanky panky.... What is most dam-
> aging is the FBI swashbuckling at the time of the plebiscite
> (is that self determination?) and even at the time of the 1968
> general election.
>
> *Memo, Summarizing Results of An Analysis of FBI*
> *Documents Conducted on Behalf of*
> *President Jimmy Carter*[1]

It was an unorthodox request: Not only did the entire population of
Vieques have to leave their island forever but, said Secretary of Defense
Robert McNamara, they also had to take their cemeteries with them. In
another reevaluation of Vieques's role, the navy planned to use the
island "for overt and covert training and/or staging of U.S. and foreign
forces."[2] That meant Vieques would be permanently closed to Puerto
Ricans civilians, especially those who on All Saints Day put flowers on
the graves of loved ones. The secretary's plans included digging up the
corpses of dead Viequesans and (presumably) reburying them wherever
McNamara and the president decided the 8,000 displaced Viequesans
would live.

The plan was vitally important to the navy because beginning in 1957,
it had decided to use the Roosevelt Roads complex (which included
Vieques) "as the primary center for Fleet Guided Missile Training Operations in the Atlantic." Vieques was, for its people, yet again the wrong

place, at the wrong time. After Sputnik, missiles received the highest priority classification, so the new facility was instantly at the center of the U.S. drive to beat the Soviets. Or as the navy put it, "Roosevelt Roads has expanded since 1957 with a rapidity characteristic of war time operations, and should continue to expand for some time."[3]

The Dracula Plan was part of the navy's continued expansion. The stumbling block was world opinion. What would people say about Americans moving bones in order to fire missiles meant to kill people?

The "real estate negotiations" (the navy's words) put Governor Luis Muñoz Marín in a difficult spot. Only two weeks after the inauguration he was in Washington requesting President John Kennedy's immediate assistance on everything from enhanced Commonwealth to helping possessions corporations keep all the profits they deemed necessary.[4]

Muñoz wanted, needed, and got the president's cooperation in a variety of areas. As early as July 25, 1961, for example, the president issued a memo Muñoz had requested. Kennedy said that "it is essential that the executive departments and agencies be completely aware of the unique position of the Commonwealth, and that policies, actions, reports on legislation, and other activities affecting the Commonwealth should be consistent with the structure and basic principles of the Commonwealth."[5] Those basic principles were "in the nature of a compact" Kennedy deftly affirmed in a thoroughly ambiguous manner. Muñoz, however, could legitimately feel that the memo was the first step on the road to the permanent agreements denied him by Senator Henry Jackson and his colleagues in 1959.

Thus, it was difficult to say no to the navy, especially when the first request came from two "specially armed, personnel messengers" sent by the secretary of defense. Muñoz got the message and immediately went to Washington, where he agreed to turn over the people and their graves "if it was really, absolutely, and unequivocally necessary for the security of the United States."[6] When the secretary said that the people had to go, the negotiations proceeded to the next stage.

However, before additional negotiations took place, the mayor of Vieques had the audacity to write to President Kennedy. He apparently had no idea he was on the verge of leaving his homeland, for the mayor complained that the navy "has taken possession of 26,000 acres of the total of 33,000 acres and for these its pays no land tax nor does it furnish jobs for the population." The mayor asked for the navy to return lands it held but didn't use and to provide jobs for the civilian population.[7]

The White House didn't know what to do with the mayor's letter. The citizens of Vieques might be upset if they knew that the governor was negotiating their departure, so a special assistant in the Defense Department contacted a special assistant in La Fortaleza; the Puerto Rican told the American not to reply to the mayor of Vieques. "He promised that the Governor would inform the mayor that these matters to which he addressed himself were being appropriately handled by the current administration of Puerto Rico."[8]

That administration was also negotiating the departure of Culebra's 570 citizens. The navy wanted the remainder of that tiny island "to provide a suitable impact area for the rapidly increasing missile training of our fleet and naval air units."[9] In exchange for Vieques and Culebra the navy was willing to swap some land. As Governor Muñoz put it:

The idea was that the armed forces, especially the Navy but not the Navy alone, would give up a number of properties [i.e., the lands they refused to give back in 1948] they held in Puerto Rico that were no longer considered necessary for defense, so that Puerto Rico would be compensated for the loss of Vieques. And some money would be available to compensate the actual people of Vieques, to transport them to some region in the island of Puerto Rico, itself, and provide them with housing and other facilities.[10]

The Defense Department had also generously agreed to give back, for a dollar, the lands it had expropriated during World War II and to sell back to the Commonwealth, "either for cost or for the present appraisal price" the land it had purchased from private owners. To Muñoz, "this was economically speaking, very flattering, very good." But, he declared,

I thought it was very wrong. It had some constitutional difficulties. You cannot abolish a municipality in Puerto Rico without the vote of the people. And you'd never get the people of Vieques to vote for the abolishment of its own municipality. It could create . . . the very strange situation of Vieques having a government in exile with no citizens on the island of Vieques, itself, because the mayor had been elected for four years.[11]

So the mayor who didn't know he was leaving would be chief executive of a municipality he was forbidden even to visit. It was very strange. In the negotiations between the navy and the secretary of state, Roberto Sanchez Vilella, sailors told President Kennedy, "Mr. Sanchez was either unwilling or unable to discuss our proposals with a view to reaching firm positions that could be embodied in a proposed agreement for final acceptance by the Governor and Secretary McNamara."[12]

The navy understood that "this represented a major and difficult political commitment" for the Puerto Rican government, but the United States still required a place to fire its missiles and train its covert forces. The United States had to take Vieques. To make sure the nation got what it wanted, sailors suggested that the president offer the following set of incentives: "Affirmative improvement of the economic lot of the residents of the two islands through a resettlement program that would provide equal opportunity with the other people of Puerto Rico"; return of valuable urban property, and, thirteen years after Admiral Leahy suggested it, "return of historic monuments and buildings to the people of Puerto Rico. Every old Spanish building or historic site occupied by the military would be relinquished, including all of F. Brooke which adjoins El Morro Castle."[13]

Confident about its offer, the navy told the president it would "clarify the basis upon which Puerto Rico will join in this undertaking" in a subsequent meeting. But before anyone even scheduled a date for the continued negotiations, Muñoz wrote a letter to Kennedy. It was dated December 28, 1961. In it Muñoz agreed that constitutional problem or not, he would go along with the president's request. However, he did think that "the political, social and human effects of the Department's plans . . . will be so profoundly destructive that the project should be abandoned unless it is not merely desireable, but clearly, critically and urgently necessary for the military defense of the Nation."[14]

In support of his plea Muñoz noted, "The political and human dismemberment which the project involves will be a fundamental shock. We know of no truly comparable action in American history." Moreover, "the project is peculiarly subject to widespread denunciation and to hostile propaganda use. . . . The United States is still charged by some people with colonial rule over Puerto Rico, a charge which is unjustified but can be made effective if given a dramatic symbol."[15]

Kennedy got the political point. In a letter to the governor dated January 16, 1962, he noted, "A new evaluation of the defense needs has been undertaken. . . . We have now concluded, largely on the basis of your argument, that we must alter our plans so as to modify the impact on the civilian community."[16]

Thus, instead of moving the population, the navy would simply bomb them. And if this sounds too cynical or sarcastic, consider this astonishing question from Kennedy's point man on Puerto Rico, Lee White, to Governor Muñoz in an oral interview conducted after President Kennedy's assassination.

Muñoz had explained all the facts cited above when White asked, "Did you think that it was important enough to take the time of the President of the United States for the problems of seven thousand people?"[17]

Somehow, Muñoz did not walk out of the room. He simply continued talking to the government official who had also been point man when Kennedy said yes, and then no, to the governor's cherished proposal for the permanent enhancement of Commonwealth status.

The scenario was recalled thus: The president very carefully read the letter (to be issued as a press release on July 25, 1962). He fully understood and even sympathized with Governor's Muñoz's efforts to perfect the Commonwealth. He was even willing to let the Puerto Ricans vote for whatever status they desired. But that didn't mean they would get what they wanted or, more precisely, that the majority ruled. Congress had ultimate authority. Lee White explained, "I recall his going over that correspondence very carefully before it left because of his awareness of the sensitivity of the way these words are handled."[18]

"Statehood" was the word that troubled the president. He told White, "Since statehood is a decision that Congress must make *without regard* [my emphasis] to whether the people want it or not,—I mean, the Congress is not going to make it if the people want it, we can't, by anything I say, commit the United States as a whole to the decision that Congress must make."[19]

Before acting, Kennedy should have remembered the example of Harry Truman and Rexford Tugwell in 1946. When the Puerto Ricans then threatened to hold a plebiscite with alternatives Congress would never approve, Truman simply vetoed the plebiscite. Case closed. Self-determination cut off at the pass before it got too embarrassing for the United States.

Kennedy's mistake was to equivocate. In his letter to Muñoz he said:

I see no reason why the Commonwealth concept, if that is the desire of the people of Puerto Rico, should not be fully developed as a permanent institution with the United States. I agree that this is a proper time to recognize the need for growth and, both as a matter of fairness to all concerned and of establishing an unequivocal record, to consult the people of Puerto Rico, as you propose to do, so that they may express any other preference, including independence, if that should be their wish.[20]

Including independence. With this partial seal of approval Kennedy gave Muñoz authority to hold a plebiscite that actually contained only two of the three proposed choices. The United States never committed itself to accept statehood, which put Kennedy in the embarrassing position Truman neatly avoided: What would Kennedy do if the Puerto Ricans voted for a status the president had said Congress would not approve "even if the people want it"?

Kennedy got lucky. When Muñoz excitedly took the plebiscite proposal back to the island, he encountered serious opposition from his own party, as well as from the statehooders, who immediately understood why the president had failed to include their option in his letter. On August 1 the statehooders publicly announced their refusal to participate in the plebiscite until and unless Congress first agreed to commit itself to whatever choice the Puerto Rican people made.[21]

The Populares hesitated because the party's 1960 platform specifically opposed a plebiscite and, even more important, because many Populares demanded that the plebiscite precisely indicate what enhanced Commonwealth did and did not include. In a party assembly held on August 1, 1962, Muñoz actually appeared on the verge of a humiliating defeat when, at the height of an opponent's speech, someone cut off the microphone and put out the lights. This "accident" silenced the opposition, who remained in the dark until Muñoz got his way. Then the lights came back on and one Populare joyously shouted, "Miracle! Miracle! When Muñoz speaks there is light!"[22]

Light yes. Agreement no. The statehooders remained adamant, so adamant that Muñoz agreed to conditions that eventually convinced John Kennedy to "betray" the governor. On November 15, 1962, the Puerto Rican legislature passed a measure that firmly and deliberately asked Washington to exert its ultimate authority. The plebiscite was on, but only if Congress clearly specified, among other things, the political and economic powers attached to Commonwealth.

When a critic asked why Muñoz agreed to this tactic, he was accused of disloyalty. How, after all, was Muñoz going to get international acceptance of Commonwealth if the island held a plebiscite without the statehooders? "To Muñoz it didn't matter what he had to do to get the statehooders to go to the plebiscite; the important thing was what occurred in Washington and Muñoz agreed to a compromise so that the statehooders would not block his efforts in Congress."[23]

Meanwhile, near one of the loveliest beaches on the island—Luquillo—U.S. and Puerto Rican officials argued about the exact meaning of Commonwealth status. On behalf of the president men like Nicholas Katzenbach told Muñoz that if he asked for too much, Congress would tire of the details and simply offer him independence. Muñoz replied, "If that happened we would always be able to reject it."[24] In reality the governor was, as in 1944, frightened by the possibility of independence. He called in his old friend Abe Fortas and, along with others, the two men produced a final text, which they sent to Harold Reis, the Justice Department attorney authorized by the president to prepare the administration's initial response to the specifics of enhanced Commonwealth.

On December 29, 1962, Reis submitted a long, intelligent, and detailed analysis of the Commonwealth proposal. His first concern was to call the president's attention to a "substantial change in the procedure heretofore proposed." Before, the Puerto Ricans were going to make a decision and Congress would then say yes or no. Now, as a result of the statehooders' efforts, Congress had to act first, and that "would amount to at least a moral commitment by Congress to take steps to implement statehood or independence if the people of Puerto Rico should favor either in the referendum."[25]

Any commitment to actual self-determination was itself cause for alarm; but once Reis analyzed the specifics of Muñoz's proposal, President Kennedy's problems multiplied. Acting on what he had told Ernest Gruening in 1936, Muñoz still wanted to have his cake and eat it too. Thus, "from the point of view of the United States, some of the most difficult problems presented by the proposed compact arise from the fact that for all practical purposes it would operate to grant independence to Puerto Rico; yet practically all of its citizens would also be citizens of the United States."[26]

Divided loyalties were understandable, divided sovereignty out of the question. For example, "theoretically Puerto Rico would be free to wage war independently or together with the United States or allied with the United States or against it. . . . It seems highly questionable whether there should be created a legal relationship which could even theoretically impose such possible conflicts on individuals holding common or dual citizenship."[27]

Reis's one overriding conclusion was that Muñoz's proposal spelled constitutional problems of the first order. In fact,

unless the concept of joint citizenship is abandoned it would seem necessary either to adopt such a course [i.e., independence] or substantially to reduce the powers in the areas of foreign relations and defense which it is now proposed Puerto Rico obtain. It may also be necessary to reduce them in the field of economic regulation.[28]

Nobody knew what to do until Lee White (apparently with Muñoz's approval) made this suggestion in a January 15, 1963, memo to the president.

Because the [Commonwealth] concepts are so novel and difficult to grasp it is our joint recommendation that this should be explored by a committee or a commission. Our principal concern is that the novelty of the proposals requires a "digestive" or "selling" process that could be done much more effectively by a distinguished commission rather than dumping the problem in Congress in the form of a bill or resolution.[29]

Kennedy agreed, if only because Muñoz did all the work. He lobbied every key member of every important committee—Lee White told the president that Muñoz pursued "what most others would regard as a completely hopeless process"[30]—and by May Congress had agreed to hearings to consider appointing a commission that would draft "a proposed compact of permanent union" between Puerto Rico and the United States; once that compact was drawn up, the island would hold a plebiscite to decide between statehood, independence, or permanently enhanced Commonwealth.[31]

Before he testified on May 16, 1963, Muñoz visited the White House. He talked with the president and he even went over the details of the

Commonwealth proposal with the president's assistants. Muñoz's aides said that he left for Congress confident that the president was on his side.[32]

The hearings began with Muñoz patiently discussing his conception of Commonwealth status; he wanted "obsolete language" removed from the Federal Relations Act. "It just remains there because that is the way it was when Puerto Rico was a territory. . . . The basic importance is to clarify a feeling, a relationship of dignity, of political dignity between Puerto Rico and the United States beyond any shadow of a doubt."[33]

Congressman John Saylor interrupted. He had been busily reading the *Congressional Records* from 1950, and he not only cited the words of Congressman Fred Crawford but angrily told Muñoz that what Crawford "said on the floor of the House on June 30, 1950, and what you are saying are as opposite as it is humanly possible to get." All the Puerto Rican people got was "the right to vote on a constitution to be submitted to the President of the United States who in turn submitted it to Congress for approval."[34]

Now Saylor's comments only reiterated the position Muñoz had repeatedly heard for the last decade. But this was a public rebuke at a crucial moment in the island's history, made all the worse because of the obvious intensity—even on the printed page—of Saylor's antagonism. He put it thus to the governor: "All of this commonwealth that you keep talking about, and the clarification, I am satisfied are things which have been built up under your administration in Puerto Rico and have not been the intention of Congress then and I hope not now."[35]

Ever the court courtier, Muñoz responded by citing his respect for Congressman Crawford. And then in a very rare admission of the truth, Muñoz said this: "If he [Crawford] was right, then Puerto Rico is still a colony of the United States. If it is still a colony of the United States it should stop being a colony as soon as possible for the honor of the United States and for the sense of self respect of the people of Puerto Rico [applause and jeers]."[36]

The chair called for order: "This committee will be moved by words but not by applause or boos." When the House soon got back to words, Representative John Kyl asked Muñoz this question: "Does the gentleman think that in anything less than statehood we can in fact create a relationship which is indissoluble except through the creation of statehood?"[37]

Perhaps Muñoz was tired? Perhaps he was upset by the confrontation with Saylor? Whatever the case, Muñoz failed to read his interrogator. The governor didn't want to get bogged down in "academic" questions. Muñoz responded, "I don't think it is worthwhile discussing it much."

Kyl disagreed. "It is in this area that I am greatly interested." In concluding his comments Kyl also tersely summarized the views of many of the men grilling Luis Muñoz Marín. Kyl stressed that "time and again" the committee had demonstrated its good intentions; "we are indeed interested in these people whom we have had to protect in some instances, to govern as incorporated or unincorporated territories, and so on."[38]

America's burdens were already quite heavy. Thus Kyl's concerns were anything but academic: "The question which we have before us is how do we do this job in keeping with the provisions of the Constitution. . . . That is the question. That is the question which will have to be resolved."[39]

At lunch Muñoz's assistants asked him to take "una actitud vertical" in the face of so much abuse. The governor refused. Kennedy, after all, was still on Puerto Rico's side, so why antagonize the men he and the president would need to achieve enhanced Commonwealth.

The president's representative was Harold Seidman, an assistant director of the Bureau of the Budget. Seidman stressed the president's good will toward the Puerto Ricans; he "favored the perfection of the existing arrangements" with one proviso: Nothing was permanent, "actions taken now cannot and should not be considered to be binding for all time and in the future."[40]

Thankfully Muñoz did not have a heart attack. Instead, as if a prisoner, he just sat in the hearing room listening to the president's representative rescind every one of the commitments Kennedy had supposedly made.

The words "permanent union" had to be deleted from the proposal; they would lead to "misunderstandings." The plebiscite should be optional rather than mandatory. The aim of resolving any doubts about Puerto Rico's "juridical equality" restricted the commission's charter. And, finally, any thought of Puerto Ricans voting for the president and vice-president of the United States was also too specific a suggestion. "We believe the Commission should be directed simply to develop proposals for a new compact or for such other arrangements as it may find to be feasible and appropriate."[41]

The chair, Leo O'Brien of New York, seemed surprised. He asked, "Mr. Seidman, would I be overstating the case if I expressed the opinion that you believe that there should be a drastic rewriting of the language of the resolution as we now have it before us?"

Seidman: I don't think that would be overstating the case. I would say we are in accord with the spirit of this bill. The specific language does give us some problems."[42]

Some problems! Stressing that he spoke for the administration, Seidman had effectively emasculated both Muñoz and any hopes for enhanced Commonwealth. Of course, soothing the governor's wounded ego was presumably an easy task; Kennedy's men would soon offer Muñoz this consolation prize: the President's Medal or Freedom.

Harder to resolve was the status of Puerto Rico. Seidman offered a series of ifs—if the commission recommends a compact, if it is first approved by Congress, if it is second approved by the Puerto Rican people, if they then want a plebiscite—then something may happen. Who knows? We shall see?[43]

What John Kennedy had done was, as in 1946, 1952, and 1959, put the Puerto Rican people on colonial hold. Nothing was done, for example, to eliminate a practice Senator Gruening called a form of colonialism worse than that practiced by King George; that is, Puerto Ricans were subject to the draft but could not vote in federal elections.[44] And nothing was done to give island administrators the political powers needed to construct a self-sustaining economy.

Frightened by the can of worms the plebiscite had opened, Kennedy said one thing and did another. Muñoz might be furious, but given his decades-long dependence on Washington, what could the governor do? He had been disappointed before. He would be disappointed again.

Congress, however, never imitated the president's flip-flops. By the end of the year the commission proposal had reached the floor of the House, and like their colleagues in 1950, representatives made certain that everyone knew that nothing threatened Congress's power over its incorporated and unincorporated territories.

Representative O'Brien, since 1954 chair of the House committee that helped decide Puerto Rico's fate, said that the commission "promises nothing more than a high level study." But just in case the commission made recommendations contrary to Congress's wishes and powers— Representative Harold Gross, for example, was afraid that "this may be opening the door somewhat to statehood for Puerto Rico"—O'Brien assured his colleagues that the commission had no authority of any sort: "I would like to underscore . . . that no Member or Members of Congress serving on this Commission have the right or authority to commit Congress in any way, shape, or form to any report or recommendations which may emanate from this Commission."[45]

And, as if that wasn't assurance enough, O'Brien emphasized, "As a matter of fact, even the four members of Congress who will serve on the Commission will not have a pen thrust in their hands and be directed to sign the report but they will sign only what they personally agree to."[46]

O'Brien, soon to be a member of the commission, ended by offering his colleagues this final bit of reassurance. The six Puerto Rican (and seven American) members of the commission would produce a historic document that had meaning only if Congress said it did. Equally important, he declared that while Congress waited for the report to be prepared, "this study will serve to calm temporarily the winds and the waves of controversy which have battered at congressional doors. Need

I say that there never was a better time for a temporary surcease of controversy in the Caribbean area?"[47]

Say no more. The commission was approved on February 20, 1964, with James Rowe, a political confidant of now president Lyndon Johnson as chair of the commission. In public Rowe was unbiased and open to all opinions. In private he kept the president informed of what was happening and why. For example, on May 6, 1964, Rowe told the president, "As you probably recall, you appointed me Chairman of the above captioned Commission." Rowe's problem was that by statute he had to call an "organizing meeting" of the commission as soon as possible. So he told the president, "My question is whether you believe there is any value in holding the morning meeting at the White House—say the Cabinet Room—where you could appear briefly?"[48]

Rowe thought the president should come. In New York and Chicago Puerto Ricans were registered to vote "and voting democratic more and more." In terms of security, none of the Puerto Ricans was likely to shoot the president; "the three Popular Democrats [Governor Muñoz's Party] and the two statehood Republican Party people were eminently respectable." Even the Independence fellow could be trusted. But "as to *policy* [emphasis in original], you should be non-committal as to statehood, 'perfected commonwealth,' or independence. Lee White (who knows far more about this than I do) can give you a memorandum and a draft of the proposed comments which will protect you on matters of substance."[49]

All in all, Rowe thought the president should come to the commission's first meeting. Tell me what you want to do, he said, but remember that "of course, you yourself would not have to devote more than ten or fifteen minutes of your own time to this, if it is politically desirable in terms of New York."[50]

Johnson decided to go, well armed with that memo from Lee White. White explained to the president how the commission had come into existence and he then laid out "the three basic possibilities":

Perfection of the Commonwealth—This was Muñoz's preference "but involves the most difficult and painstaking study and review in almost every aspect of government."

Statehood—"This alternative does not seem anywhere near feasible at this point. It cannot, however, be left out as a possibility for political reasons. Muñoz's opposition party uses this as their chief means of holding the group together."

Independence—Small support "but this too has to be regarded as a possibility to offset charges of "colonialism made by Castro and other Communist elements in the Caribbean and South America."[51]

With the alternatives laid out, White then explained that "this Commission includes Congressional representation in order to provide the Commission with some guide as to what would be acceptable to Congress and how to present it, and secondly to provide a natural body of support for it when the recommendations are submitted."[52]

One of White's final recommendations to the president—which Johnson accepted—was a contradiction in terms. The president should stress America's firm dedication to the principles of self-determination even though "statehood does not seem anywhere near feasible at this time"; even more importantly, the commission was deliberately designed to "guide" members to only the status options acceptable to Congress. This was done for the same political reasons Harry Truman had rejected the plebiscite in 1946. White told the President that "it is generally agreed that the U.S. could suffer some international loss of prestige if a program supported by the Administration to grant greater autonomy and freedom to Puerto Rico were defeated in the Congress."[53] But as in 1946, those reasons had nothing to do with self-determination and everything to do with a president's desire to avoid an international inspection of the canyon that separated democratic ideals from colonial realities.

Lyndon Johnson went to the meeting; he spent his fifteen minutes, and, again following the advice of Lee White, he "minimized any description of the Commission's duties, and took a completely impartial stand on the three basic alternatives."[54]

As the president proudly noted, "I am sure the work of the Commission will reflect the objectivity and creativity—the scholarly ability and practical experience—and, above all, the idealistic recognition of human aspirations of you who have agreed to undertake this important assignment."[55]

While the committee worked, J. Edgar Hoover supervised an assignment every bit as important as the perfection of Commonwealth. Puerto Rican independence activists were once again at work, and despite their polling only 25,000 votes in the 1960 elections, Hoover and his subordinates knew the truth. The director read it in a memo from the Federal Bureau of Investigation's (FBI's) San Juan office: "This number is no measure of the independentistas in Puerto Rico and the low figure can be largely attributed to the successful campaign of "electoral abstinence" conducted by the MPI [Movement for Independence] and joined by the pro-independence organizations, just prior to the elections."[56]

Hoover decided to take charge. He advised his people in San Juan that "a more positive effort must be made not only to curtail but to actively disrupt the activities of Puerto Rican nationalists." Use informants, create dissension within the groups, disseminate handwritten notes that plant the seeds of dissension between factions, and mail, anonymously, cartoons ridiculing the efforts of successful *independentistas*.[57]

The endless possibilities excited the agents assigned to this work. By June of 1961 Hoover was told that "as it pertains to our efforts to disrupt their activities and compromise their effectiveness," we need to know more about the psychological makeup of the Independence leaders. Why did they have such an "intense desire" for Puerto Rican independence? What did they hope to gain? And, most important of all, "we must have information concerning their weaknesses, morals, criminal records, spouses, children, family life, educational qualifications, and personal activities other than independence activities."[58]

The FBI was thorough, determined, and absolutely intent on undermining Juan Mari Bras's (he was then head of the MPI) chances of success. Mari Bras, after all, had a long history of "subversive" activities. He had been a leader of the student movement that tried to welcome Albizu in 1948; he had gone on to become a lawyer, and, by 1961, the man had contracted the dreaded "supermarket complex." The San Juan office told Hoover, "In many of his speeches Mari has attacked the growing number of supermarkets in Puerto Rico as the symbol of the menace of Yankee imperialism and the threat of an economic takeover of the island by American interests. Probably some of this conviction stems from the fact that his father is a small grocery operator."[59]

Sigmund Freud was popular in FBI circles. And so too were activities that had nothing to do with self-determination or human decency. For years the FBI tried to create dissension within Mari Bras's family; agents made concerted efforts to undermine the relationships between Mari and his most trusted colleagues; and in May 1964 about 300 people received an anonymous (FBI) letter from a phantom front group. This letter first libeled the leadership of the MPI and it then proceeded to an especially vicious personal attack on Juan Mari Bras.

The result? Mari Bras had a heart attack. Although the FBI felt it could not take full credit for the attack—Mari Bras was a hard worker under great strain—"the anonymous letter certainly did nothing to ease his tensions. . . . Our anonymous letter has seriously disrupted the MPI ranks and created a climate of distrust and dissension from which it will take them some time to recover."[60]

Mari Bras, however, was on his feet in a matter of weeks; so in the hopes of precipitating another heart attack, agents sent an anonymous letter to another *independentista*, telling him that Mari Bras and the man's wife were lovers: "If you are too much of a fool to resent a cuckold, I, as a friend, will not allow it go to on."[61]

But it did go on. Hoover continued to undermine independence ac-

tivists in every nook and cranny of the island, while at La Fortaleza Luis
Muñoz Marín made a decision that changed the shape of Puerto Rican
politics.

Muñoz retired for a variety of reasons. His humiliation at the hands
of President Kennedy moved many to question his abilities. How could
he have misread, so badly, both Congress and the president? Meanwhile, within the party a new generation of well-educated and very
intelligent Populares openly questioned the wisdom of the island's economic and political strategies. At the 1964 meeting of the entire party,
opponents asked for changes in virtually every facet of Puerto Rican life.
They wanted emphasis on cultural ties to Central and Latin America,
more capital from Puerto Rican rather than absentee owners, a merit
system in civil service, a reorganization of the university, a greater rate
of savings, and a reevaluation of the role of agriculture in Puerto Rican
life.[62]

Muñoz's anointed successor was Roberto Sanchez Vilella. According
to a memo prepared for President Johnson, he was "a doer rather than
a thinker." He had a "computer-type mind and a notably retentive
memory," he liked dominoes and horse racing, and he was a founder
of the Popular Democratic party. In his inauguration speech—Sanchez
won the 1964 election with over 62 percent of the vote; the statehooders
got 34 percent—the new governor "stressed that he could never hope
to equal Muñoz Marín" and that he could make no promises of achievement other than "to act as a partner with the Puerto Rican people in
attempting to reach their goals."[63]

What were those goals? Well, they keyed on revitalizing an economy
that despite many achievements was still plagued by double-digit unemployment, the abandonment of agriculture, and excessive dependence on tax exemptions to replace the jobs lost to liquidations and
"cheap" foreign labor.

A 1964 Commonwealth report to Congress stressed the difficulties
encountered by Puerto Rican economic planners. Over 40 percent (and
this was a conservative estimate) of the plants opened as a result of
Fomento's efforts closed their doors when the company's tax exemption
expired. The companies that stayed and the new ones that came bought
most of their goods and services abroad; thus, the island was a pit stop
on the way to market, never an economy producing the forward and
backward linkages so essential to self-sustaining growth. Finally, the
companies that stayed sent their profits to Guam and then to Europe.
The island got little chance to invest the fruits of its people's labor.[64]

One response to this problem was to increase the number of people
on the government's payroll. Between 1960 and 1965 the number of
manufacturing jobs increased by 26,000; the number in agriculture de-

creased by 39,000 and the government did its best to help: It hired 20,000 new employees.[65]

Another response to the stalled economy was to cut corners that were never very sharp in the first place. The hearings held for applicants requesting a tax exemption "became staged events"; petitioners were told beforehand what questions would be asked, they received help filling out troublesome application forms, and company lawyers were sometimes allowed to draft special provisions containing extra exemptions for their clients. Meanwhile, Fomento also played musical chairs with the companies who agreed to stay beyond their first exemption period. What happened was that a large company, say General Electric, closed one of its subsidiaries, brought home the money tax free, and then opened a new subsidiary in the old building.[66]

What was good for General Electric was not good for Puerto Rico. Governor Sanchez understood the problem; however, as a colony Puerto Rico was dependent on the mainland. And as a Populare, Sanchez, and the new generation that surrounded him, urged reforms based "on the models belonging to the same generation they so energetically criticized." One honest man wrote, "We saw it as an internal struggle between young and old, between conservatives and renovators."[67]

Nobody challenged the colonial system. Instead, as in the arrival of Textron in 1948, the Populares were delighted when in early 1965 Secretary of the Interior Stewart Udall allowed the governor to make an astonishing announcement: Puerto Rico had discovered oil! Black gold was the catalyst that would finally turn the Populares' dreams into everyday reality. As the head of Fomento told the media, "I foresee the development here of a scientific and technological complex on the style of Cambridge, Massachusetts and Palo Alto, California. This would give Puerto Rico new direction and new dimensions."[68]

Except for one thing: The entire plan—all the dreams—depended on the will of Congress. As with sugar in 1934, the petroleum companies that came to Puerto Rico after 1964 produced only what Washington said was an appropriate amount; each company received a quota that was never permanent because all quotas were themselves based on controversial exemptions to rules that had a powerful mainland constituency, linked to an even more powerful national purpose: defense, the security of the United States.

In the 1950s Americans refused to be dependent on anyone, so among others, President Eisenhower established strict quotas on the amount of foreign oil permitted to reach U.S. shores. The program initially contained voluntary restrictions, but when these didn't work, the president imposed mandatory limits based on the level of imports in 1958.[69]

One territory harshly affected by the president's quotas was Puerto Rico. Indeed, when he testified on behalf of the companies coming in the 1960s, Resident Commissioner Santiago Polanco-Abreu explained how Eisenhower's restrictions had destroyed the plans and facilities established in the 1950s.

The freeze [on the amount of oil imported] came at a particularly critical period. Fomento had invested nearly eight years' time and Government in excess of $8 million attempting to formulate an entirely new industrial concept and the experiment was far from complete. The immediate condition of the industry and the lack of flexibility imposed by the controls indicated the full potentials envisioned for petrochemicals would never be realized.[70]

In short, no new refineries were built, no new jobs provided.

Thus, when in 1965 Phillips Petroleum finally received permission to establish a new facility in Puerto Rico, no one could argue that Fomento planners never knew what they were getting into. Why, then, did they come back for more? Equally important, why did Washington agree to exemptions for Puerto Rico in the face of opposition from oil companies like Standard and Continental Oil, and from powerful senators like Russell Long of Louisiana, Rogers Morton of Kentucky, and Everett Dirksen of Illinois?

Sleeze politics was one explanation for the Phillips exemption. As Senator Morton stressed in angry speech on August 3, 1965:

Two of the President's close friends helped steer the proposal through the Interior Department. Oscar Chapman, Secretary of the Interior under President Truman, acted as an attorney for Phillips, and Abe Fortas, a former Interior official and frequently the President's personal attorney, acted as attorney for the Commonwealth of Puerto Rico."[71]

Clearly, it does help to have friends in high places. But the exemption for Phillips (and soon after for Union Carbide, Texaco, and Sun Oil) nevertheless had roots that cut to the essential dilemma faced (and still faced) by Puerto Rico and the United States.

Before and after Muñoz, the Populares agreed, however reluctantly, that all roads led to Washington. No matter how many times Congress refused to enhance Commonwealth, the Populares refused to opt for any other significant alternative. Their dependence on the United States was total, even to the point of reducing their reliance on U.S. capital by pleading for more of it and by trying to reestablish an industry Washington had (in 1959) just destroyed.

The White House, and the few congressmen who knew anything about Puerto Rico, were also neck deep in a hole they had dug. By refusing to grant independence, statehood, or enhanced Commonwealth, they guaranteed perpetual dependence on the United States. The only alternative was to redesign the island's failed economic program; but for any new program to have any chance of producing self-sustaining growth, Washington had to concede political powers the Constitution delegated to Congress. The choice was simple: Free the colony (either independence or statehood was possible) or shore up the economy with whatever program offered some hope of keeping disaster at bay.

Luis Muñoz Marín made this clear in a "last request" letter (December 8, 1964) to President Johnson. He called the president's attention to this fact: "The establishment in Puerto Rico of this petrochemical complex is essential to fulfillment of our goal of eradicating poverty in Puerto Rico." As always, the island was relying on private capital, but for that capital to come there was one requirement: The president had to authorize the project through grant of the application for an import exemption.[72]

Muñoz hoped, he wrote, that the president would authorize Secretary [Stewart] Udall to consider, as a major factor in his deliberations on the Phillips application, the relationship of this oil import application to [the] War on Poverty as it affects Puerto Rico."[73]

Udall agreed with Muñoz, to the point of making poverty the most significant variable affecting his decision to grant the import exemption. In a February 2, 1965, letter to the director of the budget he wrote that "the Island will soon be in serious difficulties unless new approaches are taken to assure sustained economic growth." In his mind Commonwealth officials had made a convincing case for the petrochemical complex; he hoped the director of the budget agreed because "it seems evident that Puerto Rico must promptly attract industries that will afford greatly increased opportunities for employment if the well-being of its citizens is to be promoted and a rising tide of unemployment checked."[74]

The tragedy—perceived at the time—was that the petrochemical complex included all the elements that assured, not sustained growth, but sustained dependence on outside capital, accompanied by sustained dependence on Washington, accompanied by sustained levels of tortuously high unemployment. Phillips, for example, had a sweetheart deal every bit as enticing as the one offered to Royal Little in 1948. Estimates of its initial extra profits ranged from $15 million to $30 million a year; this was itself tax free, and even though the secretary literally demanded that Phillips agree to reinvest portions of its windfall, the contract also included escape clauses: As Senator Morton told his colleagues in Congress, the deal between Phillips and Puerto Rico "provides that, in the event such [import] protection is withdrawn and the market opened up to all through lifting of import controls, Phillips can pull out of Puerto Rico entirely. What a brazen condition. And what a bonanza to Phillips."[75]

The Phillips deal also failed to reverse what Milton Taylor had called, in 1953, the perverse impact of the tax exemption incentive. What Puerto Rico had was people. To give the exemption to businesses that were capital intensive—the Resident Commissioner noted that a $400,000,000 investment had so far produced only 4,000 jobs[76]—was to assure that the profits went to the companies who would provide the fewest jobs as they simultaneously made the largest profits.

Theoretically, the complex was to provide "spin off" work for Puerto Rico's unemployed. Plastics, insecticides, synthetic fibers, resins: Puerto Ricans would work in these satellite factories only if Congress agreed to increase the quotas that were, even at their initial levels, extraordinarily difficult to obtain. By 1967 President Johnson's Special Counsel reported that twenty-eight senators had introduced a bill "to severely limit the movement to the States of petroleum products other than crude oil, *including the shipment of such products from Puerto Rico to the United States* [emphasis in original]." To Harry McPherson, "this bill would hurt the Commonwealth boys badly," since "in stifling Puerto Rico's petroleum industry, the bill would destroy the major, and perhaps only means now available to Puerto Rico to cope in a substantial fashion with the island's critical unemployment problem."[77]

The Johnson administration helped defeat the restrictive legislation by agreeing to restrict the amount of oil imported into Puerto Rico. Senator Long held a gun—his legislation—to Secretary Udall's head, and the same man who promised sustained growth also stopped it. By late 1967 Udall agreed that "he would grant no more quotas that would result in a significant amount of petroleum products flowing to the East Coast from the Caribbean Area."[78]

By making its oil more expensive than U.S. crude, the Organization of Petroleum Exporting Countries (OPEC)—and Puerto Rico's "ally" Venezuela was part of OPEC—eventually destroyed Puerto Rico's petrochemical dreams. But long before OPEC appeared on the scene, those dreams were threatened, not by the poverty of the Puerto Rican people, but by the poverty of the ideas the Populares and the Americans employed. One failure followed another, and as the economic hold grew deeper, both sides filled it with more dependence on strategies that were as perversely effective in 1965 as they were in 1948.

Nobody wanted to make fundamental changes, least of all the Status Commission appointed by President Lyndon Johnson.

Commission Chairman James Rowe wrote to the president on July 28, 1966. Apparently that first fifteen minutes at the inaugural White House meeting was all the time Johnson ever devoted to the commission's work, for Rowe began his memo by telling the president, "You may recall you appointed me Chairman of the Commission. Its function was to recommend whether Puerto Rico should stay as a Commonwealth, become a State or become an independent nation."[79]

Well, the commission had now finished its work, and Rowe needed to know if the President wanted a formal presentation of the report or "did he just want to duck it." Ever the politician, Rowe asked, "What if anything would a formal presentation of the Report do to *help* [emphasis in original] President Johnson?" The Puerto Ricans were "a formal lot, loving ceremony and ritual." Even more important, "they were fast becoming a balance of power in New York State politics, and a minority group which occasionally, but not often, mutter about favoritism toward the Negroes. Certainly they are not alienated today like the Mexican-Americans. But they are sensitive and proud."[80]

Rowe had no particular suggestion, such as distributing pens or autographed pictures with a concerned President, but he did say, "My personal judgement is that collectively they would not be offended if there is no ceremony, but would be pleased if there is one."

With the essential issues settled, Rowe also added three sentences about the commission's work. First, "the Report is, I think, a safe one. It does *not* recommend to the President or the Congress that he or they *do* anything [emphasis in original]." Another sentence says that each of the three—Commonwealth, statehood, independence—are possible and that all three are "equal in dignity." (Very important!) However, if the people of Puerto Rico and the Congress were eventually to select statehood or independence, "a transition period from fifteen to an indefinite number of years would be necessary."[81]

End of the president's briefing. Back to politics. Rowe explained that because of the "irreconcilable conflict" between Senator Jackson and Muñoz, Jackson would have a short accompanying statement when the report was issued. Rowe had done his best to "fuzz" this over, but Jackson meant to stress that English had to be the language of the Commonwealth and, more importantly, "that Congress could act unilaterally without the consent of Puerto Rico."

One final point: "There are United Nation undertones in all of this but we have watched them very carefully."[82]

Johnson decided to duck the report. The memos suggest that he had nothing to gain politically from a formal presentation of a perfectly "safe" report. His aides said he was already popular with Puerto Ricans, and to call attention to the report was to call attention to the remarks of Senator Jackson. The Cubans kept raising the Puerto Rican issue in the United Nations, and even though Ambassador Arthur Goldberg "pulled out all the stops to block" the Cubans,[83] publicity about Senator Jackson's position would underline the validity of the Cubans' argument and, just possibly, make it impossible for Goldberg to stop them. As another memo noted, "When colonial issues arise even the Latins desert us."[84]

A Johnson assistant accepted the report as the president's proxy. Despite Rowe's assurances, however, the report did make one tentative recommendation: An expression of the will of the people would be "helpful."

The plebiscite was once again on the table, and as in 1962, the statehooders tenaciously (if you were a Populare the word would be *stubbornly*) held to the principles set out when Muñoz first called for a vote on status. For example, Governor Sanchez sent the island's legislature the draft of a plebiscite bill on December 6, 1966; that same day the statehooders literally walked out of the legislature. They had repeatedly asked Muñoz in 1962, and the commission from 1964 to 1966, to "clearly define" Commonwealth before submitting the status question to the will of the people. The commission did nothing to satisfy their understandable demands—after all, what sense did it make for the people to vote for a word (*Commonwealth*) that, as the presentation of the Report proved, meant very different things to Senator Jackson and Luis Muñoz Marín. So they refused to participate in a process that would simply certify the totally confusing status quo.[85]

Since the Populares controlled the legislature, they passed a plebiscite bill on December 23, 1966, which called for a vote the following July. The statehooders, now fighting among themselves, tried to reach a consensus about their position. Eventually they agreed to disagree—many statehooders voted in the plebiscite, a relatively equal number abstained—but the Populares had neatly put them between a rock and a hard place. If the statehooders didn't participate, Commonwealth was even more likely to receive an overwhelming endorsement; and if they did participate, the statehooders essentially legitimated a procedure they knew to be farcical, namely, to vote without a precise definition of enhanced commonwealth.

Meanwhile, the *independentistas* had sent shivers down the spine of J. Edgar Hoover. In August 1966 Juan Mari Bras, head of the MPI, had been invited to the home of Concepción de Gracia, head of the Puerto Rican Independence party. For years these men had been unable to work together but the prospect of a plebiscite moved them to join forces, a situation the FBI founded intolerable. In a memo dated September 2, 1966, headquarters instructed all relevant agents to "be alert for an opportunity to disrupt this budding alliance between these two individuals and their organizations while it is in the formative stage. The development of suitable counter-intelligence measures to accomplish this should receive close and continual attention by your office."[86]

Agents immediately and creatively followed orders. In February 1967 they added to their typewritten letters "brief handwritten paragraphs in order to personalize" the attacks on independence officials. This personal touch was designed to allay the suspicions of *independentistas* who, through the 1960s, had received so many FBI communications that they were always skeptical of attacks made by one member of the group on another. The FBI noted, "It is expected that they [the handwritten paragraphs] will enhance prospects of positive results."[87]

The FBI was wrong. By June a memo titled "Groups Seeking Independence for Puerto Rico" noted that "the various groups advocating independence have greatly increased their activities with the approaching plebiscite." However, this dangerous situation could be remedied if headquarters accepted this suggestion: The proindependence groups all used the same printing presses. So "the San Juan office proposes that a chemical agent, available to the Bureau, be placed in the printer's ink which, activated by the heat of the presses, will emit a strong odor and prohibit the use of the presses."[88]

Its inventors claimed that the agent would make a skunk proud; despite this endorsement, however, headquarters said no to the use of stink bombs. This sound idea had to be rejected because the FBI no longer had the keys to the building that housed the independence printing presses. The fellow who was the FBI's double agent had been caught sneaking into the building only days before, and the FBI refused to risk getting caught in the act with the plebiscite now only weeks away.[89]

The vote occurred on July 23, 1967, and as expected, Commonwealth received an overwhelming endorsement: 60 percent for continuation of the present status, 39 percent for statehood. As Governor Sanchez soon put it in a letter to Johnson, 99.39 percent of islanders favored a permanent union with the United States, so wasn't it time to finally define the actual meaning of Commonwealth status?

As a matter of record that process was already under way the day before the Puerto Rican people voted. In a handwritten note (dated July 22, 1967) to Supreme Court Justice Abe Fortas, Luis Muñoz Marín submitted two drafts of the statement the administration should use, in Muñoz's words, "to extend our most affectionate congratulations to our fellow citizens in Puerto Rico upon their chosen form of political status. We are convinced that the relationships they have endorsed so decisively will continue to flourish and improve in the years ahead."[90]

Perhaps Muñoz had access to private polls? In any event he certainly knew what would happen in Puerto Rico. What he could not control was the reaction of Abe Fortas. Muñoz had said, "Here are two drafts to choose from, mix, discard, substitute." Fortas did as he was asked and more because he told Johnson's aides to use draft A for background and in draft B Fortas crossed out a statement central to Muñoz's position.

Muñoz had written "the people of Puerto Rico have earned and deserve our fullest cooperation in the further development of their close and now unalterable relationship to the United States." Fortas wrote in a capital *No* next to the words "and now unalterable." He refused to endorse any statement suggesting that as a result of a plebiscite that had not yet taken place, Congress had somehow relinquished its right to make all needful rules and regulations for Puerto Rico and its people. Fortas's own suggestion, scribbled in at the bottom of Muñoz's draft B, was that the president simply show his "pride and pleasure" that __ percent of the people had endorsed a "definite continuation of the warm and mutually beneficial association between the U.S. and Puerto Rico."[91]

The president did as he was asked. But in expressing his "deep gratification" about the plebiscite's results, Johnson endorsed a position that harked back to the granting of citizenship in 1917. The president expressed his pleasure that "those who went to the polls expressed an abiding loyalty to the permanent union of Puerto Rico and the United States *on the basis of our common American citizenship* [my emphasis]."[92] That, after all, was why Puerto Ricans were made citizens in the first place: to show that the island permanently belonged to the United States.

But when it came to Commonwealth, the president substituted ambiguity for any mention of permanence. He noted that "it is especially gratifying that Commonwealth status—a form of association between Puerto Rico and the Federal Union, mutually created by the Congress of the United States and the people of Puerto Rico—has received a clear endorsement."[93]

Perfect. There was no mention of a compact and no mention of ultimate authority. Congress was listed first, but the Puerto Rican people were also included, so everybody—except Muñoz and anyone else to whom he showed drafts A and B—could read into the statement whatever they pleased.

Johnson also agreed to appoint members to an advisory commission that would discuss perfecting Commonwealth. Seemingly, despite the FBI's activities, he could not resist this closing line: "Self determination is an historic goal of the United States policy. Thus we sought—and have received—an expression of the will of the Puerto Rican people. Having done so, we can move forward together to achieve our hopes for the island, guided by the will of the people."[94]

Years later an internal memo of the Jimmy Carter administration would effectively argue that Johnson's statement smelled as bad as one of the FBI's proposed stink bombs. Carter's people were worried about what to say at the United Nations in 1978. Puerto Rican activists had obtained copies of the FBI's memos and threatened to use them at the United Nations. Carter had an assistant review the documents, and this is what he reported. "In all probability documents have been withheld" and many contain inked-out deletions. But the documents nevertheless showed that "the tactics employed were of the dirty tricks variety: enlisting informant disrupters, circulating rumors, flyers, pamphlets, and anonymous letters; planting stories and cartoons in newspapers; possibly buying off a newspaper columnist; and conducting what were referred to as 'aggressive interviews' of suspects."[95]

The Carter official noted, "That was not an exhaustive list," but

the entire record leaves the United States highly vulnerable to an attack by both independence parties. . . . The U.S. has repeatedly and pridefully declared its policy on political status to be that of self-determination. Yet here is a record of a decade of hanky-panky. . . . What is not acceptable is a campaign of disruption of what functioned as a legally constituted party, a campaign that spread to the non-violence prone independence party.[96]

What President Carter's aides called unacceptable in 1978 was, in 1967, a clear and unequivocal undermining of the Puerto Rican people's right to self-determination. If the absence of a precise definition of Commonwealth and the statehooders' and independence boycott by themselves cast no doubt on the legitimacy of the 1967 plebiscite, presidential confirmation of FBI interference should finally silence those who claim that the 1967 plebiscite was anything other than a shameful episode in U.S.– Puerto Rican relations.

With the 1967 plebiscite victory in its pockets, the FBI turned its attention to the 1968 elections. Headquarters notified the San Juan office that as of December 1967 they should continue to "confuse the independentista leaders, exploit group rivalries and jealousy, inflame personality conflicts, emasculate the strength of these organizations, and thwart any possibility of pro-independence unity."[97]

Hoover was especially concerned about a split among the Populares. None of the old guard wanted to remove their *capacetes* (helmets worn by plantation overseers); they resisted even the minor changes proposed by Governor Sanchez. So when the party voted on its new candidate for governor, Sanchez was booed as he took the podium. The result was the formation of a new party, the People's party, and a split that prompted Hoover to write a special memo in July 1968. He told his agents, "You should closely follow the activities of the various independence seeking groups to determine their plans concerning this election. Be especially alert to any plans of these groups to take advantage of the current problems within the PPD."[98]

Hoover's men returned to their old tactics, spreading, for example, rumors about sexual relationships between one independence activist and the wife of another. The electoral impact of this harassment and interference was felt in two primary areas. First, by creating dissension within the groups, agents helped avert the possibility that as in 1946, or even in 1952 (when they won 19% of the vote), independence activists would once again become a significant force in island politics.

Second, and more important for any understanding of the island from 1968 until today, the FBI continued a policy of harassment that "began" with Muñoz's enactment of La Mordaza in 1948. A youngster born in 1950 or 1960 grew up fearing the consequences of any independence activity. That fear became (and remains) an institutionalized part of Puerto Rican political life, and the FBI must assume a good degree of responsibility for helping the Populares strike fear into the heart of anyone considering an independence posture. No one knows what the Puerto Rican people really believe because to this day few islanders will ever openly discuss independence leanings—especially with an American.

Beside FBI interference, another noteworthy result of the 1968 elections was the victory—first in island history—of the statehood, or New Progressive, party. Granted, the statehooders won only because the Populares split their votes—42 percent for Muñoz's man, 10 percent for Sanchez's People's party—but their victory still represented far more than a one election aberration. In fact, the victory of Luis Ferre signified a marked change in the political allegiance of many Puerto Ricans, especially poor Puerto Ricans; it also was a fundamental about-face in the claims of those who advocated statehood.

In the 1940s islanders asked for statehood; and despite one rejection after another, they continued to plead for what Congress refused to give.

After 1968 islanders demanded statehood; they claimed it as a *right* of citizenship, and they directed their appeals to the many thousands of unemployed Puerto Ricans squashed into the island's cities.

Industrialization, accompanied by the Populares' neglect of agriculture, urbanized the Puerto Rican people. They waited for jobs in San Juan, Ponce, or Mayagüez while the Populares highlighted the industries, like petrochemicals, that not only provided few jobs but gave those jobs to the minority of islanders with a good education.

Statehooders saw a hole, which they filled with a message that was, supposedly, anathema to citizens who ardently defended the Republican party ideals of Richard Nixon; the message was that statehood is for the poor. Or as Carlos Romero Barcelo proudly told prospective supporters:

The logical—and accurate—conclusion that we can draw from the above observations is that Puerto Rico's per capita contribution to the Federal Treasury, were we a state, would come to less that of any other state in the Union. At the same time, the per capita benefits we'd reap from federal aid programs would be greater than those of any other state in the Union.[99]

The statehooders were never subtle. Vote to be the fifty-first star because the federal government would assist islanders in every important aspect of life. Food stamps, housing, unemployment insurance, jobs: The list got longer when Puerto Rico's economy took an especially bad turn; but whether short or long, the list always produced the same bottom line: Ask not what you can do for yourself, ask what the state can do for you.

The Ferre administration, for example, began a "massive expansion of the public sector's commitment." From a small thing like annual Christmas (not Three Kings Day) bonuses for all government employees, to pressuring the federal government to extend food stamps to the island, to a substantial increase in the number of jobs in state-supported construction projects, Ferre and his associates helped change the tone of island politics.[100]

Statehood, once a political ideal, was transformed into an economic tool; it became the theoretical salvation of a failed economy while Congress, with no analysis whatsoever, offered statehooders (and Populares) the food stamp program that perversely complimented the statehooders' message.

As a poor islander would soon tell the wife of ex-Governor Sanchez Vilella, "This is worse than Hiroshima."

"Why?" asked Jeanette Sanchez Vilella.

"Because," said the old lady, "we have no dignity left."

"But how can you not give it to them?" asked Guillermo Rodríguez Benitez, head of the Government Development Bank.[101]

NOTES

1. President Carter Library, Atlanta, Georgia, President's Personal Files, Box 80, memo dated May 9, 1978.

2. President Lyndon Johnson Library, Austin, Texas, National Security File, Country File—Latin America, Puerto Rico, Vol. 1, January 1962–March 1965, memo titled "Puerto Rico Real Estate Negotiations" and dated December 14, 1961.

3. Naval Historical Center, Operational Archives Division, Roosevelt Roads, U.S. Naval Station, Command History File, 1943–1973, p. 2.

4. President Kennedy Library, Boston, Massachusetts, White House Central Files, ST 51–2, memo dated February 13, 1961.

5. Kennedy Library, WHCF, 51–2, memo dated July 25, 1961.

6. Kennedy Library, Oral History Interview with Governor Muñoz Marín, June 11, 1965, p. 3.

7. Kennedy Library, National Security Files, Box 335, September 28, 1961.

8. Ibid., September 17, 1961.

9. Johnson Library, p. 2.

10. See Kennedy Library, Muñoz interview, p. 3.

11. Ibid., p. 4.

12. Johnson Library, p. 2.

13. Ibid., p. 2.

14. Kennedy Library, National Security Files, Box 329, p. 1 of the four-page letter.

15. Ibid., p. 2.

16. Kennedy Library, National Security Files, Box 329.

17. Kennedy Library, Muñoz interview, p. 5.

18. Ibid., p. 12.

19. Ibid.

20. Kennedy Library, WHCF, 51–2, July 24, 1962.

21. Juan García Passalacqua, *La Crisis Política en Puerto Rico*, 2nd ed. (Río Piedras: Edil, 1983), p. 26.

22. Ibid., pp. 26–27.

23. Ibid., p. 33.

24. Ibid., p. 36.

25. Kennedy Library, WHCF, Box 18, Reis's memo was directed to Arthur Schlesinger and it is dated December 29, 1962; see pp. 2–3.

26. Ibid., p. 12.

27. Ibid., pp. 14–15.

28. Ibid., p. 18.

29. Kennedy Library, WHCF, 51–2, pp. 1 and 2 of the memo.

30. Ibid., p. 2.

31. *Puerto Rico–1963, Hearings before a Subcommittee on Territorial and Insular Affairs of the Committee on Interior and Insular Affairs*, House, 88th Congress, 1st session, 1963, pp. 1–2.

32. García Passalacqua, *La Crisis Política*, p. 38.

33. Hearings, 1963, p. 50.

34. Ibid.

35. Ibid.

36. Ibid.

37. Ibid.

38. Ibid., p. 51.

39. Ibid.

40. Ibid., pp. 193–194.

41. Ibid., p. 194.

42. Ibid., p. 196.

43. Ibid., p. 200.

44. See *Puerto Rico Federal Relations Act, Hearings before the Committee on Interior and Insular Affairs*, Senate, 86th Congress, 1st session, 1959, p. 52.

45. *Congressional Record*, House, 88th Congress, 1st session, October 23, 1963, p. 19120; for Representative Gross's remark see p. 19118.

46. Ibid., p. 19120.

47. Ibid.

48. Johnson Library, Ex.File Group 759, Box 408.

49. Ibid., p. 1.

50. Ibid., p. 2.

51. Ibid. Memo is three pages.

52. Ibid., p. 2.

53. Ibid.

54. Ibid., p. 3.

55. Johnson Library, Ex.Files Group 759, Box 408, press release dated June 9, 1964.

56. Marie Merrill Ramírez, *The Other Side of Colonialism: Cointelpro Activities in Puerto Rico in the 1960's*, University of Texas at Austin, 1990, p. 494.

57. Ronald Fernández, *Los Macheteros* (New York: Prentice Hall, 1987), p. 54.

58. Merrill Ramírez, *The Other Side of Colonialism*, p. 482.

59. Ibid., p. 483.

60. Ibid., p. 528.

61. Ibid., p. 529.

62. See García Passalacqua, *La Crisis Política*, p. 60; also Robert Anderson, "The Party System: Change or Stagnation," pp. 3–27, in Jorge Heine, ed., *Time for Decision* (Lanham, Md.: North-South, 1983).

63. Johnson Library, Office Files of H. McPherson, Box 27.

64. See *Tax Treatment of U.S. Concerns with Puerto Rican Affiliates, Hearings before the Select Committee on Small Business*, Senate, 88th Congress, 2nd session, 1964, esp. p. 84.

65. Department of the Treasury, *The Operation and Effect of the Possessions Corporation System of Taxation*, Sixth Report, Washington, D.C., GPO, 1989, p. 21.

66. See Luis P. Costas Elena," I.R.C. Section 936 and Fomento Income Tax Exemptions in Puerto Rico," *Revista del Colegio de Abogados de Puerto Rico* 42 (November 1981): esp. pp. 637–639.

67. García Passalacqua, *La Crisis Política*, p. 188.

68. *U.S. News And World Report*, March 15, 1965, pp. 90–92.

69. *Hearings before the Subcommittee on Mines and Mining*, Committee on Interior and Insular Affairs, House, 90th Congress, 2nd session, 1968, pp. 23–24.

70. Ibid., p. 265.

71. *Congressional Record*, 89th Congress, 1st session, August 3, 1965, p. 19079.

72. Johnson Library, Office Files of Harry McPherson, Box 27, pp. 1–2.

73. Ibid.

74. Ibid.

75. *Congressional Record*, 1965, p. 19078.

76. See *Hearings*, 1968, 261.

77. Johnson Library, Papers of Harry McPherson, memo and summary of the legislation dated October 13, 1967.

78. See, for example, *U.S. News and World Report*, December 4, 1967, p. 106; see, too, *Economic Study of Puerto Rico*, Commerce Department (Washington, D.C.: Government Printing Office, 1979); Vol. 2 has a good summary of federal policies regarding the oil industry.

79. Johnson Library, Office Files of Harry McPherson, Box 27.

80. Ibid., p. 1 of the Rowe memo.

81. Ibid., pp. 1 and 2 of the memo.

82. Ibid., p. 2.

83. Johnson Library, Office Files of Harry McPherson, Box 27, Memo to W. W. Rostow, dated January 10, 1968.

84. Johnson Library, Office Files of Harry McPherson, Box 27; this is a memo about the United Nations to Lee White, dated November 30, 1964.

85. For the administration's history of the plebiscite see Johnson Library, White House Central Files, Box 30 (1593).

86. See Merrill Ramírez, *The Other Side of Colonialism*, p. 542.

87. Ibid., p. 545.

88. See Document 16, "Informe of the Puerto Rican Civil Rights Commission," Washington, D.C.: Commonwealth of Puerto Rico, 1989, Appendix.

89. Merrill Ramírez, *The Other Side of Colonialism*, pp. 548–549.

90. Johnson Library, White House Central Files, Box 30 (1593).

91. Ibid.; Fortas's comments appear on the bottom of draft B.

92. Johnson Library, White House Central Files, ST51–2.

93. Ibid., p. 1 of the president's statement.

94. Ibid., p. 2 of the statement.

95. Carter Library, see note 1; this is from p. 2 of the three-page summary.

96. Ibid., p. 3.

97. Merrill Ramirez, *The Other Side of Colonialism*, p. 577.

98. The Hoover memo, dated July 25, 1968, can be found in the Appendix to the Report of the Puerto Rican Civil Rights Commission.

99. Carlos Romero Barcelo, *Statehood Is for the Poor* (San Juan, 1974), p. 87.

100. The massive expansion comment is from Jorge Heine, ed., *Time for Decision* (Lanham, Md.: North-South, 1983), p. xxiv; on the Christmas bonuses see Kal Wagenheim, *Puerto Rico: A Profile* (New York: Praeger, 1972), p. 86.

101. See President Gerald Ford Library, Ann Arbor, Michigan, Domestic Council, Papers of James M. Cannon, Box 28. The quote is from a long report prepared by Sam Halper.

Chapter 9

Continued Colonialism

No provision of law bestows a constitutional status on the
U.S. citizenship held by persons born in Puerto Rico.
Attorney General Dick Thornburgh, February 5, 1991

I also want to compliment you, Mr. Chairman, for your
perseverance. You are almost solely responsible for bringing
this issue to the attention of both the Senate and the House.
Quite frankly, my first impression in the last Congress was
that both you and Senator McClure must have spent too
much time in the sun.
Senator Malcolm Wallop, January 30, 1991[1]

A Republican brought food stamps to Puerto Rico. In a laudable attempt
to forever end hunger in the United States, President Richard Nixon
argued that the poorest Americans should have free food stamps and
that allotments should be substantially increased. After many calls from
men like Governor Luis Ferre, Nixon (and Congress) also agreed to
extend the food stamp program to Puerto Rico, Guam, and the Virgin
Islands in 1971. An effort that cost $228 million in 1969, food stamp
allocations grew so fast that by 1973 the program cost more than $2
billion a year.[2]

For a variety of political and administrative reasons, Puerto Ricans
initially received less than their fair share of stamps. But Congress had
a problem: The price of commodities was rising so fast in 1973 that the
cost of delivering actual food to the poor promised to be "prohibitively

expensive." What to do? A young lawyer whispered into the ear of now-Speaker of the House Tom Foley: "Phase in foodstamps nationwide and phase commodities out."[3]

One whisper equaled one simple solution that, together, equaled a federal mandate to extend food stamps into every state and territory and possession of the United States. By law the program was to be phased in over time, but Carlos Romero Barcelo, mayor of San Juan and author of *Statehood Is for the Poor*, sued and beat the federal government in federal court. As of September 1974 the Court ordered that the food stamp program be extended at once to every city and town and *barrio* (neighborhood) in Puerto Rico.

Because the island's per capita income was half again as small as the nation's poorest state, fully 75 percent of Puerto Rico's population qualified for food stamps. So with good intentions but absolutely no analysis of the impact of so much money—$500 million within a year of its implementation—food stamps came to Puerto Rico, met by an avalanche of requests that was so great that some "certifying centers" in San Juan handled more clients than the entire state of Texas. Within twelve months *cupones* penetrated more deeply into the poor person's house than any federal program in the twentieth century; and if food stamps helped people weather the temporary economic storms caused by the oil crisis of 1973, and the perpetual failure of Operation Bootstrap, they also created negative consequences that remain an institutionalized part of island life.

First came the underground economy. If people worked in legitimate occupations, they showed income that made them ineligible for stamps. Thus, more and more Puerto Ricans either refused to work or, if they did so, bartered with one another or accepted cash payments "under the table."

Second, especially in the 1970s, came the new cars. The U.S. and local banks suddenly had hundreds of millions of dollars of "costless, risk-free government money."[4] One alternative was to invest in projects that offered some hope of long-term benefits. Another, the one chosen, was to loan the money to finance companies, who loaned it back to the Puerto Rican people, who paid for the loans with the money from food stamps and the income earned under the table. So as workers lost their jobs in Detroit, subsidiaries of Chase Manhattan and Citibank used federal food stamp funds to underwrite the purchase of Japanese automobiles.

The cars point to a third unintended consequence of the stamps. So much money could have had substantial ripple effects in the local economy if people used the money to buy food produced and goods manufactured in Puerto Rico. Tragically, the Japanese cars suggest what happened to the money: Whether for food from the States or cars from the Orient, the increased demand created by the stamps had its principal sales impact—except, of course, for the banks—outside of the island. The food stamp millions did little to help an economy that was increasingly dependent on the stamps as a principal source of the island's rising per capita income.[5]

Recall the message of the statehooders; they wanted to use federal funds to help the island's poor. The Populares, seeing the political impact of this message, also caught the federal bug, and in the 1972 election one party competed with the other to root economic growth not only in private capital from the mainland but also in *public* capital from the mainland.

The Populares, for example, won the 1972 election—the new governor was Rafael Hernández Colón—but that had no impact on federal funding: It continued to climb so fast that between 1970 and 1975 the increase in net transfer payments (e.g., the food stamps and unemployment insurance) was 649 percent and the rise in total federal assistance 207 percent; the percentage of the GNP derived from federal assistance had also doubled, from 10 percent to fully 20 percent of the island's gross product.[6]

What about the Congress that time and again claimed responsibility for setting Puerto Rico's short- and long-term course? Well, as the food stamp program proved, Congress sometimes acted without thinking; more often, however, Congress simply accepted the consequences created by the inherent contradictions of its Puerto Rican policy. After all, if Puerto Ricans were Americans, then you had to extend to the island most, if not all, of the programs that real Americans received. To say no to the island was to underline its colonial status; thus when a new program was created, or an old one received additional funding on the mainland, Puerto Ricans also got their share of the public pie. It was policy by default, a plastic-coated bandage that dramatically increased the island's already significant dependence on the United States.

Hope for change was difficult to find. The oil crisis murdered the already-weakened petrochemical complex, so despite massive increases in federal funding, both statehood and Populare governments kept catastrophe at bay only by substantially increasing public sector borrowing and public sector employment. Never more than $100 million a year before 1968, public sector borrowing climbed to $600 million in 1975; and while the number of people employed in manufacturing fell by 2,000, the number employed by government increased by 37,000 between 1970 and 1975.[7]

It was a disastrous situation made all the worse by yet another refusal to enhance Commonwealth. After years of study, and arguably the most thorough, honest, and conscientious review by any U.S. president, Gerald Ford reluctantly told Congress that it was impossible to agree to the latest Puerto Rican proposals. The Interior Department advised him in a memo, "Admittedly, the argument can be made that this [Commonwealth status] is continued 'colonialism' and falls short of full self government and self determination; but we do not believe that the constitutional mechanism exists to do more without admitting Puerto Rico as a State of the Union or granting it its independence."[8]

President Gerald Ford inherited the problems created by, especially, Presidents John Kennedy and Lyndon Johnson. The former delivered a "let's delay a decision" commission and the latter a plebiscite invalidated by, among other things, FBI "swashbuckling."

President Richard Nixon's role was to appoint the advisory commissions mandated by the victory of Commonwealth in the 1967 plebiscite. The first of these commissions was appointed in 1970, but Congress refused to accept its recommendations (e.g., that islanders vote in presidential elections). In September 1973 with the Populares back in the governor's mansion, President Nixon appointed another advisory group to potentially enhance Commonwealth. Senator Marlow Cook of Kentucky headed the U.S. delegation, former governor Luis Muñoz headed Puerto Rico's contingent of mostly Populare politicians.

The "Ad Hoc Advisory Group on Puerto Rico" was still at work when Gerald Ford assumed the presidency on August 9, 1974. He inherited the issues ducked by his immediate predecessors, but when Ford forthrightly tried to face those issues, he immediately confronted the problems left by all his presidential predecessors: After 76 years holding Puerto Rico as a U.S. possession, the White House still "had no permanent records or knowledge of Puerto Rico." In one administration after another, policy had been decided in a social and historical vacuum, a situation Ford tried to change by recommending the creation of "some institutional permanency" in the White House.[9]

Ford also hired Samuel Halper, a longtime editor of *Time* and a former consultant to the Puerto Rican government. Halper knew the island quite well and soon presented the president with a long, informative, and utterly pessimistic analysis of Puerto Rican society. Guillermo Rodríguez Benítez, then head of the Government Development Bank, told Halper:

After 25 years what have we to show? Our industrialization program has been anything but a success. If we had been competitive here, with this great tax incentive we have, we'd have been smothered by factories. Where are they? The wage differential is completely wiped out. . . . We couldn't even attempt a Khmer Rouge. There are no cane fields to drive our people back to. What's the answer? I don't know.[10]

Talks with Teodoro Moscoso underlined the point made by Rodríguez: To turn around the economy the government rehired the architect of its admittedly failed program! Equally important, Halper was struck by this small but nevertheless meaningful contradiction: The Puerto Rican members of the advisory commission demanded control over immigration to the island. They were especially concerned by the wave of immigrants from the Dominican Republic. But what did Halper find when he went to Moscoso's home? Despite widespread unemployment, a Dominican was doing the housework in the residence of the man charged with putting Puerto Ricans back to work.[11]

In a section of his report labeled "Search for a Solution" Halper stressed a danger that underlined the contradictions of U.S. policy: For change to occur islanders had to take charge of their own affairs, but that meant an "upsurge of nationalism" and "the danger that the growth in nationalism could slop over into independentismo." Halper reminded the president that "there is a strong independentista unconscious among the Puerto Rican people," so President Ford somehow had to encourage the nationalism that would produce change but not stimulate it so much that it would "slop over" into independence sentiment.

Halper never explained why independence was slop. What he did do was criticize the proposal presented by the Puerto Rican members of the advisory commission. When Halper asked about the costs of tariff changes suggested by Muñoz and his associates, "the upshot of many phone calls on the island and to me [Halper] in New York City from the Governor and the Undersecretary [of Agriculture] was that the costs to Puerto Rico had not been quantified." Halper understandably thought this "raised some questions as to the wisdom" of the proposed changes. But he was even more bothered by what he called the Puerto Rican "spirit of uniqueness": They wanted to set their own wage and environmental standards yet they also wanted to share in the prevailing U.S. benefits in education, housing, and social welfare. In Halper's words, "It's nice if they can get it, and maybe they are entitled to try, but the logic eludes one."[12]

Not really. Luis Muñoz Marín chaired the Puerto Rican advisory group. As always, he wanted his cake and he wanted to eat it too, so when President Ford finally received the recommendations of the Puerto Rican contingent, he discovered a document filled with constitutional problems, accompanied by a threat from Governor Rafael Hernández Colón. As Halper summed it up in his report, the governor stressed that "if we face closed doors we'll find ourselves in a hell of a situation. I'm not saying we'll go independentista. But if they close doors, in a number of years we could be so bad off economically you don't know what will happen here in Puerto Rico."[13]

What a line! A colonial governor had effectively told the president of the United States to give us what we want or we give you your worst nightmare: independence.

Halper advised the president to take the governor's threat seriously. Chaos in the Caribbean was not a pleasant prospect, but unfortunately for President Ford, neither was the document that—ever so slowly— came from his advisory commission. In the first draft submitted by the Puerto Ricans, the Populares had been incredibly insensitive; they had not only drafted the document "in secrecy" but had held "no public meetings, as prescribed by the Federal Advisory Committee Act."[14]

The statehooders—and who could blame them—complained, and so Norman Ross, of the President's Domestic Council, made a suggestion similar to the one given to Presidents Kennedy and Johnson: "Diplomatically terminate the activities of the Advisory Group with an 'acceptable' report." For example, the president could simply table the document because the Populares not only did not consult the statehooders but they also did not consult any of the advisory group's mainland delegates.[15]

In sharp contrast to Presidents Kennedy and Johnson, Ford chose to confront the status issue honestly. Hoping that "the Puerto Rican delegates would be capable of swallowing their embarrassment and retreat from the far reaching position they [had] taken," he sent the document back to the total committee. Mainland and island delegates were to submit a report that would "in the shortest period of time" produce a document capable of eliciting widespread support.[16]

The president tried. Indeed, even after Sam Halper told him that "the agreement, if ratified, will do little to alter the deteriorating state of affairs in Puerto Rico,"[17] President Ford looked for some way out of the nation's colonial dilemma. He was obviously upset when Resident Commissioner Jaime Benítez introduced the compact in legislative form in December 1975, but Ford understood that Benítez, and Hernández Colón, and Muñoz Marín, had acted in such a precipitous fashion because they believed that if the compact was to have any chance of passage before the island's next gubernatorial election, it had to reach Congress as soon as possible.

Ford understood politics. His problem was the "cake and eat it too" compact. The President had, for example, asked all involved government departments to submit detailed comments about the legitimacy of enhanced Commonwealth. What the president received in return was a repeat—albeit the most thorough repeat—of the arguments Muñoz had heard since 1952.

The Interior Department: "The difficulty is that "free Associated State" does not identify with greater accuracy the precise nature of the relationship. If anything it tends to describe a relationship which may be constitutionally infeasible."

The Justice Department: Under the compact "the navigable waters of Puerto Rico would be the property of the latter rather than the United

States. . . . It should be noted that this would confer on Puerto Rico a far greater degree of autonomy than is enjoyed by the several states."

The Commerce Department: This department had "serious problems" with the compact provisions that "would permit Puerto Rico to negotiate independent trade and preferential tariff arrangements with third countries." Puerto Rico was, after all, "part of the customs territory of the United States." In a separate memo from the Commerce Department's Office of Policy Management, officials reminded the president that the island "is currently the world's largest per capita purchaser of mainland United States goods." To make any changes that threatened that trade was to suggest something "of great practical importance to the U.S. mainland business community."

The president also received critical comments from the Department of Agriculture and even from the Secretary of Health, Education, and Welfare.[18] The compact had to be rejected, so President Ford sent a detailed message to "the heads of the House and Senate" on September 24, 1976. He cited many of the problems noted above and a few others as well; for example, he couldn't figure out how an almost sovereign island would also enjoy representation in both the House and Senate of the United States?

The president's ultimate objection revolved around the issue of authority:

The compact would relinquish U.S. powers, while granting incentives, Federal benefits and guarantees and other entitlements and prerogatives. *I believe that to enter into such a relationship with Puerto Rico would constitute a fundamental and unacceptable shift in the relations which the Federal government maintains with other territorial governments* [my emphasis]. A situation such as this may increase rather than decrease existing tensions between the U.S. and Puerto Rico.[19]

The president was right. Taxpayers in the United States were sure to scream if Puerto Rico was treated better than any of the fifty states. Equally important, the compact "raised serious constitutional questions": indeed, as in the 1959 and 1962 analysis by Harold Reis of the Justice Department, yet another independent analysis had concluded that enhanced Commonwealth was a constitutional impossibility.[20]

But in rejecting the compact, the president had also reluctantly affirmed Puerto Rico's colonial status—in the very year the United States celebrated 200 years of independence. After all, if nothing fundamental changed in 1952, and the president of the United States still refused to make fundamental changes in 1976, then Puerto Rico remained, fundamentally, a colony of the United States.

Here is where President Ford differed from his predecessors. He understood the inherent impossibility of the United States ever signing an agreement like that proposed by the Populares. Thus, only two weeks before he left office, the president proposed a new commission. This one would "develop a comprehensive report on all the issues and implications involved in changing the status of Puerto Rico from that of a Commonwealth to that of a State of the Union."[21]

Many people wondered why Gerald Ford made such a proposal only two weeks before leaving office. The primary answer is in a memo to the president dated December 21, 1976. The president's advisers (among them Dick Cheney and Brent Scowcroft) said, "To those of us who have worked with this, it seems clear that the realistic choices for Puerto Rico are either statehood or independence."[22] Real power for Puerto Rico was, given Puerto Rico's military and economic significance, an impossible option for the United States; the President therefore chose statehood.

President Ford and his advisers deserve great credit for doing something no other postwar administration had done: face up to the constitutional futility of Commonwealth-colonial status. Serious problems arise, however, when an observer raises the issue of self-determination. The president hadn't even consulted the statehooders, much less the majority of the population, who, as Sam Halper told him, had "a strong independentista unconscious" running through their psyches. The Populares, for example, immediately accused the president of paying back the Republicans who had voted for him at the convention.[23] Even were this true, the records at the Ford Library indicate that the president's primary motivation was to resolve a problem that had, as he and his advisers saw it, only two solutions: statehood or independence.

Gerald Ford can be legitimately criticized for disregarding the will of the Puerto Rican people and thus acting as what he was: chief executive of a colony. But the president nonetheless confronted the essential issue. He did try to get Puerto Rico and the United States off square one of their (then) seventy-eight-year political relationship.

Congress, on the other hand, had (and still has) no intention of granting statehood; indeed, it had no intention of doing anything about status. It dealt with Puerto Rico by doing what was best for the United States: It approved in 1975 and 1976 a package of tax proposals that, even if they did nothing substantial for Puerto Rico's economy, at least reduced the likelihood that any more Puerto Ricans would come to the United States.

In March 1976 Resident Commissioner Jaime Benítez explained Puerto Rico's problem: The island "was essentially a trading post where we import what we consume and export what we produce." This dismal appraisal put Benítez in a peculiar situation; he was about to act as a lobbyist for the U.S. corporations that had, since 1948, done everything in their power to avoid reinvesting their profits in Puerto Rico. Quoting the House Ways and Means Committee, Benítez agreed that "the present Federal tax exemption of such corporations on income from sources *outside* [my emphasis] of Puerto Rico does not contribute significantly to the economy of the Commonwealth."[24]

What understatement! And what restraint on Benítez's part. When in 1973 and 1974 Congress first decided to change the "possessions corporations" tax laws, for example, it never even bothered to inform the Puerto Ricans. The House Ways and Means Committee actually voted to repeal crucial provisions of the law before the colony found out what was happening. Quick and immediate lobbying changed Congress's mind, but there was still no way to avoid the truth of the remark made by Robert Baker in 1950: "The very meaning of a line in the law is that you may intentionally go as close to it as you can if you do not pass it."

Nobody passed the line in Puerto Rico: Everyone leaped right over it. One device used by the possessions corporations was to open a subsidiary in another country; then with the tax-free profits earned in Puerto Rico their headquarters would finance the new subsidiary. Neatly, neither Puerto Rico nor the United States benefited from the jobs then flowing to Asia.[25]

Congress also discovered the funds flowing from Puerto Rico to Guam to Europe and then, upon liquidation of the possessions corporation, back to Guam, back to Puerto Rico, and finally back to the parent corporation in the United States—who, in the era of the multinational corporation, often made its new investments abroad.

Congress had, of course, long known about the flow of money to Guam. What surprised many analysts in 1975 and 1976 was the amount of money involved; by the federal government's estimate some $5 billion had been stockpiled by the possessions corporations[26] who, in being "forced" to keep the money abroad helped neither the colony nor the mainland.

Congress decided to let the corporations bring home their profits—tax-free—as soon as they pleased; this theoretically eliminated the need to stockpile the money in Guam and even enabled a company to invest its profits on the mainland, in, say, Detroit or Pittsburgh or Buffalo.

But what about the Puerto Rican economy? The purpose of the tax exemption was, after all, to stimulate development on the island. Initially the Puerto Rican government acted in a sane manner; it wanted laws that would allow the government to get its hands on some of a company's profits before they left for parts unknown. One idea—used in Singapore in this period—was to actually demand that the companies reinvest their profits in Puerto Rico.

When the representatives of the possessions corporations told the Puerto Ricans what to do with their reinvestment idea, the always desperate Populares reversed course. Opportunities in Asia made Puerto Rico less attractive than every before, and the application of minimum-wage scales made even other Caribbean islands a lure to potential U.S. investors. So the Populares saw no alternative; they gave in to the possessions corporations' threat, even to the point of agreeing that financial investments in Puerto Rican banks—even sixty- or ninety-day investments—were also free of federal taxes.

The Puerto Rican government did make one change that theoretically promised to increase its tax revenues substantially. In 1976 it added a modest so-called tollgate tax (the figure was generally 10 percent) to its arsenal of weapons designed to keep profits in Puerto Rico. Since both Congress and island representatives assumed that the corporations would bring their dividends home at once, 10 percent of, say, $2 billion or $3 billion a year was a tidy return for the Puerto Rican government and, ultimately, the island's unemployed workforce.[27]

Congress agreed to this corporate windfall for a variety of reasons. First, for almost thirty years it had never received any serious tax money from the possessions corporations, so nothing from nothing was still nothing. A tax reform checklist provided for President Ford noted that the changes in Puerto Rico were "good and not significant."[28] Second was the U.S. balance-of-payments problems. There was so much possessions corporations money abroad that if it came back to the States, the scales would tip at least a little further in the right direction. Third, "the costs and benefits of the [tax exemption] program were poorly understood." Nobody knew what was going on and nobody tried to find out.[29] Finally, there was fear. Congress had no idea what to do with Puerto Rico. It had backed itself into a colonial corner, and even though analysis suggested that the tax exemption laws should be repealed, it never did this because "repeal would lead to plant closings, accelerate Puerto Rican unemployment—which was approaching 20% of the labor force—and force many Puerto Ricans to move to the United States."[30]

The new tax legislation, called the 936 laws, went into effect in 1976. By 1977 the companies had already devised a number of ways to avoid reinvesting the money in Puerto Rico as they simultaneously avoided paying their rightful share of federal taxes.

One beautifully legal scam was the "allocation of intangibles." Say you were one of the pharmaceutical companies busily moving operations to Puerto Rico. What you did was take the rights from a drug invented on the mainland and transfer it to a Puerto Rican subsidiary. Thus, all the money earned by the drug—the so-called intangible—went to Puerto Rico and came home, if you wanted, tax free. Not satisfied with this bonanza, what the companies also did was deduct the costs of *mainland* research and development for the now Puerto Rican intangible from their—you guessed it!—mainland tax bill.[31]

Another technique was to invest funds for very short periods of time. Manuel Escobar explained that much of the money invested in island branches of Citibank and Chase Manhattan belonged to the pharmaceutical companies. Granted, pharmaceutical companies accounted for only 10 percent of the island's possessions corporations, but they still made 45 percent of the net income. In 1978 that was a net profit of $1.1 billion, 30 percent on sales alone.[32]

This much money would never be invested in Puerto Rican factories, but it could reap a healthy return if invested in tax exempt certificates of deposit (CDs). Unfortunately, given possible changes in the tax law, and the need for liquidity, corporations invested 60 percent of their funds in one- to six-month CDs and another 15 percent in six- to twelve-month CDs. The corporations thus used Puerto Rico as a banking warehouse while the island's government, and the Puerto Rican people, found themselves unable to fund long-term investments with short-term funds.[33]

Yet another surprise was the revenue garnered by the tollgate tax: A mere $5 million in 1977. One explanation was a loophole left in the law; Congress and the island legislature had actually retained a liquidation provision in the new tax exemption law. Thus, a corporation preferred to keep its money on the island until it closed up shop, the laws changed, or the government became unstable.

However, to everybody in government's surprise, another reason the corporations failed to bring their bonanza home was "the fear that they would have to provide for the 10% tollgate tax in their financial statements."[34] Mainland corporations used their Puerto Rican subsidiaries as a cash cow; such extraordinary profits substantially increased earnings, plus the value of the company's stock, plus the salary of its executives. To reduce profits by even 10 percent was bad business, so the corporations stockpiled the loot on the island until the Puerto Rican government did as it was asked: It reduced the modest tollgate tax only a year after the first legislation was passed.[35]

These tax reductions were made by the prostatehood administration of now Governor Carlos Romero Barcelo. Running on a platform that specifically put status on the back burner, Romero promised a plebiscite when he got Puerto Rico's economic house in order. However, like the Populares, he too responded to the threats made by the possessions corporations. In the tax adjustments made in 1977, he not only reduced the tollgate tax but also gave an additional exemption to textile, apparel, and shoe manufacturers whose tax exemption grants expired in the next five years. Incredibly, this grant was *automatic*, no demands made, and no serious questions asked about increases in employment or new investment.[36]

Puerto Rico was desperate, and the Carter administration knew it. As part of the Tax Reform Act of 1976, the new federal law mandated periodic reports from the Treasury Department; the theory was, let's finally discover the costs and benefits of the possession corporation system of taxation.

When the White House received a copy of the first report (published in 1978) President Jimmy Carter's adviser Al Stern provided a detailed, in-house analysis of the Treasury Department's findings. For example, he pointed out that "in one possessions corporation [Stern did not name the corporation] the Federal tax expenditure exceeded $500,000 per Puerto Rican employee." The astonishing average for the pharmaceutical companies was $34,873 per employee (by 1983 it was $57,761); this was more than three times the average compensation of employees in the pharmaceutical industry and quite important in any analysis of the Puerto Rican tax program because "corporations whose Federal tax savings per employee exceeded $10,000 per year received 71% of the total tax saving while employing 15% of all possessions corporations' employees."[37]

The Treasury Department had done a good job. Stern's ninety-page analysis was, for example, studded with one abuse after another, such as the way in which headquarters manipulated the subsidiaries' transfer costs of goods and services. Stern agreed that the program was inefficient, but he also stressed that

it can and has been argued that any change which reduced the tax expenditure in the high profit industries . . . would drive the investors out of Puerto Rico. And rather than returning to the United States and paying Federal taxes, they would move their operations abroad. In the end Puerto Rico would lose the benefits, and the Federal government would not collect any additional tax—the large tax expenditure under the current system notwithstanding."[38]

What a predicament! Get fleeced in Puerto Rico or get fleeced abroad but, always, get fleeced.

President Carter, however, had the perfect tool to foster change; fully a year before the Treasury Department study was published he and Governor Romero had asked the Commerce Department to prepare a detailed analysis of the Puerto Rican economy. Granted, "the primary concern in designing the study was to keep it politically neutral so that the Carter Administration would not become entangled in the island debate of what Puerto Rico's Constitutional Status should be."[39] But now that Carter had the Commerce Department study in hand, as well as the similar and equally pessimistic analysis from the Treasury Department,[40] the president could have tried to produce the changes that might have produced jobs. Instead, he chose neutrality while Romero chose to be angry about a report that, in his eyes, was no help toward statehood.

President's Carter's men met with Governor Romero in early November 1978. According to William Pounds, the governor "was displeased with the study." It analyzed Puerto Rico as something other than a state and thus played into the hands of the Populares. What, specifically, asked Pounds, did the governor mean? Romero hedged, but

as an illustration of what he meant—and this is the only time he was specific on the subject in the interview—he offered the observation that the Study consistently used the word "foreign" to describe mainland–Puerto Rican investment and trade flows. He allowed that we would never use the word "foreign" to describe interstate relationships if we were studying the economy of Texas, for example.[41]

The governor had a point. But Puerto Rico was an unincorporated territory; or as Romero told the United Nations only three months before he met with Pounds, "I myself am on record that Puerto Rico's relationship with the United States retains vestiges of colonialism."[42] Given the Governor's statement, how could the Commerce Department do anything else but analyze Puerto Rico as a separate entity?

Pounds felt that "what the Governor really was unhappy about was that in fact the Study was politically neutral." Romero "is appraising the study almost entirely on a political basis, and from the point of view of whether it is consistent with his image of Puerto Rico as a candidate for statehood." In fact, Pounds believed that "there may be little understanding of *or regard for the substantive findings* [my emphasis] of the Study and the value of the Study as a way of getting the Puerto Ricans started in a deliberate process of thinking out what they want for their economy and how to achieve it."[43]

OK. The Puerto Rican government didn't want to face the music. But what about Jimmy Carter? He, after all, now had two studies that demonstrated the extent of the corporate abuses and the ineffectual impact of the tax exemption program. He might have forced the issue; he might have tried to make it something for the nation to debate seriously. Instead, Carter allowed the tax abuses to continue and so too Puerto Rico's ever-increasing dependence on federal funds to keep the economy afloat. From 15 percent of personal income in 1970, transfer payments (e.g., food stamps, social security, veterans benefits) increased to 29 percent of personal income by 1980.[44]

The facts were there. The Treasury and Commerce Departments had done their homework. It's just that no one listened. Or, perhaps more accurately, it is that no U.S. President was willing to take "extraordinary" political chances for Puerto Rico unless the issue was Fidel Castro's twenty-year campaign of (in Washington's eyes) abuse at the United Nations.

In 1961 the United Nations created the Committee on Decolonization. From the formation of the committee until today, the Cubans have diligently tried to make Puerto Rico a part of the committee's work, and just as diligently the U.S. has tried to hamper Puerto Rico's efforts. In 1968, for example, Ambassador Arthur Goldberg "pulled out all the stops" to keep Puerto Rico off the committee's agenda; and in 1975 Ambassador Patrick Moynihan proudly noted that the way to stop the Cubans was "to inform the members of the Decolonization Committee in their capitals that we would regard voting against us on this matter [i.e., a resolution reaffirming the right of the Puerto Rican people to self-determination and independence] to be an unfriendly act."[45]

The UN meeting in 1978 was especially interesting for at least two reasons. First, all island political parties came to the UN sessions and all loudly criticized U.S. policy. Even Romero Barcelo talked about colonialism, although his arguments were quite contradictory. For example, in *Statehood Is for the Poor* Romero wrote, "The results of the general elections held every four years hinge on a great many issues, most of which have little or no direct bearing on the ultimate resolution of Puerto Rico's status question."[46] Yet when Romero wanted to attack the U.N. sessions, he noted that their prime support came from a "political faction [i.e., the independence advocates] in Puerto Rico whose electoral strength has remained at less than eight percent of the voting public for two decades."[47]

If the elections had little or no direct bearing on the issue of political status, then the 8 percent for the *independentistas*, or the 48 percent for the statehooders, was no indication of what Puerto Ricans actually wanted. The electoral returns were not the issue. Colonialism was.

Because the Carter administration understood the real issue, it had, "for the past two years, taken extraordinary diplomatic measures to counter the Cuban campaign."[48] Carter believed that the United Nations had no role to play because Puerto Ricans had freely chosen, in "an act of self determination" to establish links with the United States. Of course, the president's own survey of FBI documents indicated that the bureau had interfered in Puerto Rican politics in general and the 1967 plebiscite in particular.

Equally important, Zbigniew Brzezinski had written a White House memo that noted that "the free associated state may in fact be a contradiction in terms." Brzezinski also added that

from the U.S. perspective Puerto Rico's free elections may suggest a self governing democracy; from the perspective of its Caribbean neighbors or other newly independent and small developing countries, however, Puerto Rico's peculiar relationship with the U.S. doubtless is suggestive of a special variety of neo-colonialism. Cuba is not alone in this interpretation, and the support

Cuba has received at the United Nations on behalf of Puerto Rican independence is at least partly explained by that.[49]

So in private Carter and his men talked of neocolonialism, peculiar relationships, and interference in free elections. In the United Nations, however, they took the extraordinary measures they refused to take in relation to the island's economy. Shortly before the Committee on Decolonization session, on the anniversary of the U.S. invasion, the president issued yet another presidential assurance of self-determination; meanwhile at the United Nations Carter aide Robert Pastor reported that the administration first refused to acknowledge the debate; it then sought to preempt it; it then tried to discourage Puerto Rican leaders from participating in the debate it could not preempt; and, finally, it tried to protest the resolution that "endorsed independence and any form of free association between Puerto Rico and the U.S. based on political equality and a recognition of the sovereignty of the people of Puerto Rico."[50]

The amazing thing about the 1978 UN session was that the Carter administration spent so much time and effort denying reality when it could have been expending extraordinary efforts to implement its own economic suggestions; or just as necessary, it could have been doing something extraordinary to stem the violence that had suddenly appeared on the beaches of Vieques, a jail in Tallahassee, and the streets of San Juan.

The navy lied. It lied so many times and in so many places that the governor of Puerto Rico sued the United States of America. Asked why he had resorted to such a surprising tactic, Carlos Romero Barcelo told Congress that the navy was now using Vieques more heavily than ever before; "in every instance they have been carrying it out over our objections." When asked if he was satisfied with the consultative process between the navy and his administration, Romero explained, "There has been no consultative process about the operations of the Navy."[51]

The navy's lies, and indifference to the expressed will of the Puerto Rican people, dated back to the 1940s. However, like the problem confronted by President Ford when he tried to find the island's permanent White House records, Congress normally discussed Puerto Rico in a social and historical vacuum. The past never had to be erased because no one had written it down in the first place.

This time Congress had to confront, not the navy's distant, but the navy's all too recent war record. On June 22, 1974, after a long and bitter confrontation, President Nixon ordered the navy to leave Culebra. They had to terminate their weapons training activities by July 1, 1975.[52] When that date rolled around, the navy still had set no date for ending its activities, so Culebra's lawyer, Richard Copaken, sent an angry letter to the National Security Council.

Copaken explained that the navy appeared to be lying to everyone. They told him they wanted more time to plan for a final departure from Culebra because they had "not been altogether candid with Congress." For at least a decade they had told the House and Senate that Culebra was "absolutely essential" to the nation's security and now, if they admitted the truth, they would "suffer a loss of credibility on the hill." Copaken hated but understood the navy's predicament. However, he was not "truly shocked" until he found out that the navy was also lying to him and to the people of Puerto Rico: "All the time the Navy was stonewalling it knew full well that Secretary Jack Bowers already had gone on record with a key Congressional Committee to the effect that Navy training at the Culebra Cays as well as at Culebra proper was no longer essential."[53]

The navy eventually obeyed the president's orders. What bothered the Puerto Rican people was that the navy simply transferred to Vieques the bombing that used to occur at Culebra. As Admiral Arthur Knoizen explained to Congress, Vieques was the "tie-in-ingredient" that made the Roosevelt Roads complex the "best Naval training area in the world"; it was America's "university of the sea" and "absolutely essential" to the nation's security because it was the only place in the Atlantic Ocean where planes could "scrimmage" while marines stormed the beach, while boats fired surface-to-air missiles at aerial drones, while submarines patrolled the waters nearby, while North Atlantic Treaty Organization (NATO) forces also participated in the aerial and sea bombardment.[54]

Translated into human terms the navy dropped roughly 3,400 bombs a month, or approximately 5 million pounds of ordnance a year, on an island that was home to 9,000 people.[55] It admitted that "fifty percent of the daylight hours was the approximate usage of the target range of Vieques for either gunfire support or aerial operations." Of course, there was also night bombing—it sounds like persistent thunder if you are on the island—which added up to 158 days a year of naval gunfire, 200 days a year of air-to-ground combat firing, 228 days on the underwater range, 21 days of marine assaults, and a variety of unenumerated NATO attacks.[56]

When the navy said that Vieques was absolutely essential to the national security, the Puerto Rican government understandably remained skeptical. But when islanders discovered the birds were more important than they, a few feathers were ruffled. The navy could have used Bloodsworth Island in the Chesapeake, but it was difficult to conduct coordinated activities so close to people who voted in national elections (i.e., the citizens of Delaware); the sounds from the bombing bothered the nearby residents; and, equally important, "Bloodsworth was closed 3 months of the year to provide habitat for migratory waterfowl." Admiral G.E.R. Kinnear told Congress, "When the geese are moving there are times of the year we cannot use it for that purpose."[57]

Money and time were the real reasons the navy refused to move. As Assistant Secretary of the Navy Jack Bowers told Congress in closed session, "The vast majority of the sites [i.e., alternatives to Culebra and Vieques] were eliminated from consideration because they were beyond the practical range in which logistic support could be provided from Naval Station, Roosevelt Roads."[58] For example, the navy could have used Dog Island, also in the Caribbean. But the navy's study "concluded that the Dog Island location is too far from existing weapons training sites for coordinated exercises."[59] On Vieques, only seven miles from the Roosevelt complex, the boats spent substantially less money on fuel and, each night, they returned to the base for rest and relaxation. This was too perfect a facility to relinquish, so as in the 1940s, the Puerto Ricans could put up with it or move to Alaska.

The governor sued the United States, but long before the case was settled, islanders decided to imitate Dr. Martin Luther King, Jr. In 1978 they blocked the marines with "beach-ins," while island fishermen placed their tiny vessels in front of the fleet's destroyers and over the fleet's submarines. The resisters were arrested, and one young man, Angel Rodríguez Cristóbal, was sentenced to serve time in federal prison in Tallahassee, Florida.

Rodríguez was murdered in prison. Guards were the suspected assailants, but no one was arrested. In retaliation for what happened to Rodríguez, a Puerto Rican revolutionary group, Los Macheteros (the cane cutters), attacked a navy bus on December 9, 1979. Two sailors were killed and ten injured in an attack that was immediately labeled a terrorist assault.[60]

This label created a consistency problem for U.S. policy makers because only three months before the attack on the bus President Jimmy Carter had pardoned Oscar Collazo (the Nationalist who attacked President Harry Truman's residence in 1950) and the four Nationalists who opened fire on the House of Representatives in 1954. Following the example set by Pedro Albizu Campos in the 1940s, all five had refused to leave prison unless they were granted an unconditional pardon. Carter agreed to free them because as, Zbigniew Brzezinski put it,

there are compelling humanitarian, foreign policy and political reasons for releasing from *prison the Puerto Rican nationalists* [emphasis in original]. Lolita Lebron and three other Puerto Rican nationalists have been in Federal prison for 24 years. No other woman in the Hemisphere has been in prison on such charges for so long a period; a fact which Communist critics of your human rights policy are fond of pointing out.[61]

Other than the partially cynical basis for the humanitarian gesture, the fascinating thing about the internal debate in the Carter White House was the label attached to the prisoners: They were "Puerto Rican Independence Fighters."[62] They were revolutionaries who had attacked agents of colonial authority, and whatever one thought about the use of violence, the Carter administration understood, in relation to assault on Blair House or the House of Representatives, the difference between revolution and terrorism.

The consistency problem appeared when U.S. policy makers described Los Macheteros and the other revolutionary groups that were also active on the island and on the mainland.[63] For example, again in retaliation for activities on Vieques, Los Macheteros took credit for killing one sailor and wounding three others in a May 1982 attack in San Juan. Before the attack Los Macheteros had publicly announced that if the navy held maneuvers off Vieques, it would retaliate for the navy's disregard of the Puerto Rican people's protest of their activities.[64]

In Senate testimony in 1983 then FBI director William Webster defined a terrorist for the American people. He said terrorism was "the unlawful use of force or violence against persons or property to intimidate or force a government, the civilian population, or any segment thereof in furtherance of political or social objectives."[65]

Now by that definition any one of the five Puerto Rican Nationalists was certainly a terrorist. But using that definition so too was George Washington to the British in 1776 and Menachim Begin to the British in 1946. Begin, for example, was cheered by both the Carter and Reagan administration, but he had, in 1946, bombed the King David Hotel, killing or injuring more than 200 people; and in 1977 he not only defended that bombing, in *The Revolt*, but also noted that "substantial quantities of explosives were the main weapon in the struggle for liberation."[66]

A cynic might argue that only after twenty-five years in prison, or twenty-five years in political obscurity, did yesterday's terrorist become today's freedom fighter. However, the consistency gap on the part of the Carter and Reagan administrations nevertheless points to an issue that cuts through the century-long history of contact between the United States and Puerto Rico.

Violence, for example, cannot—logically—be the main issue when North-Americans condemn Puerto Rican revolutionaries. From President Dwight Eisenhower to President George Bush's recent request to regain authority for assassinations, U.S. presidents have had few compunctions about using violence to intimidate or force legal governments to do what the United States wanted.[67] And President Reagan proudly supported a counterrevolution in Nicaragua for eight years—to the point of buying weapons from the Iranians he called terrorists—so if revolutionary violence was always wrong or unlawful, how could he have supported such a violent struggle?

In relation to Puerto Rico, the FBI's definition of terrorism serves four important purposes. First, by defining terrorism in such a broad fashion the government intentionally or unintentionally says that all attacks against the United States are illegitimate. By definition, there must be something wrong with the attackers rather than with the institutions or individuals they assault. Thus, although the issues vary, there is a direct cultural link between the behavior of William Taft in 1909, Woodrow Wilson in 1917, Franklin Delano Roosevelt in 1936, Harry Truman in 1950, and Ronald Reagan in 1983. All are united by their ability to shift the blame for any attacks on U.S. policy or personnel from us to them.

What is also avoided by such a broad-brush definition of terrorism is the direct link between generations of Puerto Rican revolutionaries. For example, on September 12, 1983, Los Macheteros robbed $7.1 million from a West Hartford, Connecticut, branch of Wells Fargo. They deliberately chose September 12 because that is the birthdate of Pedro Albizu Campos. Now, for reasonable men and women four generations of revolutionaries might signal a good reason to pause for thought. What happens in the United States is that by using the terrorism label U.S. authorities can immediately dismiss the revolutionaries because by definition terrorism is beyond the human pale. The causal links of a century-long struggle are thus neatly disregarded.

A third consequence of using the FBI's definition of terrorism is that it justifies what would otherwise be described as cruel and unusual punishment. As of mid–1991, for example, there were nineteen Puerto Ricans in U.S. jails because of political "crimes." These individuals receive not only special treatment but are subjected—because they are terrorists—to conditions that supposedly occur only in Argentina or Iraq. It is not unusual for some prisoners to receive four to six "full body cavity" searches a day. At Lexington, Kentucky, the women were housed in a specially constructed "cellar" facility. The walls, the floors, the ceilings—everything was white. Any attempt to personalize or individualize their tiny living space was forbidden. Doctor Stewart Grassian, professor of psychology at Harvard, recently testified that the first suggestions for this type of facility came from Nazi jailers.[68]

The final consequence of using the FBI definition of terrorism is that it focuses attention on *what* the Puerto Ricans did, rather than *why* they resorted to revolutionary acts of violence. As with President Carter's policy at the United Nations, the task is to avoid dealing with a reality admitted by, among others, the Ford administration, namely, that U.S. policy toward Puerto Rico is "continued colonialism."

What, for example, would U.S. citizens do if, as on Culebra and Vieques, they had been lied to for what is now half a century? Would the descendants of Tom Paine and Patrick Henry docilely accept such a situation? And given the last century of U.S. policy toward Puerto Rico, isn't the surprising thing not the amount of violence that has occurred, but its relative absence?

Questions like these must become part of a nationwide debate if the United States is ever to eliminate the moral and constitutional contradictions associated with owning a colony. However, instead of facing the difficult questions, the reaction of many U.S. officials is to imitate President Taft's behavior in 1909. As Representative Richard Schulze of Pennsylvania told his colleagues in 1982, Puerto Rico is "America's Problem Child in the Caribbean."[69]

Puerto Rico is not a child. It is a nation. And it is also, as President Reagan well understood, a costly possession of the United States of America.

In 1985 President Reagan avidly sought ways to save federal dollars. His promised balanced budget had turned into three times the largest federal deficit in the nation's history. The president needed help. So he turned to Puerto Rico, or, more accurately, to the pharmaceutical and other corporations making a tax-free bundle as a result of their unique business status: a Puerto Rican–based possessions corporation.

The president had what seemed to many a genuinely good idea. He wanted to replace the tax credit with a wage credit because almost a decade of experience with the 936 laws indicated that even though the inflation-adjusted tax-exempt income of possessions corporations had more than doubled since 1972, employment levels had remained flat.[70]

Actually the president was being kind. From 1972 to 1986, Puerto Rico had seen the number of its people employed in manufacturing drop by 2,000. However, the number of people employed by the government (with the statehooders in control for eight of these fourteen years, the Populares for six) had risen by 49,000; the state now employed 23 percent of the workforce—the figure for 1972 was 18 percent—and despite anywhere from $10 *billion* to $15 *billion* of available possessions corporation funds, there had been more real investment in the 1970s, when the funds were not available, than in the 1980s, when they were.[71]

Based on the president's suggestion, and the dismal state of the island's economy, the House of Representatives held hearings in 1986. The Populares once again controlled the governor's mansion, and they stressed the absolute indispensability of the 936 program. Fomento chief

Antonio Colorado told Congress the official rate of unemployment was 21 percent, among youth sixteen to nineteen it was 53 percent, among twenty- to twenty-four-year-olds it was 40 percent and "fifty-one percent of our unemployed persons had 13 or more years of school."[72]

Perhaps to avoid scaring the representatives, Colorado never mentioned the two central preoccupations of the Puerto Rican people: crime and drugs.[73] Except for Washington, D.C., Puerto Rico (i.e., San Juan) was "number one" on almost any list of states and cities with high murder and drug addiction rates.

Colorado seemed to agree that Puerto Rico's economic misery had structural origins, but to rebuild the society, he could offer only the same old building blocks. First, "the extension of federally financed social welfare programs to the island had reduced the pressure for persons to migrate to the mainland in search of employment." And second, for long-term development, Congress had to understand that "section 936 has been the essential vehicle for the economic development of the Commonwealth of Puerto Rico."[74] Now, a congressman who had studied the island might have offered the evidence presented by the president. What economic development was Colorado talking about? For example, even the government-sponsored *Puerto Rico Business Review* admitted that from 1977 through 1985 the net growth in manufacturing was 227 additional jobs.[75]

Nobody pushed Fomento chief Colorado. And nobody was amazed or appalled when he repeated the strategy first announced by Teodoro Moscosco in the 1940s. Colorado openly admitted that "as far as the government of Puerto Rico our policy within Puerto Rico and outside of Puerto Rico is that private industry is the one that decides what project they go into and where they go into. We do not push one company one place or the other."[76]

In an era in which successful capitalists in every part of the globe—from Singapore to West Germany, from Korea to France—underlined the crucial significance not only of strategic planning but also of close control of those plans,[77] the Populares swam against the capitalist stream. They preached laissez-faire, and if Congress and the pharmaceutical companies liked that approach, the statehooders literally sounded the deathknell of the island's economy.

Baltasar Corrada, president of the statehood party, said that "the clock has struck midnight for Puerto Rico's Cinderella economy. We are in a straightjacket, in a dead end." How, for example, could "anyone say that the economic stability and future of Puerto Rico depends on a provision in the Internal Revenue code that has resulted in the loss of four thousand manufacturing sector jobs for 13 years?"[78]

How anyone could say that was indeed difficult to understand. Yet in 1982 statehood governor Carlos Romero Barcelo told Congress that

"Section 936 works. In a relatively efficient way it creates jobs in Puerto Rico." In fact, "I am writing today to ask that Section 936, which is the backbone of Puerto Rico's attempt to create jobs and reduce our dependence on transfer payments, not be changed in any way. As long as Puerto Rico is not a state, special incentives are necessary and should be retained in Federal statue."[79]

Now Romero had written that letter in July of 1982. But until his defeat in 1984 he had pressed for the continuation of Section 936. Had someone broken Puerto Rico's backbone between 1984 and 1986? Or was the party out of power simply trying to discredit the party in power?

Congress didn't seem to care. It had listened to the president's arguments. And as with the study done by the Carter administration in 1978, it had all the facts at its disposal. The only thing Congress had no intention of doing was acting on the overwhelming evidence presented by the president, the Treasury Department, and (depending on whether you were talking to Corrada or Romero) the statehooders.

So in 1986 Congress lost yet another opportunity to face up to Puerto Rico's structural woes. Meanwhile, Baxter Laboratories reported tax savings of $73 million in 1988 and $75 million in 1989. Abbott Laboratories boasted of tax savings (from Puerto Rico and Ireland) of $78 million in 1987, $76 million in 1988, and $79 million in 1989. And, as a final example, Smith Kline Beckman said that its tax savings (again from Puerto Rico and Ireland) were $53 million in 1988 and $76 million in 1989.[80]

Meanwhile, from 1982 through 1989 the drug companies created less than 3,000 jobs in Puerto Rico. In a report on long-term trends and structural problems, the Puerto Rican government reported that "the proportion of capital-intensive manufacturing operations, particularly in the high tech industries has expanded, fostering increased dependence on the U.S. economy for capital inflow and trade."[81]

A congressman once asked Luis Muñoz Marín if any particular event constituted a turning point in Puerto Rico's relations with the United States. Muñoz answered that "when you are traveling in a circle, every point is a turning point."[82]

The irony in 1989 was that Muñoz's protege, Governor Rafael Hernández Colón, decided once again to stay within the confines of the colonial circle. After his reelection in 1988 Hernández went to the Virgin Islands to see the vacationing Senator J. Bennett Johnston. A Democrat from Louisiana, Johnston was also the powerful and well-respected chair of the Senate committee that, as Senator Johnston's mentor Henry Jackson put it in 1959, oversaw all needful rules and regulations for Puerto Rico.[83]

Hernández apparently had two good reasons to push for a plebiscite. One was that it would be the capstone of his political career. Despite his experiences in the 1960s and his complete failure in 1975, Hernández still believed he could get Congress to approve "enhanced Commonwealth." A second reason to push for a plebiscite was the statehooders. In an economy on the verge of collapse, the "statehood is for the poor" message had caught on. Granted, even Romero stressed that the elections were no indication of status sentiment, but the almost forty-year failure to enhance Commonwealth suggested the need for immediate action. Something had to be done before Puerto Ricans agreed with President Ford that only independence and statehood were constitutionally possible.[84]

With the approval of the statehood and independence parties, in his 1989 inaugural address Hernández announced plans to petition Congress for a plebiscite. On February 9, President Bush also approved of the plebiscite proposal. Although his personal preference was statehood, in concert with a long line of U.S. presidents, he ardently defended the right of the Puerto Rican people to decide their own destiny.

One of Hernández's first mistakes was to forget Senator Johnston's personal and legislative past. The senator was not only an honest and intelligent man, but also a member of the 1975 commission whose U.S. members sharply edited the Commonwealth proposal submitted by, among others, Governor Rafael Hernández Colón. The edited version was itself deemed constitutionally impossible by President Ford; despite his protestations, therefore, Hernández had no cause for surprise when, before the hearings even began, Senator Johnston echoed the sentiments of Senator Jackson: Commonwealth could never be permanent. The constitution gave Congress ultimate authority over all U.S. territories (unincorporated as well as incorporated), and even if Senator Johnston wanted to, there was no honorable way he and his colleagues could refuse to accept their constitutional responsibilities.[85]

Strike 1 for Commonwealth. Strikes 2 through 18 came when Senator Johnston eliminated seventeen of the twenty specific proposals made by Hernández and his Populare associates. The *San Juan Star* said that Senator Johnston was "shocked" by the breadth of the Populares demands.[86] If that was so, Johnston, like Hernández, had no reason to be surprised. The 1989 demands were similar to those made in 1975, 1962, and 1959. It was the same old merry-go-round because Congress, the Populares, and any other Puerto Ricans willing to participate apparently liked the ride.

In the hearings themselves Senator Johnston consistently tried to remind everyone that for the plebiscite to have any meaning for the Puerto Rican people, islanders needed precise definitions of the three alternatives. Taxes, citizenship, the military bases, tariffs: Without answers to these questions the proposed plebiscite, even without the FBI's interference, would be as meaningless as the vote in 1967.

Senator Johnston was a determined man. And also a bit testy when President Bush's representative presented the administration's position. The senator interrupted the Treasury Department's Kenneth Gideon to ask, "Are you saying that the people of Puerto Rico should choose their status without knowing what their tax status will be, . . . just leave aside the economics until they choose?"[87]

Gideon: "We think any of those choices, Senator Johnston, will be very complex."

Johnston: "Well, no kidding. No kidding, I mean what do you think we have been writing to you since February 9th [the date of the President's address] about? Of course it is complex. That is why we called you up here. And you are saying that they ought to just make those choices without knowing what the economic effect on Puerto Rico is going to be?"[88]

Every administration has its flak catcher. Gideon assumed that chore for President Bush, a leader who chose a funny way to guide islanders toward statehood. Cynics said that like President Lyndon Johnson in 1966 and 1967, President Bush simply made his Puerto Rican proposal to court the Hispanic vote. My own guess is that Bush and his people simply had no idea what they were getting into; they were in fact so intellectually lazy that Senator Johnston brought up U.S. colonial policy.

Again in response to a less than specific proposal from Gideon, Senator Johnston said:

You know, what is really colonial is to tell the people of Puerto Rico, do not worry. Big Brother up here is going to do what is fair, what is nice, what is even handed, what is appropriate. Just mush words. . . . But we cannot just give them mush words. I mean, they want to know what is going to happen, and that is a daunting task. It is a big task.[89]

And it was a task Congress meant to perform before the people voted. General M. J. Bryon, for example, had testified that "we fully support the right of the people of Puerto Rico to choose their political status, but under any option we would need to retain and use the facilities listed above" (e.g., the Roosevelt Roads complex).[90] To an outsider that might seem to infringe on the right the Puerto Rican people supposedly had: If they were free to determine their destiny, were they not also free to eliminate the bases? After all, according to the promises made by representatives of President Franklin Roosevelt, those bases were temporary.

Even the thought of losing the bases upset Senator James McClure (R., Idaho). When the State Department's Mary Mochary suggested that the international norm was to first grant independence and then negotiate military bases,[91] Senator McClure explained, "From my standpoint, you are not going to get the Congress of the United States to grant a blank check with respect to these issues, which it seems to be what is considered here."[92]

When Mochary responded, "Well, strange as it may seem, I think that is the norm—that independence comes first, and then the bilateral arrangements are negotiated afterwards," even Senator Johnston felt compelled to make a statement. "If we do not have the right to do defense, then contrary wise, all we would have the right to do is give them independence and then that is it. And then whatever flows after that is whoever makes a coup of the government, or whose got the loudest voice, or whatever. Is that not true?"[93]

Of course it was true! But what did self-determination mean if Congress first foreclosed the rights that, as Mochary stressed, normally came with independence? To Senator Dale Bumpers (D., Alabama) this was a moot issue anyway. As the senator told the Treasury Department's Gideon, "I do not think you need to bother yourself, Mr. Gideon, with independence. That is not going to happen. I do not think there is a person in this room or in Puerto Rico that thinks that."[94]

Senator Johnston immediately edited his colleague's peculiar definition of self-determination. The Louisiana senator stressed that all three options would get a fair shot in the plebiscite; but in the proposals that eventually left the Senator's committee, the United States not only guaranteed its rights to the twelve installations cited by General Bryon but also stressed that even an independent Puerto Rico had to deny all countries "access to or use of the territory of Puerto Rico for military purposes, except as specifically authorized by the Government of the United States."[95]

Puerto Rico would be free. Except of congressional control.

On August 2, 1989, Senator Johnston's committee approved specific and detailed definitions of the three alternatives. Critics like Senator Malcolm Wallop argued that the "bill was unbalanced because it frontloaded the benefits under the statehood option,"[96] but the specific proposals were nonetheless a basis for debate. Everybody had some idea what the future would and would not mean.

The Senate Finance Committee soon raised constitutional questions about the tax options proposed,[97] but these were mild compared to the objections that came from the House of Representatives. Acting like Big Brother, the House wanted no detailed definition of the status options, and like Harry Truman in 1946, it absolutely refused to commit Congress to the winning status.

As chairman of the House Committee—what irony!—Delegate Ron De Lugo of the Virgin Islands noted when he introduced the House bill in May 1990:

Our bill would require the development of legislation to implement a winning status the next year after the referendum in consultation with the Puerto Rican party advocating that status, with the other two parties, and with the President. It would commit the Federal government to quick action on that legislation in early 1992. But it would provide that this final federal action would only take effect if it is approved by the people of Puerto Rico in a second vote in July of 1992, so that they make the final decision on this issue. The status development would then be effective in October of 1992.[98]

The House meant to keep the reins of power in Washington. Speaker Tom Foley agreed that islanders got nothing until Congress first negotiated the terms of the status islanders had, theoretically, already accepted.[99] Even then, Congress made no promises about approval of the final federal version of the bill. In a remark that could have easily been made by Senator Joseph Foraker in 1900, Senator William Jones in 1914, or Representative Fred Crawford in 1952, the powerful Representative Morris Udall (Democrat of Arizona and a former presidential candidate) told the Puerto Rican people on May 9, 1990, "I do not wish to raise the expectations of the Puerto Rican people. . . . It must be made very clear that the exact details of status-implementing legislation cannot be determined in advance, and that while we can assure through this legislation that a winning status will be considered by both Houses of Congress, we cannot assure enactment or that the bill will be what the winning political party would prefer."[100]

Give Udall this: He pulled no punches. He clearly indicated who was in charge, and he thus made a mockery of the president's and Congress's repeated protestations that the Puerto Rican people were free to choose their own destiny. They were free to take what Congress offered. That and nothing more.

To his credit Senator Johnston, in 1990, refused to accept the House's bill. Even after Delegate De Lugo's legislation received unanimous approval by the House (on October 10, 1990), Senator Johnston held fast. He was bothered by the lack of specificity and by the absence of a self-executing provision in the plebiscite bill. In October 1990 Senator Johnston knew that without a self-executing provision Congress had, as in 1967, committed itself to nothing, and the Puerto Rican people to another worthless expression of time and energy.[101]

By February 1991 Senator Johnston had changed his mind. He was now willing to go along with a bill like the one described by Morris Udall. Johnston's colleagues, however, still had grave reservations about taking any action on Puerto Rico. Even a non-self-executing bill died a quick and decisive death in the 102nd U.S. Congress.

But the 1991 debates nevertheless made points that underline both Puerto Rico's colonial status and the hundred years of U.S. involvement in creating and perpetuating that status.

Testifying on February 7, 1991, Attorney General Dick Thornburgh sounded very much like President Taft in 1909 and Supreme Court Justice Taft in 1922. Thornburgh noted

Citizenship of persons born in the several states is *constitutionally* guaranteed by section one of the Fourteenth Amendment. The citizenship of persons born in Puerto Rico is [and under the Commonwealth option would remain] "guaranteed" and "secured" by *statute....* In the latter case, citizenship status could be modified or revoked by statute. No provision of law bestows a constitutional *status* on the U.S. citizenship held by persons born in Puerto Rico [emphasis and quotation marks in original].[102]

This perfectly accurate comment was rooted in an even more important assertion made by President Bush's representative: "We consider it imperative that it be made clear beyond peradventure that the Commonwealth is and must remain under the sovereignty of the United States. This is necessary to avoid the continuation of the uncertainties and controversies that have plagued the existing commonwealth relationship."[103]

What uncertainties! Thornburgh had just repeated the arguments made by Congress in 1952, 1959, 1963, and, most forcefully by President Ford, in 1975.

The only uncertainty was in the mind of the Populares, who refused to believe what they were time and again told. They complained to President Ford when he called them a territory in 1974, but Thornburgh made the exact same statement in 1991: "It [Puerto Rico] remains, for constitutional purposes, a territory subject to Congress' authority under the Territory Clause."[104]

And when Senator Johnston submitted the plebiscite legislation, he too stressed that "the Principles of Commonwealth have been modified so as to maintain the fundamental relationship which currently exists between Puerto Rico and the Federal Government."[105]

Nothing fundamental has changed. Puerto Rico was a colony in 1900. A colony in 1952. And it is still a colony—of citizens by statute no less—in 1992. What islanders do is, by natural law, only for the Puerto Rican people to decide. What Americans do is another question. We can finally erase what Senator Millard Tydings called a blot on the American system. Or we can continue to live with a terrible contradiction: The United States of America, the oldest representative democracy on earth, owns Puerto Rico, the oldest colony on earth.

NOTES

1. Committee on Energy and Natural Resources, Senate, 102nd Congress, 1st session, 1991, pp. 102 and 212.

2. E. G., Maurice McDonald, *Food Stamps and Income Maintenance* (New York: Academic Press, 1977), pp. 1–5, also p. 12.

3. Richard Weisskoff, *Crops vs. Coupons: Agricultural Development and Food Stamps in Puerto Rico*, in Jorge Heine, ed., *Time for Decision* (Lanham, Md.: North-South, 1983), pp. 135–136; Richard Weisskoff, *Factories and Foodstamps* (Baltimore: Johns Hopkins University Press, 1985).

4. Weisskoff, *Crops vs. Coupons*, p. 143; 1985, pp. 60–64.

5. See, for example, Fernando Pico, *Historia General de Puerto Rico* (Río Piedras: Huracán, 1988), pp. 287–289.

6. See *Puerto Rico's Political Future*, Report to Congress by the Comptroller General, Washington, D.C., March 1981, p. 53.

7. Department of the Treasury, *The Operation and Effect of the Possessions Corporation System of Taxation*, First Report, Washington, D.C., 1978, p. 27; for employment see Sixth Report, 1989, p. 21.

8. President Gerald Ford Library, Ann Arbor, Papers of Jim Cannon, Box 27, the eight-page Interior Department letter is signed by Under Secretary Kent Fruzzell; it is dated December 30, 1975.

9. Ford Library, Papers of General Alexander Haig, Box 1.

10. Ford Library, Papers of Jim Cannon, Box 27; this quote is from pp. 4–5 of Halper's report to the president.

11. Ibid., p. 31.

12. Ibid., esp. pp. 33–34.

13. Ibid., p. 39.

14. Ford Library, Papers of Norman E. Ross, Box 6, see memo dated May 2, 1975.

15. Ibid., p. 3.

16. Ibid., p. 4.

17. Ford Library, Papers of James Cannon, memo dated August 2, 1975.

18. Ford Library, Papers of Jim Cannon, Boxes 27 and 28; the critical comments are a package of roughly sixty pages of documents, submitted under the particular department's letterhead, primarily through the months of November and December of 1975.

19. Ford Library, Papers of Norman Ross, Box 6; the president's five-page memo is dated September 24, 1976; my quote is from p. 3.

20. Ibid., p. 5.

21. Ford Library, Papers of James Cannon, Box 8, for the proposal.

22. Ford Library, Papers of Jim Cannon, Box 8; there is a three-page memo and, attached, a suggested statement for the president.

23. Roberta Johnson, *Commonwealth or Colony* (New York: Praeger, 1979), p. 158.

24. *Tax Reform Act of 1975, Hearings before the Committee on Finance*, Senate, 94th Congress, 2nd session, 1976, see pp. 1039 and 1042.

25. See Thomas St. G. Bissell, "The Changing Structure of the United States–Puerto Rican Tax Relationship," *Georgia Journal of International and Comparative Law* 8 (1978): p. 901.

26. See Department of the Treasury, First Report, p. 64.

27. See Bissell, "Changing Structure," esp. pp. 903–908.

28. President Ford Library, Special Files Unit, Box 6.

29. See President Carter Library, Atlanta, Georgia, Domestic Policy Staff, Papers of Al Stern; the ninety-one-page analysis of the tax laws is dated June 23, 1978; my quote is from p. 2.

30. See Ibid., p. 1.

31. See Leo Rockas, "Recent Changes in the Possessions Corporation System of Taxation," *Cornell International Law Journal* 16 (1983) pp. 431–453, esp. see p. 443; also see Department of the Treasury, *The Operation and Effect of the Possession Corporation System of Taxation*, Fourth Report, February 1983, esp. pp. 14–15.

32. Manuel Escobar, *The 936 Market* (San Juan, 1980), pp. 21–23.

33. Ibid., p. 52.

34. Bissell, "Changing Structure," p. 909.

35. Ibid., p. 910.

36. Department of the Treasury, First Report, pp. 17–18.

37. See Carter Library, Papers of Al Stern, p. 6.

38. Ibid., p. 89.

39. Carter Library, WHCF, ST51–2, memo dated March 1, 1977.

40. See *Economic Study of Puerto Rico*, Washington, D.C.: 1979.

41. Carter Library, Domestic Policy Staff, Papers of Al Stern; the memo is dated November 7, 1978, and is labeled "Meetings with the Puerto Rican Government"; the quote is from p. 6 of the memo.

42. Carter Library, WHCF, ST51–2; Romero sent a copy of his statement to the president.

43. Ibid., p. 7 of Pounds's summary.

44. See Jorge Heine, ed., *Time for Decision* (Lanham, Md.: North-South, 1983), p. xxvii.

45. For the Goldberg remark see President Johnson Library, Office Files–Puerto Rico, Box 27; for Ambassador Moynihan's remark see Daniel Moynihan, *A Dangerous Place* (N.Y.: Berkeley, 1978), pp. 120–121.

46. Carlos Romero Barcelo, *Statehood Is for the Poor* (San Juan, 1978), p. 104.

47. See Carlos Romero Barcelo, Carter Library, WHCF, ST51–2, p. 2.

48. Carter Library, White House Official Files, ST51–2; this is from a memo labeled "Talking Points on Puerto Rico."

49. This memo from Brzezinski is dated February 17, 1977; it is at the Carter Library, White House Central Files, 51–2.

50. Robert A. Pastor, "Puerto Rico as an International Issue: A Motive for a Movement?" in Richard J. Bloomfield, ed., *Puerto Rico* (Boulder, Colo.: Westview, 1985), pp. 99–140. See, too, Pastor's "International Debate on Puerto Rico: The Costs of Being an Agenda Taker," *International Organization* 38, no. 3 (1984):esp. p. 584.

51. *Status of Navy Training Activities on the Island of Vieques, Hearings before the Committee on Armed Services*, House, 96th Congress, 2nd session, 1980, p. 166.

52. Ford Library, White House Staff Files of Bobbie Kilberg, Box 3.

53. Ibid. Attorney Coapken's letter to the National Security Council is dated June 26, 1975; my quote is taken from p. 2 of the letter; as an attachment to the letter there is the then secret testimony of Secretary Bowers.

54. See, *Hearings*, 1980, p. 100.

55. See *Naval Training Activities on the Island of Vieques, Hearings before the*

Committee on Armed Services, House, 97th Congress, 1st session, 1981, p. 1; for the 5 million figures see Hearings, 1980, p. 162.

56. Hearings, 1980, pp. 8–9.

57. Ibid., p. 72; Hearings, 1981, p. 5.

58. Ford Library, Staff Files of Bobbie Kilberg, Box 3, p. 2 of Bowers testimony.

59. See Hearings, 1980, p. 325.

60. See, for example, Newsweek, December 17, 1979, p. 55.

61. Carter Library, Counsel's Office Files, Box 43; the Brzezinski memo is undated.

62. See ibid.; see a memo from Al Stern to Bob Pastor dated June 5, 1978; another from Pastor to Joseph Aragon and Stern is dated May 31, 1978.

63. Domestic Security Guidelines, Hearings before the Subcommittee on Security and Terrorism, Senate, 97th Congress, 2nd session, 1982, esp. pp. 65–71.

64. See, for example, Ronald Fernández, Los Macheteros (Englewood Cliffs, N.J.: Prentice Hall, 1987).

65. FBI Oversight and Authorization Hearings before the Subcommittee on Security and Terrorism, Senate, 98th Congress, 1st session, February 2, 1983, p. 18.

66. Menachim Begin, The Revolt (New York: Dell Books, 1977), rev. ed., p. 90; see, too, Amos Perlmutter, The Life and Times of Menachem Begin (New York: Doubleday, 1987).

67. For Eisenhower see Madeleine Kalb, The Congo Cables (New York: Macmillan, 1982); for Kennedy see Ellen Hammer, A Death in November (New York: E. P. Dutton, 1987).

68. Richard Kohn, "The Effects of Confinement in the High Security Unit at Lexington," Social Justice 15, no. 1 (Spring 1988):pp. 8–29.

69. Congressional Record, 97th Congress, 2nd session, July 19, 1982, p. 16958.

70. See Puerto Rico's Economy, Oversight Hearing before the Committee on Interior and Insular Affairs, House, 99th Congress, 2nd session, 1986, p. 131.

71. Department of the Treasury, Sixth Report, p. 80 for the investment comment and p. 73 for the funds available. No one seems to know the exact sum the corporations have stockpiled.

72. Hearings, 1986, p. 18.

73. See, for example, a Nuevo Día poll of January 14, 1986; and an El Mundo poll of July 24, 1990. Both place crime and drugs as the central public preoccupations of the Puerto Rican people.

74. Hearings, 1986, pp. 18–19.

75. Puerto Rico Business Review 13, no. 8 (August 1988):pp. 7–11.

76. Hearings, 1986, p. 60.

77. For example, Hafiz Mirza, Multinationals and the Growth of the Singapore Economy (New York: St. Martin's Press, 1986); Peter Berger, The Capitalist Revolution (New York: Basic Books, 1986).

78. Hearings, 1986, p. 90.

79. Congressional Record, Senate, 97th Congress, 2nd session, July 21, 1982, p. 17234.

80. See Baxter International, Form 10k for 1990, p. 43; Abbott Laboratories, Annual Report, 1989, p. 30; Smithkline Beckman Annual Report, 1989, p. 69.

Smithkline's profits are reported in pounds. I multiplied by the exchange rate on May 14, 1990, $1.7 to the pound.

81. *Puerto Rico Business Review*, Special Supplement (March 1987): p. 3.

82. See Pastor, "International Issue," 1985, p. 101.

83. A fine overview of the plebiscite process is Harry Turner's "Odyssey of Puerto Rico's Plebiscite, 1988–1990," *San Juan Star*, December 23, 1990; see, too, Carmen Gautier Mayoral, ed. *Poder Y Plebiscito: Puerto Rico en 1991* (Río Piedras: Centro de Investigaciones Sociales, 1991).

84. Turner, "Odyssey," 22.

85. Ibid., pp. 24–25.

86. Ibid., p. 25.

87. *Political Status of Puerto Rico, Committee on Interior and Insular Affairs*, Senate, 101st Congress, 1st session, 1989, Vol. 3, p. 195.

88. Ibid., p. 195.

89. Ibid., p. 197.

90. Ibid., p. 143; for the full testimony of General M. J. Byron see pp. 131–151.

91. Ibid., p. 168.

92. Ibid.

93. Ibid., p. 169.

94. Ibid., p. 225.

95. See *Puerto Rico Status Referendum Act, Report from the Committee on Energy and Natural Resources*, Senate, Report no. 101–120, 101st Congress, 1st session, September 1989, p. 11.

96. Ibid., p. 63.

97. See *Tax Rules Relating to Puerto Rico under Present Law and Under Statehood, Independence, and Enhanced Commonwealth Status*, Senate Committee on Finance, 101st Congress, 1st session, November 1989.

98. See H.R. 4765, House, 101st Congress, 2nd session, May 9, 1990. This was a committee packet sent to anyone who asked. The quote is from p. 5 of Delegate De Lugo's attached statement.

99. Ibid.; see portions of a Foley press conference attached to the House bill.

100. *Congressional Record*, 101st Congress, 2nd session, May 9, 1990, E1439.

101. Turner, "Odyssey," p. 27; I also discussed these matters with Senate staffers but agreed that their comments were not for attribution.

102. See *statement of Dick Thornburgh, Hearings before the Committee on Energy and Natural Resources*, Senate, 102nd Congress, 1st session, February 7, 1991, p. 34.

103. Ibid., p. 31.

104. Ibid.; for the complaints to President Ford see Ford Library, Papers of Kenneth Cole, Box 3.

105. See *Puerto Rico State Referendum Act*, p. 28.

Epilogue

Where do we go from here? This inevitable question is as easy to ask as it is difficult to answer. Nevertheless, I will offer this assessment of Puerto Rico's future.

First, Congress will never significantly enhance Commonwealth. It is constitutionally impossible to offer the island what the Populares have tried, for almost fifty years, to obtain. So if the goal is to break out of the colonial circle, independence and statehood are the island's only meaningful options.

Second, and following Pedro Albizu Campos, Americans will never act unless there is a crisis. Our ignorance about the island is appalling, our indifferences to its colonial condition a century-long constant. On a recent plane ride from Washington a student at one of America's most prestigious universities asked, "What kind of currency do they use down there?"

Third, if the crisis is violent, it will be militarily suppressed by Americans who will profess to be shocked at Puerto Rico's ingratitude. From Cuba in 1903 to Cuba in 1961, and from Haiti in 1915 to the Dominican Republic in 1965, to Grenada in 1983, U.S. officials have self-righteously eliminated (or tried to eliminate) governments or movements that threatened U.S. interests or U.S. perceptions of right and wrong.

Fourth, a movement that seeks serious change will use the United Nations as a forum for debate. Successive U.S. administrations have shown real and serious concern about having to confront colonial realities in an international setting. The United Nations offers a forum to peacefully resolve what Senator Millard Tydings rightfully called "one of the most unsatisfactory relationships between two governments that I have ever encountered, on the face of the earth."

Finally, whatever course islanders choose, for change to be self-sustaining it must be rooted—again following Albizu Campos—in an utter rejection of the self-depreciating mentality shaped by 400 years of Spanish and 100 years of U.S. colonialism. Statehood, for example, will solve nothing if it is based on a crude calculation of even greater economic dependence on the mainland.

As in Singapore, Puerto Rico's greatest natural resource is its own people, a people who are among the most decent, intelligent, and admirable on earth.

Build a movement on the legitimate but still latent pride of the Puerto Rican people, and significant yet peaceful change is possible.

Build that movement on mainland dependence, and the island will enter the twenty-first century as it entered the twentieth: as a colony of the United States of America.

Selected Bibliography

Acosta, Ivonne. *La Mordaza*. Río Piedras: Edil, 1987.
Albizu Campos, Pedro. *Obras Escojidas*, Vols. 1–3. San Juan: Editorial Jelofe, 1981.
Bernabe, Rafael. *Prehistory of the Partido Popular Democrático: Muñoz Marín, the Partido Liberal and the Crisis of Sugar in Puerto Rico*. Ph.D. thesis, State University of New York at Binghamton, 1989.
Cabranes, José. *Citizenship and the American Empire*. New Haven, Conn.: Yale University Press, 1979.
Clark, Truman. *Puerto Rico and the U.S., 1917–1933*. Pittsburgh University of Pittsburgh Press, 1975.
Delgado Pasapera, German. *Puerto Rico: Sus Luchas Emancipadoras*. Río Piedras: Editorial Cultural, 1984.
Dietz, James. *Economic History of Puerto Rico: Institutional Change and Capitalist Developments*. Princeton, N.J.: Princeton University Press, 1986.
Diffie, Bailey, and Justine Diffie. *Porto Rico: A Broken Pledge*. New York: Vanguard Press, 1932.
Ferrao, Luis Ángel. *Pedro Albizu Campos y el Nacionalismo Puertorriqueno*. Río Piedras: Editorial Cultural, 1990.
García Passalacqua, Juan. *La Crisis Política en Puerto Rico*. San Juan: Edil, 1983.
Gautier Mayoral, Carmen. *Puerto Rico y ONU*. Río Piedras: Edil, 1978.
González, José Luis. *El País de Cuatro Pisos*. Río Piedras: Huracán, 1985.
Gould, Lyman. *La Ley Foraker*. Río Piedras: Editorial University of Puerto Rico Press, 1969.
Heine, Jorge, ed. *Time for Decision*. Lanham, Md.: North-South, 1983.
Hunt, Michael. *Ideology and U.S. Foreign Policy*. New Haven, Conn.: Yale University Press, 1987.

Lewis, Gordon. *Puerto Rico: Freedom and Power in the Caribbean*. New York: Harper & Row, 1963.

Matthews, Thomas. *Puerto Rican Politics and the New Deal*. Gainesville: University of Florida Press, 1960.

Meléndez López, Arturo. *La Batalla de Vieques*. 2nd edition. Río Piedras: Edil, 1989.

Negron de Montilla, Aida. *Americanization in Puerto Rico and the Public School System*. Río Piedras: Editorial Edil, 1970.

Nieves Falcon, Luis. *Diagnóstico de Puerto Rico*. Río Piedras: Edil, 1970.

Pantojas García, Emilio. *Development Strategies as Ideology*. Boulder, Colo.: Lynne Rienner, 1990.

Pico, Fernando. *Historia General de Puerto Rico*. Río Piedras: Huracán, 1988.

Santana Rabell, Leonardo. *Planificación y Política*. Río Piedras: Editorial Cultural, 1989.

Scarano, Francisco, ed. *Inmigración y Clases Sociales*. Río Piedras: Huracán, 1985.

Suarez, Manuel. *Requiem for Ceroo Maravilla*. Maplewood, N.J.: Waterfront, 1987.

Weisskoff, Richard. *Factories and Foodstamps*. Baltimore: Johns Hopkins University Press, 1985.

Zapata Oliveras, Carlos Ramón. *United States–Puerto Rico Relations in the Early Cold War Years*. Ph.D. Dissertation, University of Pennsylvania, 1986.

Index

ABOUT THE AUTHOR

RONALD FERNANDEZ is Professor of Sociology at Central Connecticut State University. The author of *Los Macheteros: The Violent Struggle for Puerto Rican Independence* (1988), he has spent the last seven years researching Puerto Rico.